Managing Change: Sustainable Approaches to the Conservation of the Built Environment

4th Annual US/ICOMOS International
Symposium Organized by US/ICOMOS,
the Graduate Program in Historic Preservation
of the University of Pennsylvania, and
the Getty Conservation Institute

Philadelphia, Pennsylvania
April 2001

*Edited by Jeanne Marie Teutonico
and Frank Matero*

THE GETTY CONSERVATION INSTITUTE

LOS ANGELES

Getty Conservation Institute
Proceedings series

© 2003 J. Paul Getty Trust

Getty Publications
1200 Getty Center Drive, Suite 500
Los Angeles, California 90049-1682
www.getty.edu

Timothy P. Whalen, *Director, Getty Conservation Institute*
Jeanne Marie Teutonico, *Associate Director, Field Projects and Science*

Sheila U. Berg, *Project Manager and Manuscript Editor*
Pamela Heath, *Production Coordinator*
Hespenheide Design, *Designer*

Printed in the United States by Edwards Brothers, Inc.
Cover and color insert printed in Canada by Transcontinental Printing

The Getty Conservation Institute works internationally to advance conservation and to enhance and encourage the preservation and understanding of the visual arts in all of their dimensions—objects, collections, architecture, and sites. The Institute serves the conservation community through scientific research, education and training, field projects, and the dissemination of the results of both its work and the work of others in the field. In all its endeavors, the Institute is committed to addressing unanswered questions and promoting the highest standards of conservation practice.

The Getty Conservation Institute is a program of the J. Paul Getty Trust, an international cultural and philanthropic organization devoted to the visual arts and the humanities that includes an art museum as well as programs for education, scholarship, and conservation.

Library of Congress Cataloging-in-Publication Data

US/ICOMOS International Symposium (4th : 2001 : Philadelphia, Pa.)
    Managing change : sustainable approaches to the conservation of the built environment : 4th Annual US/ICOMOS International Symposium organized by US/ICOMOS, Program in Historic Preservation of the University of Pennsylvania, and the Getty Conservation Institute 6–8 April 2001, Philadelphia, Pennsylvania / Jeanne Marie Teutonico and Frank Matero.
        p. cm.
Includes bibliographical references.
        ISBN 0-89236-692-3 (pbk.)
1. Historic preservation—Congresses. 2. Historic sites—Conservation and restoration—Congresses. 3. Cultural property—Protection—Congresses. 4. Sustainable architecture—Congresses. I. Teutonico, Jeanne Marie. II. Matero, F. G. (Frank G.) III. Title.
CC135U8 2003
363.6'9—dc21

                                                                    2003010324

Contents

PART THREE

Practicing Sustainability: Case Studies

Sustainable Approaches to the Conservation of Archaeological Sites

Sustainable Approaches to Building Conservation

Sustainable Approaches to Historic Cities

Sustainability and Tradition

Foreword

IT IS MY PLEASURE to introduce this publication in the Getty Conservation Institute's Proceedings series which brings together the thinking, discussion, and conclusions of the 4th US/ICOMOS International Symposium held in Philadelphia from April 6 to 8, 2001, under the theme "Managing Change: Sustainable Approaches to the Conservation of the Built Environment." In 2001, US/ICOMOS had the great pleasure of partnering with the Getty Conservation Institute and the Graduate Program in Historic Preservation at the University of Pennsylvania to cosponsor the event.

International and transcultural professional exchanges are the core mission of US/ICOMOS and of its parent organization, the International Council on Monuments and Sites. ICOMOS is a worldwide alliance of individuals, agencies, and institutions dedicated to preserving and protecting the built heritage of all humanity. The annual US/ICOMOS symposium is but one of the instruments we see for the fulfillment of our mission. Through publications and periodicals, through the electronic dissemination of information, through technical assistance projects, and by ensuring the presence of the expertise of members in all important international heritage forums, US/ICOMOS is a major gateway for all American preservationists to develop a global dimension. Perhaps more than any other program, our twenty-year-old International Summer Intern Program best exemplifies our commitment to the import and export of best practices in heritage conservation. Through this program, more than five hundred young preservationists from sixty-one countries have been ushered into the world of international preservation practice.

This global vision for the practice of heritage conservation is shared by the Getty Conservation Institute and the University of Pennsylvania Graduate Program in Historic Preservation. That common vision set the ideal foundation for our partnership in the 4th International Symposium.

In its few short years, the US/ICOMOS symposium has become a central element in the annual preservation calendar of the United States, as the only programmed forum that regularly connects our national preservation community with colleagues from overseas through a single topic. Drawing from important experiences from abroad, as well as from the international professional involvement of American preservationists, the US/ICOMOS symposium aims to elevate our stewardship of the built environment by opening new visions to innovative approaches from all continents and cultures.

These *Proceedings* of the 2001 symposium, like those of other years, may be treated as a stand-alone document that delves into its theme. But more than isolated efforts, each US/ICOMOS symposium builds on those that have preceded it. In this sense, there is a common thread that links the proceedings from all symposia into an important in-depth opus on the major issues and challenges that local preservation communities all over the world are facing.

The success of the 4th International Symposium was a result of the indefatigable dedication of Jeanne Marie Teutonico and Frank Matero, who constituted the Scientific Committee that devised the theme, content, and structure of the event. Both Ms. Teutonico and Mr. Matero are members of the US/ICOMOS Board of Trustees and longtime supporters of our mission. In addition to their talent and knowledge, they brought with them the generous support of the Getty Conservation Institute and the University of Pennsylvania, whose human, physical, and financial resources were perfect complements to those of US/ICOMOS. This volume is a testimonial to the larger commitment of the Getty Conservation Institute to the success of the symposium.

Many others at the university, the Getty Conservation Institute, and other organizations contributed selflessly to the event. At the Getty Conservation Institute, US/ICOMOS owes special gratitude to its director, Timothy P. Whalen, for the continued support and encouragement he has given us for many years. At the University of Pennsylvania, special mention must be made of Suzanne Hyndman and the members of the Historic Preservation Class of 2002, who miraculously caused the many logistical obstacles to disappear before they were noticed. We would also be remiss if we did not mention the support given by the Association for Preservation Technology International (APT), driven largely by the effort of President-elect Kent Dieboldt and Stephen J Kelley.

Finally, a word of special thanks to the Samuel H. Kress Foundation and the National Park Service for their support of this symposium. The success that US/ICOMOS has achieved in the past is attributable, in large part, to their trust and sustained generosity over many years.

Robert C. Wilburn
CHAIRMAN
US/ICOMOS

Preface

Frank Matero

OVER THE PAST DECADE heritage has come center stage in the discourse on place, cultural identity, and ownership of the past.[1] This has been due in part to the development of historic preservation into a field many now consider among the most significant and influential sociocultural movements that affect the built environment. Yet for all its direct impact on public life, heritage conservation has lagged behind in its involvement in the larger debate on the quality of life and the environment. Conservation's theoretical and methodological approach as a transdisciplinary field based on the humanities and the social and physical sciences renders it a powerful vehicle into the questions of form, meaning, and value of past human works. If we accept the most basic definition of conservation as protection from loss and depletion, then conservation of all cultural heritage—tangible and intangible—addresses and contributes to memory, itself basic to all human existence. Conservation is predicated on the belief that memory, knowledge, and experience are tied to cultural constructs, especially material culture. Conservation helps to extend places and things of the past into the present and establishes a form of mediation critical to the interpretive process that reinforces these important aspects of human existence.

The fundamental objectives of conservation concern ways of evaluating and interpreting cultural heritage for its preservation and safeguarding now and for the future. Yet all conservation is a critical act in that the decisions regarding what is conserved, and who presents these decisions and how, are a product of contemporary values and beliefs about the past's relationship to the present. The role of value in the determination and preservation of heritage has long been recognized; who determines that value and how it plays out through "appropriate" methods of use, presentation, intervention, and ownership has become one of the major issues of our time.

Since the 1970s sustainability has evolved as a significant mode of thought in nearly every field of intellectual activity. The highly publicized United Nations Conference on Environment and Development (UNCED) in Rio de Janeiro in 1992 brought the ideas of sustainability and development to the forefront of global politics. In UNCED's Agenda 21, principles of sustainable development were formalized, stipulating that both environmental quality and economic growth must be considered equal partners for viable long-term development strategies. With their origins in the nature conservation movement of the early twentieth century, sustainability and sustainable development are about finding ways to design and manage that allow essential or desirable resources to be renewed faster than they are destroyed.[2] In the building industry, sustainability has become synonymous with "green architecture," or buildings designed with healthy work environments, energy conserving systems, and environmentally sensitive materials. For historic tangible resources—whether cultural landscape, town, building, or work of art—the aim is notably different, as the physical resource is finite and cannot be easily regenerated. Instead, sustainability in this context means ensuring the continuing contribution of heritage to the present through the thoughtful management of change responsive to the historic environment and to the social and cultural processes that created it. By shifting the focus to perception and valuation, conservation becomes a dynamic process involving public participation, dialogue and consensus, and an understanding of the associated traditions and meanings in the creation, use, and re-creation of heritage.

Sustainability emphasizes the need for a long-term view. If conservation is to develop as a viable strategy, the economic dimension needs to be addressed, while at the local level community education and participation is central to sustaining conservation initiatives. Unless we understand how cultural heritage is being lost or affected and what factors are contributing to those processes, we will not be able to manage it, let alone pass it on. Effective heritage site management involves both knowing what is important and understanding how that importance is vulnerable to loss.

If sustainability ultimately means learning to think and act in terms of guaranteeing the prosperity of interdependent natural, social, and economic systems, then heritage with its unique values and experiences must be contextualized and integrated with this view. In the transformation of our physical environment, what relationships should exist between change and continuity, between the old and the new? Only when history is rightly viewed as continuous change can conservation affect an integrated and sustainable environment.

The US/ICOMOS 2001 International Symposium explores the issues of sustainability through conservation as a new model for stewardship as it relates to design, technology, economics, development, and social viability. These aspects are examined across diverse cultural heritage ranging in scale from individual buildings and sites to cities, landscapes, and other historic environments. Through the lens of sustainability, it is hoped that heritage conservation ultimately can be expanded into culturally responsive strategies that provide an alternative to imported solutions that do not relate to or grow out of the existing cultural context. As both a means and an end, heritage conservation should provide a dynamic vehicle by which individuals and communities can explore, reinforce, interpret, and share their historical and traditional past and present, through community membership as well as through input as a professional or non-professional affiliate. In this view, conservation can and should facilitate a sustainable, long-term relationship with the natural and cultural resources of a place and its people and their associated memories and lifeways.

Notes

1   The term "heritage" is used here specifically to mean all cultural property that is intentionally constructed and biased toward a particular group or issue. See D. Lowenthal, *The Heritage Crusade and the Spoils of History* (London: Viking Press, 1997).

2   G. Fairclough, "The 'S' word—Sustaining conservation," in *Conservation Plans in Action: Proceedings of the Oxford Conference,* ed. K. Clark (London: English Heritage, 1999), 127.

PART ONE

Thinking Sustainability: Concepts and Principles

Sustainability in the Conservation of the Built Environment: An Economist's Perspective

David Throsby

DECISIONS CONCERNING CONSERVATION of the built environment have in the past been the domain largely of architectural historians, urban planners, conservation specialists, and related professionals. In recent years, however, rising costs and the increasing scarcity of funds have led to heightened attention to the financial aspects of these decisions. As a result, accountants, economists, and financial analysts have been drawn more and more into the decision-making process. Broadly, we can identify two extreme positions that might be taken in approaching the economic questions raised by the conservation of cultural heritage in an urban context. On the one hand, the principles and practices of the conservation profession might be taken as constant and non-negotiable, providing a fixed framework onto which can be grafted an assessment of the economic consequences of decisions made on terms determined solely by the conservation issues under discussion. On the other hand, the economic environment might be assumed as a given, and conservation practice might be interpreted as having to adapt to what are seen as inevitable changes in the economy; these changes include an increasing emphasis on financial incentives and market-driven resource allocation and an inexorable shift from serving the collective public good to the satisfaction of the demands of individual consumers. In other words, this position would see conservation decisions as subject to immutable constraints imposed by an economic agenda that, whether we like it or not, is increasingly influential in local, national, and international affairs.

Neither of these extreme approaches makes much sense. Conservation cannot remain a closed and solely self-referential profession, and indeed it has not.[1] At the same time the inexorable rise of global markets and the ascendancy of economic imperatives in policy formulation around the world does not mean that social, cultural, environmental, and other humanistic values have no role to play in shaping decisions about our futures. It is precisely because neither of these extreme positions is tenable that sustainability emerges as such an important concept, not just in guiding decisions about conservation of the built heritage, but more generally in providing a holistic framework for interpreting how economic, social, cultural, and biological systems fit together.[2]

To demonstrate how sustainability comes to the fore as an important concept in an economist's approach to urban conservation, I shall construct a simple illustration. Suppose a local authority or community group in some town or city, which could be almost anywhere, owns a historic building or site. It might be a town hall, a marketplace, or an industrial building. Whatever it is, it is deemed to have a degree of cultural significance for the town's residents and might hold some interest for out-of-town visitors as well. The local group wants some advice about how to restore the site, perhaps to adapt the use of the building to meet contemporary needs. They are concerned about the financial consequences of any redevelopment project, so they decide to call in an economic consultant to help them put together a conservation strategy. The type of consultant they might engage falls into one of three categories.

The first type is the large commercial consulting firm that can turn its hand to anything—investment advice, financial planning, marketing strategy, product development, and so on. Let us suppose that the local committee in our hypothetical example brings in such a firm. The economist assigned by the firm to the heritage conservation project advises the committee that the focus has to be on profitability. The redevelopment must be positioned to generate maximum revenue, and in doing so, it will stimulate the town's economy by generating new jobs and income. The ideal proposal, it is suggested, will entail significant modification of the building to allow for retail development, advertising placement, and the installation of extensive facilities catering to tourists. The consultant admits that some compromises may have to be made along the way but argues that when there is a conflict between, say, historical authenticity and profit potential, the latter must take precedence, or the project will be a financial disaster. Needless to say, the strategy proposed by such a consultant is likely to be crass, tasteless, and insensitive.

The second category of economic consultant that could be brought in is typified by the small team of economists assembled from the nearby university's economics department. These people are a lot smarter than the commercially driven consultant from the big accounting firm. They recognize that there is more to the economic benefits of a heritage project than is simply reflected in the bottom line and that maximizing only the tangible financial returns overlooks a major contribution that the project would make to the community. They point out to the committee that the principal benefits of built cultural heritage are in fact intangible in nature and include, for example, local residents' pride in their town's cultural facilities, the links with local history that a heritage building represents, the educational value of presenting heritage to the public, and the symbolic role that heritage plays in representing people to themselves. The economists go further and suggest that the beneficiaries of this heritage building extend beyond the town's boundaries, that the fate of the site is a matter of concern not just to local residents but to the region as a whole and indeed to the nation, since the building comprises an element of the country's overall inventory of cultural resources. To impress the committee, the team uses a lot of jargon, including terms such as "public goods" and "external benefits" and "nonmarket effects," but their intention is clear enough—to broaden the concept of benefit beyond that which accountants identify when they look only at monetary profit and loss.

These economists propose to undertake both a financial analysis of the project and what they refer to as a "contingent valuation study."[3] In this study, residents, tourists, and others will be surveyed to evaluate the extent to which the intangible benefits mentioned above actually exist in the minds of the community and to find out how much these recipients of intangible benefits would be willing to pay (for example, out of local taxes, by donation, or through some other means) for these benefits. From the results of the survey sample it will be possible to infer the total amount that the population as a whole would be prepared to contribute to the project. This monetary valuation of the aggregate demand for the intangible benefits of the project can then be included in the overall assessment of the project's economic worth. The economists acknowledge that their estimates of willingness to pay remain hypothetical and do not contribute to the *realized* financial outcomes of the project, unless some means can be found to "capture" all or part of this willingness in the form of actual payments. They suggest some options for achieving this end, including a small levy on local government rates that could be earmarked for the project or the establishment of a foundation fund to which people would be asked to contribute.

Even without such capture, an evaluation of the intangible benefits of a heritage project can provide some comfort to a local government authority. To illustrate, in the early 1980s a colleague and I undertook an economic study of a cultural center occupying a historic house in a town in rural Australia.[4] The local council was concerned that the center imposed a continuing cost burden on ratepayers, which had to be financed each year out of general council revenue. However, when the value of the intangible benefits of the arts center to the local community was added in, measured by means of a contingent valuation exercise that we undertook, the rate of return on capital was shown to be quite healthy. This result persuaded the council that its operating expenditures for maintaining this heritage project were justified in terms of the nonmarket benefits enjoyed in the community as demonstrated by the residents' willingness to pay.

In our present example, the extension of the concept of economic benefit proposed by the second group of consultants—that is, augmenting the assessment of direct use values of the project with an evaluation of benefits to a wider constituency—is certainly a big step forward. In recent years an increasing number of such studies have appeared that have focused considerable attention on the measurement of the intangible benefits of built heritage. These studies represent an extension into the cultural heritage field of empirical methods that have been widely applied in valuing the intangible benefits of environmental amenities and resources. Examples are a study of the restoration of Bulgarian monasteries (Mourato and Danchev 1999); an estimate of the public-good benefits of a range of heritage sites in Naples (Santagata and Signorello 2000); a study of the preservation of the historic Northern Hotel in Fort Collins, Colorado (Kling, Revier, and Sable 2000); and an assessment of a project involving the cleaning of Lincoln Cathedral in England (Pollicino and Maddison 2001).

But the question remains as to whether all the values attributable to a heritage project can be expressed in a single monetary measure. While it is true that the enjoyment of both the direct and the indirect benefits of cultural heritage may spring from any number of individual motivations, including aesthetic, social, and spiritual concerns, there are doubts about whether an expression of such values in terms of willingness to pay fully captures the nature of the benefits involved. To widen the focus from an individualistic economic model to a broader assessment that accepts that some aspects of cultural worth may not be expressible in terms of market prices or of willingness to pay, we need new ways to conceptualize heritage that comprehend both economic and cultural dimensions. One such approach is to interpret items of cultural heritage as *cultural capital*, whose management can be cast in the framework of sustainability. Let me explain briefly what these terms mean.

Consider an item of tangible heritage such as a historic building. As an asset, it may have much the same outward or physical characteristics as any ordinary building: it was created by human activity, it lasts for a certain time, it will decay if it is not maintained, it gives rise to a flow of services over time, it can be bought and sold, and its financial value can be measured. In short, it is an economic asset like any other piece of real estate. But its value extends further. Because of its historical connections, because of what the building may mean as a symbol of the culture of the surrounding community, because of its aesthetic qualities as an example of a particular architectural style, and for a host of other reasons, the value of the building transcends its purely functional economic worth. We can refer to these latter sources of value of the building as comprising its cultural value. Clearly this value will be related to economic value.[5] Generally, the higher the cultural value of an asset—that is, the more cultural significance it embodies—the more people might be prepared to pay to acquire it, to use its services, or simply to preserve it. But there is no reason to suppose a one-to-one relationship between economic and cultural value, and indeed examples can readily be cited in which there is a disjunction between the two; for instance, listing a building judged to be of high cultural worth may actually depress the amount people will pay to buy or to use it, if listing were to entail significant regulation limiting the building's reuse.

The virtue of identifying cultural goods as items of cultural capital in this way lies in the fact that this concept can provide a coherent and rigorous framework within which both the economic and the cultural contribution of the cultural resource can be analyzed and assessed. Intervention involving expenditure of public or private funds can then be seen as a capital investment project. In the present example, in which the asset is a historic urban building and the project is the restoration and reuse of the site, we can suggest that treating the cultural resource as an item of cultural capital enables the familiar tools of investment appraisal to be applied. The identification of cultural value alongside the economic value generated by the project means that the economic evaluation can be augmented by a cultural appraisal carried out along the same lines, that is, as a parallel benefit-cost analysis wherein the time-stream of both economic and cultural value can be assessed.

This brings us back to sustainability, because viewing a heritage building as an item of cultural capital immediately invites consideration of the long term, and the concept of sustainability provides a framework for evaluating the long-term problems of dealing with capital assets. As is well known, the term "sustainable development" is most frequently heard in the context of the environment following the work of the World Commission on Environment and Development (WCED), known as the Brundtland Commission.[6] We can go on to argue that just as natural capital (the stock of natural resources and ecosystems) provides long-term benefits for successive generations, so also does cultural capital exist as a source of cultural goods and services that provide benefits both now and in the future. As individuals or as a society, we can allow cultural capital to deteriorate over time, we can maintain it, we can add to it, in short, we can *manage* it in a way that suits our individual or collective purpose. What principles should guide our management decisions? By articulating more precisely what sustainability entails when applied to cultural heritage, such a set of principles emerges. In this way, rather than attempt to *define* sustainability—an enterprise fraught with problems because of its multifaceted nature—we could provide instead a basis for judging whether an action (a project, a policy decision, etc.) might or might not lead to a sustainable result.

And so we come finally to the third type of economic consultant that the local committee might call on. This is an economist who works for a firm with a name like Sustainable Solutions, Inc. The firm comprises a group of professionals accustomed to working together as an interdisciplinary team. Indeed, the first thing this economist says to the committee is that the analysis of the economic and financial aspects of the project has to be integrated with a full and equal cultural value assessment and that this can only be done effectively on a team basis, so that all the ramifications of the project—economic, social, cultural, historical, environmental, and so on—can be taken into consideration. She suggests that the principles of sustainability provide the appropriate set of benchmarks for bringing these concerns together and for guiding the formulation of an optimal restoration strategy.

Broadly, the principles of sustainability that might be particularly relevant to my illustrative example would include the following:

- *Generation of material and nonmaterial benefits.* This principle implies a careful assessment of both the tangible and the intangible benefits, that is, the sorts of effects discussed above that would be measured in a comprehensive economic evaluation of the project.
- *Intergenerational equity.* A key principle of sustainability is the need to recognize the ethical responsibility of the present generation to care for resources in a manner that does not compromise the welfare of future generations; thus, for example, in

adding up the time-stream of benefits and costs generated by a project in the future, more weight should be given to more distant outcomes than might be warranted in a purely commercially oriented assessment. In other words, this principle suggests leaning toward long-term nurturing of resources rather than short-term exploitation for immediate gains.

- *Intragenerational equity.* Society recognizes a principle of fairness in the distribution of access to income and wealth among the present generation, a principle often neglected or sidelined in the pursuit of economic efficiency. As a component of sustainability, this principle indicates in the present example that the project's equity effects would be considered, for example, by asking whether the direct benefits of the project are equally accessible to all social groups in the community.

- *Precautionary principle.* This principle states that decisions leading to irreversible change should not be taken lightly but rather that an added duty of care is imposed if, for example, a major structural modification were proposed that could not be undone if it were subsequently found to have been misguided.

- *Diversity and the interconnectedness of systems.* In a sense the whole concept of sustainability can be encapsulated in this principle, which asserts that a holistic view is required, recognizing that all elements of any system are interconnected in some way. In the present case, the principle suggests that the various dimensions of the local committee's heritage project—its economic, social, cultural, and environmental effects—cannot be treated in isolation and that no one dimension can be privileged over any other. In particular, the principle implies that a complete evaluation would try to come to grips with both interpretations of value, economic and cultural; if successful, this process would enable identification of whether and to what extent an assessment of the economic value incorporating both use and nonuse values might fall short of a full understanding of the cultural significance of the project.

It need hardly be added that the sort of investigations that would be required to provide a comprehensive sustainability analysis of a given heritage project along these lines, paying attention to all the considerations discussed above, would be both more extensive and more complex than, say, a simple financial assessment. Indeed, the application of these ideas to real cultural heritage projects is still in its infancy. A recent research project undertaken at the Getty Conservation Institute has clarified a number of the problems involved, especially in regard to the assessment of value interpreted from economic and noneconomic perspectives, the treatment of heritage as cultural capital, and the principles of sustainability that are relevant to conservation decisions. But full-scale empirical applications undertaken on a multidisciplinary basis have yet to appear; to an economist, such applications could be very useful, for example, in highlighting both the strengths and the shortcomings of economic evaluations involving contingent valuation and other assessment methods.

To conclude, we might ask, what hope is there for the local committee in our example, indeed for the thousands of such coalitions of community interests around the globe that are confronted with similar problems of how to conserve cultural resources in a world increasingly subservient to the demands of the marketplace? I have suggested here that the related concepts of sustainability and of cultural capital can provide a way forward in integrating the economic and the cultural ramifications of conservation decisions, in the same way that ideas about sustainable development have proved so powerful in allowing the economic use of natural resources to be seen in a broader ecological context. In the analysis of sustainability and cultural capital, much theoretical progress has been made. What is now urgently needed is a more extensive empirical testing of these propositions in real-world applications.

Notes

1 For a recent reassessment, see Mason and de la Torre (2000).

2 The relationship between the economy and natural ecosystems is dealt with in the emerging subdiscipline of ecological economics, in which sustainability is a central concept (see, e.g., Costanza 1991). For a sociological view, see the treatment of social capital summarized in Dasgupta and Serageldin (2000). For the relationship between sustainability and culture, see Throsby (1997; 2001:chap. 3).

3 See Hausman (1993); for a critical assessment from an economic viewpoint, see Portney et al. (1994).

4 The full report of this study is contained in Throsby and O'Shea (1980); for a summary, see Throsby (1982).

5 Remember that *economic value* here refers to the value as measured by economic analysis, including both tangible and intangible benefits, expressed in monetary terms. *Cultural value* is more difficult to define, as it is multidimensional and lacks a common unit of account. For some ramifications of notions of value in conservation, see the contributions in Avrami, Mason, and de la Torre (2000).

6 The familiar definition of "sustainable development" that was put forward by the Brundtland Commission may be found in WCED (1987:43).

References

Avrami, E., R. Mason, and M. de la Torre, eds. 2000. *Values and Heritage Conservation.* Los Angeles: Getty Conservation Institute.

Costanza, R., ed. 1991. *Ecological Economics: The Science and Management of Sustainability.* New York: Columbia University Press.

Dasgupta, P., and I. Serageldin, eds. 2000. *Social Capital: A Multi-faceted Perspective.* Washington, D.C.: World Bank.

Hausman, J. A., ed. 1993. *Contingent Valuation: A Critical Assessment.* Amsterdam: North Holland.

Kling, R., C. Revier, and K. Sable. 2000. Estimating the public good value of preserving a local historic landmark. Paper presented at the 11th International Conference on Cultural Economics, Minneapolis, 28–31 May.

Mason, R., and M. de la Torre. 2000. Heritage conservation and values in globalizing societies. In UNESCO, *Cultural Diversity, Conflict and Pluralism, World Culture Report 2000,* 164–79. Paris: UNESCO.

Mourato, S., and A. Danchev. 1999. Preserving cultural heritage in transition economies: A contingent valuation study of Bulgarian monasteries. Paper presented at the ICCROM Forum, Valuing Heritage, Beyond Economics, Rome, 30 September–2 October.

Pollicino, M., and D. Maddison. 2001. Valuing the benefits of cleaning Lincoln Cathedral. *Journal of Cultural Economics* 25:131–48.

Portney, P. R., et al. 1994. Contributions to the symposium Contingent Valuation. *Journal of Economic Perspectives* 8(4):3–64.

Santagata, W., and G. Signorello. 2000. Contingent valuation of a cultural public good and policy design: The case of "Napoli Musei Aperti." *Journal of Cultural Economics* 24:181–204.

Throsby, D. 1982. Social and economic benefits from regional investment in arts facilities: Theory and application. *Journal of Cultural Economics* 6:1–14.

Throsby, D. 1997. Sustainability and culture: Some theoretical issues. *International Journal of Cultural Policy* 4:7–20.

Throsby, D. 2001. *Economics and Culture.* Cambridge: Cambridge University Press.

Throsby, D., and M. O'Shea. 1980. *The Regional Economic Impact of the Mildura Arts Centre.* Research Paper No. 210. Sydney: Macquarie University, School of Economic and Financial Studies.

World Commission on Environment and Development (WCED). 1987. *Our Common Future.* Oxford: Oxford University Press.

The Links between Historic Preservation and Sustainability: An Urbanist's Perspective

John C. Keene

HUMAN SOCIETY HAS EMBARKED on a course that will bring us into collision with the capacity of our natural systems to sustain us. Those involved in historic preservation and cultural conservation can work to ameliorate some of the contributing causes to the unsustainability of metropolitan areas across the world.

Sustainability: Definition and Substantive Content

In the United States, the roots of concern about the impacts of human civilization on the natural environment extend far back into our history. The Progressive movement of the late nineteenth and early twentieth century, the muckrakers, the Regional Planning Association of America, the planners and lawyers who began the city planning movement in the United States in the first decade of the last century, the garden city movement, the Tennessee Valley Authority, and the other environmental initiatives of the New Deal—all stand as antecedents to the environmental movement that burst on the American scene in 1970 with the signing of the National Environmental Policy Act on January 1 and the first Earth Day on April 22 (Scott 1969).

But the recognition of the serious and growing impacts of human activities on the environment and the development of the concept of sustainability as we now know it first became widespread in the 1970s. The Club of Rome's *Limits of Growth*, published in 1972, sounded a widely heard warning (Meadows et al. 1972). The United Nations instituted its Environment Program in 1972, and the Cocoyoc Declaration in 1974 recognized that humanity was at a critical turning point. The declaration stated: "Environmental degradation and the rising pressure on resources raise the question whether the 'outer limits' of the planet's physical integrity may not be at risk" (cited in Friedman 1992:2). Satisfying the basic needs of the world's poor was proclaimed more important than simple growth maximization.

The General Assembly of the United Nations established the World Commission on Environment and Development (WCED) in 1983. Its report, *Our Common Future*, articulated the widely quoted definition of sustainability: "Sustainable development is development that meets the

needs of the present without compromising the ability of future generations to meet their own needs" (WCED 1987:8).

The United Nations Conference on Environment and
Development (the Earth Summit) in Rio de Janeiro in 1992 was an important and influential international conference. It adopted two major documents. The Rio Declaration recognized that social equity must coexist
with economic development and called on the polluting nations to contribute to cleaning up the environment. President George W. Bush
recently refused to implement the Kyoto Accord, which grew out of the
Rio Declaration, much to the consternation of the leaders of the
European Community. The second major document, *Agenda 21*, formu-
lated a full set of goals and more than one hundred twenty strategies for
achieving them. Again, it recognized that "[h]umanity stands at a defining
moment in history. We are confronted with a perpetuation of disparities
between and within nations, a worsening of poverty, hunger, ill health and
illiteracy, and the continuing deterioration of the ecosystems on which we
depend for our well-being" (Sitarz 1993:28). The 1996 Habitat II Conference in Istanbul continued that line of thinking and confirmed that social
equity and human resource development are essential components of a
truly sustainable development process.

We have come to understand that we must find a way to promote
technological innovation, social learning, and social change that increases
social equity. We must bring our patterns of production, reproduction,
consumption, and disposal in concert with the capacity of the ecological
system to perform life-giving functions over the long run. We must find
ways to renew the raw materials that we use to generate energy and produce goods, to recycle more successfully, and to absorb the wastes we produce without jeopardizing fundamental natural balances. This is what we
mean by sustainable development.

As urban conservationists, the field of concern to us can be conceived of as the intersection of four areas:

(1) the culture and social institutions through which our values
    are transmitted from one generation to the next;
(2) the economic and technological sectors that shape the produc-
    tion and disposition of goods and services, especially the built
    environment;
(3) the legal institutions and planning procedures that give teeth
    to societal norms; and
(4) the built environment that embodies the social and aesthetic
    traditions of the past.

Aldo Leopold (1966:253) observed in *A Sand County Almanac*, with
respect to natural systems, "Land . . . is a fountain of energy flowing
through a circuit of soils, plants, and animals." We can paraphrase
Leopold thus: The economy of man is a flow of energy and materials
through the social, cultural, religious, economic, and legal institutions that
each of our societies has constructed. Clearly, the link between the two is

the energy flow. If we are consuming energy at an unsustainable rate, sooner or later the human economy will collapse.

The historic preservation and cultural conservation movements can be seen as antientropic efforts that seek to maintain variety and difference in both the built environment of buildings and places and the cultural environment of values as they are reflected in distinct societies and neighborhoods. By analogy to natural systems, they can be viewed as maintaining cultural diversity, in much the same way that environmentalists seek to maintain biological diversity. Each monument, each landmark, each site, each urban neighborhood, each city center, each natural setting is a special creation that may be worthy of conservation. Conservationists seek to resist the homogenization of style and culture that results from the overpowering technology of the Internet, communications, television, and other mass media, the cell phone, "big box" commercialism, and the globalization of so many aspects of our twenty-first-century lives.

The Unsustainability of Human Activities

Over the past two centuries, human activities have had an increasingly disruptive impact on the natural ecosystems of every continent. They have thrown a worldwide ecosystem that was once more or less in rough equilibrium into disequilibrium.

The rapid growth in human population, from less than 1 billion in 1800 to 6 billion in 2000, is one of the causes of this disequilibrium. Fortunately, the rate of population growth has declined in recent years, to a little over 80 million per year. Still, we will add another billion people to the world population by the end of 2012.

Technology, whose power and extent are increasing at a rapid rate, enables us to transform the face of the earth, whether by cutting down major parts of our tropical rain forests; consuming nonrenewable resources; discharging large volumes of carbon dioxide, methane, and other "greenhouse gases" that may be contributing to global warming; or polluting the planet's air, water, and soil. The ambient levels of carbon dioxide in the atmosphere have increased from 280 to over 360 parts per million in the past one hundred years. Mean sea level rose 4 to 8 inches in the twentieth century. The polar ice caps are melting. And the earth's average temperature has risen more than 1 degree Fahrenheit in the past one hundred years (U.S. Environmental Protection Agency 2001). The question is one of causation: Are the carbon dioxide levels rising because the earth is getting warmer as a result of receiving more energy from the sun, or is the earth getting warmer because human activities are creating higher levels of the so-called greenhouse gases? More and more scientists are concluding that anthropogenic factors are having at least a discernible influence on global warming.

The increased affluence of at least the first world nations and the upper tier of the peoples of other "worlds" is reflected in rapid increases in per capita consumption of natural resources, energy, and human services and products. If developing countries raise their standards of living, they will also gain increased capacity to consume more material goods and energy, and, because of their large populations, their impacts on the ecosystem will be more dramatic.

Humankind's assault on the natural environment is resulting in a mass extinction of species on a par with the five other mass extinctions that have taken place over the past half billion years, such as the one 65 million years ago caused by the impact of an asteroid that ended the dinosaur age. In fact, E. O. Wilson (1992) estimates that if we do not modify our ways drastically, as many as one-fifth of the world's species may become extinct by 2025 as a result of anthropogenic causes.

I have cited these examples to show that humanity's current course of action, premised on a growing population's pollution of the earth and profligate consumption of nonrenewable resources, is not sustainable and that the current trajectory will lead to a collapse of human society as we now know it within a few centuries.

But what, you may ask, does this have to do with historic preservation and sustainability? What obligations do historic preservationists have? Since there are many causes for our rashly unsustainable course of action, the remedy has many components, some of the most important of which are within the purview of the historic preservation movement. In my view, there are two major areas of appropriate concern. The first addresses the management of the broad processes of development and redevelopment of urban centers in a way that promotes sustainability. The second addresses the specific, economically sound and politically feasible programs for maintaining and rehabilitating the built environment that have come down to us from times past.

Sustainable Approaches to the Conservation of the Built Environment: The Link between Sustainable Development and the Conservation of Urban Settlements and Monuments

With regard to the conservation of historic neighborhoods and city centers, as well as individual monuments and sites of unique natural beauty, we wish to maintain cultural diversity in much the same ways that environmentalists aim to protect biological diversity. We seek to conserve and remediate components of the built environment that were constructed decades or centuries ago and that embody the values and aesthetics of times gone by. The medinas of the Arab world, the medieval walled towns of Europe, the frontier settlements of the United States, the mission towns of Mexico and Peru, even the suburban subdivisions that surround American cities—each constitutes something analogous to a species of urban settlement. While we should guard against making facile comparisons between cultural diversity and biological diversity and against drawing unwarranted conclusions for one field based on findings from the other, the analogy is instructive.

For example, sites such as Morelia in Mexico, New Orleans's French Quarter, Philadelphia's Society Hill, the urban cores of European cities such as Santiago de Compostela, Grasse, and Rothenburg, and the medinas of North African cities such as Fez and Kairouan, just to mention a few places with which I am familiar, communicate to future generations a special aesthetic, a perception of the built environment, a view of the relationships between humankind and our environment, and a tangible, materialized expression of long-treasured values. They also embody substantial material resources. They required energy to build and would consume energy were they to be demolished and replaced with contemporary town sections. The same is true of the infrastructure that serves them.

Thus, both because these urban settlements embody the cultural values of different eras (and thus, to pursue the biological analogy, constitute different species of urban places) and because of the raw materials and energy that went into their construction and maintenance over the years, these historic settlements should be conserved. The same is true of less distinctive urban areas, and, for the same reasons, they should also be conserved. It is this embodiment that links urban conservation and sustainable development (Hawken 1993). However, because resources are limited, the challenge facing the conservation community is to develop a set of strategies and priorities that will permit it to focus its efforts on the conservation of those resources where the benefit-cost ratio is most favorable.

The challenge of maintaining urban resources takes different forms in different societies because the processes of urban development and redevelopment vary from place to place. In the United States, for instance, suburban sprawl and downtown decline have been the dominant mode of metropolitan growth. Whole new communities grow up on the periphery of our metropolitan areas, while the inner cores of our cities lose jobs and residents and their inhabitants are disproportionately poor and belong to minority groups. In North Africa, urban development is characterized by the movement of rural families to the oldest parts of cities and to squatter settlements that are often located near downtown areas—the "habitats spontanés" of the region. In other parts of the world, such as western Europe where national populations are stable or declining, the process of urban development and redevelopment takes still other forms.

To demolish the distinctive neighborhoods that characterize the world's cities and replace them with uniform twenty-first-century settlements is analogous to cutting down a rain forest and replacing it with pasture or monocrop tillage. It reduces cultural diversity and increases entropy.

The Broader Strategy: The U.S. Experience

In the United States, at least since World War II, national urban development policy has focused on promoting suburban sprawl, as have current state and local statutes, economic incentives, and, perhaps, consumer preferences. This policy has been exemplified at the federal level by the interstate highway program, mortgage insurance and guarantees for suburban housing, and federal grants for the construction of suburban water supply, sewerage, and sewage treatment systems. At the metropolitan level, it has taken the form of low-density suburban and exurban residential zoning ordinances designed to encourage sprawling development at the edges of our metropolitan areas and a virtual abandonment of inner-city areas. Local governments have overzoned for industry, underzoned for townhouses, apartments, and mobile homes, restricted large areas to single-family detached housing on lots of one acre or more, and created burdensome and costly subdivision requirements. Their objective is to protect the municipal fisc by limiting new development to commercial and industrial uses and relatively expensive homes, all of which generate tax revenues that more nearly approach their allocated share of municipal expenditures. In many cases at least, they also have the effect of excluding low- and moderate-income families whom they perceive to be a threat.

The policy operates in furtherance of the Norman Rockwellian dream of a young husband and his wife raising their two children in a small house in the suburbs, with the mother busy around the home and the children playing happily in the backyard. But more and more families do not meet this stereotype. With later marriage, fewer children, higher divorce rates, and increased longevity, the number of households composed of a mother and father and children has declined to about 25 percent of the total.

The policy of promoting suburban sprawl produces an unsustainable society. It squanders our precious resources and jeopardizes our nation's ability to compete in the world marketplace. Low-density, dispersed residential development destroys a valuable portion of our capital stock of natural resources, such as prime farmland, temperate forests, and areas of ecological significance. Furthermore, automobile-powered suburban sprawl generates traffic congestion and air pollution and requires inordinate amounts of time to travel to work, school, and shopping centers. Urbanists have come to realize that land use, transportation, and air and water quality (the "LUTRAQ Connection") are intimately interrelated. Distributed patterns of residential development generate more automobile travel. The additional automobile use creates greater emissions of nitrogen oxides (NOx), sulfur oxides (SOx), and particulates, which in turn exacerbate the ground-level ozone problem and acid rain deposition.

In addition, our metropolitan urban development policy raises the cost of the public infrastructure on which the economy is based, in two ways:

1. The centrifugal urban sprawl it spawns requires massive investment in schools, roads, water and sewer systems, sewage treatment plants, and all the other elements of needed infrastructure.
2. The depopulation of our center cities results in abandonment of large areas and an uneconomical underutilization of their vast infrastructure. Many cities have excess water and system capacity. Furthermore, the partially abandoned areas of our older cities lie fallow, and the resources used to construct them serve no public purpose.

In short, we are doubly wasteful: we raise the real cost of providing new homes, commercial facilities, industries, and public buildings to meet the needs of our families and our businesses, and we underutilize the built stock that we have instead of finding ways to reuse it. We raise our costs of production and therefore diminish our capacity to compete in the world economy.

In its starkest form, urban sprawl results in an ever-widening ring of land conversion from agricultural, forest, and other open uses to suburban land uses and the underutilization or abandonment of the housing and infrastructural facilities—to say nothing of the residents of the communities and the human resources they represent—located at the cores of metropolitan areas. Historic preservation, with its emphasis on the conservation and renewal of historic components of our building stock and infrastructure and on the cultures that support their continuation can contribute substantially to the reduction of sprawl and the creation of a more sustainable metropolitan development process.

Sustainable Metropolitan Development: An Alternative to Suburban Sprawl

A sustainable form of metropolitan development, one that seeks to minimize impacts on natural resources on the edge and maximize returns on investments in infrastructure in the center, would limit centrifugal movement and turn development pressures back to the aging cores of metropolitan areas. It would conserve important natural resources such as farm- and forestland and make use of facilities in existing developed areas.

The many undesirable characteristics of suburban sprawl compel us to formulate and implement a different policy for metropolitan development, one that seeks to benefit from the recent efforts to find ways of moving toward sustainability in our national and state policies for land development and environmental protection. Such a policy leads to a steady state in which there is a dynamic redirection of urban development pressures from the edges of metropolitan areas inward to the centers, coupled with a continuous renewal of older suburban sectors as they age. We can conceive of a metropolitan area as consisting of three broad types of sub-areas: the older core areas that were largely built before World War II, the postwar suburbs, and the rural-urban fringe. The shadow of obsolescence moves out from the core and is beginning to affect some of the older, close-in suburbs.

We should seek to reshape national and metropolitan urban development policies so as to create a different pattern of metropolitan development that results in essentially stable, sustainable metropolitan areas, characterized by (1) continuous redevelopment of older urban areas as they age, (2) in-fill development in the interstices of existing suburban areas, and (3) where new development is appropriate on the urban fringe, a pattern of nodes and corridors that creates denser communities while reducing the consumption of farmland, wooded areas, and other valuable resource land.

Such a policy faces a number of substantial hurdles: deteriorated housing stock, poor inner-city school systems, neighborhood crime, relative paucity of rewarding jobs, high real property taxes, Brownfields in need of unascertained levels of remediation, and so on. Yet because of the imperative need for more sustainable development we must find ways to accomplish this objective.

Recommendations of the President's Council on Sustainable Development

The President's Council on Sustainable Development was formed in 1993 and charged with recommending a national action strategy for sustainable development. It issued two major reports: *Sustainable Development: A New Consensus for Prosperity, Opportunity, and a Healthy Environment for the Future* (1996) and *Towards a Sustainable America* (1999). The latter, final report set out major goals and a number of implementation strategies and sought to create a process for generating consensus concerning the need to reshape a wide range of American policies in order to move toward the goal of sustainable development.

Towards a Sustainable America covers several major areas ranging from climate change and environmental management to international issues. The one most relevant for my purposes here concerns metropolitan and rural strategies for sustainable communities. It, in turn, identified five strategic areas of sustainable community development:

1. Green infrastructure: the "network of open space, air sheds, watersheds, woodlands, wildlife habitat, parks, and other natural areas that provides many vital services that sustain life and enrich the quality of life."

2. Land use and development and the desirability of pursuing "smart growth" policies: the congeries of policies that minimizes "urban sprawl, conserves open space, reverses disinvestment in existing communities, respects nature's carrying capacity, increases social interaction, and provides protection from natural hazards."

3. Community revitalization and reinvestment: a natural complement to smart growth, it promotes the "use of local economic, ecological, and social resources and assets, such as undercounted purchasing power, vacant housing stock, transportation access, vacant and underutilized land, and biodiversity."

4. Rural enterprise and community development: also a complement to smart growth, this embraces new strategies such as "community-supported agriculture, organic farming, conservation tillage, forest conservation, ecotourism, and other sustainable enterprises."

5. Materials reuse and resource efficiency: "strategies that conserve resources and minimize waste by retaining, recycling, reusing, and remanufacturing materials." It also includes "deconstruction," the process of systematic dismantling of buildings and the salvage of construction materials and "eco-industrial" parks, such as the one in Cape Charles, Virginia. (President's Council on Sustainable Development 1999:64–66)

Towards a Sustainable America recognized the need to conserve the existing historic stock of buildings and community facilities, to refurbish existing infrastructure, to internalize the applicable real and environmental costs of doing business in our cities, to promote the expanded use of market-based incentives as contrasted to continuing heavy reliance on "command and control" techniques, to explore the use of innovative tax incentives to promote urban conservation and revitalization, and to strengthen community development corporations and other local neighborhood leadership groups. The report also recognized, as have many other thoughtful analyses of smart growth programs, that regional institutions and partnerships should play an important role in the process of growth management because of the larger-than-local nature of most urban development processes.

Conclusion

In the United States, preservation planners must work generally to slow urban sprawl and to encourage the rehabilitation of older urban areas. To do this, they must focus their efforts specifically on using traditional conservation techniques such as historic district and historic landmark ordinances and tax incentives, for example, low- and moderate-income housing and historic preservation tax credits, transferable development rights, and flexible zoning. They should also seek to develop innovative measures, such as those that rely more on market-based incentives than on command-and-control techniques. Such actions will maintain cultural diversity, as well as the traditional built environment, an accomplishment analogous to maintaining biodiversity by preventing the destruction of neighborhoods and buildings that embody the values of different times.

References

Friedman, J. 1992. *Empowerment: The Politics of Alternative Development.* Cambridge, Mass.: Blackwell.

Hawken, P. 1993. *The Ecology of Commerce: A Declaration of Sustainability.* New York: HarperCollins.

Leopold, A. 1966. *A Sand County Almanac.* New York: Ballantine.

Meadows, D. H., D. L. Meadows, J. Randers, and W. W. Behrens III. 1972. *The Limits of Growth.* New York: Universe Books.

Newman, P., and J. Kenworthy. 1999. *Sustainability and Cities: Overcoming Automobile Dependence.* Washington, D.C.: Island Press.

Pezzoli, K. 1996. Sustainable development: A transdisciplinary overview of the literature. Paper presented at the annual meeting of the Association of Collegiate Schools of Planning, Toronto.

President's Council on Sustainable Development. 1996. *Sustainable Development: A New Consensus for Prosperity, Opportunity, and a Healthy Environment for the Future.* Washington, D.C.: U.S. Government Printing Office.

President's Council on Sustainable Development. 1999. *Towards a Sustainable America (Final Report).* Washington, D.C.: U.S. Government Printing Office.

Scott, M. 1969. *American City Planning since 1890.* Berkeley: University of California Press.

Sitarz, D., ed. 1993. *Agenda 21: The Earth Summit Strategy to Save Our Planet.* Boulder, Colo.: Earth Press.

U.S. Environmental Protection Agency. 2001. *Global Warming Site.* http://www.epa.gov/global warming/climate/index.html

Wilson, E. O. 1992. *The Diversity of Life.* New York: W. W. Norton.

World Commission on Environment and Development (WCED). 1987. *Our Common Future (The Brundtland Report).* New York: Oxford University Press.

PART TWO

Framing Sustainability: The Promise and the Paradox of Conservation

Cultural Landscape, Sustainability, and Living with Change?

Graham Fairclough

T HE CULTURAL LANDSCAPE IS CENTRAL to the debate about managing change. It is entirely the product of change and of the changing interplay of human and natural processes; our intellectual and spiritual responses to it are ever-changing; its components (tree cover, hedges, land cover) are seminatural living things, changing daily and with the seasons. Change, both past and ongoing, is one of its principal attributes, fundamental to its present character. There is no question of arresting change.

Change needs to be managed, however. Conservation should not merely be change's witness but a central part of its very process, the better to direct it sustainably. Conservation is not the "outside" activity it once was, no longer merely a fight to save fragments of the past from somebody else's bulldozer of progress. In part because of sustainable development, it is becoming socially embedded. For future historians, "conservation" will be one of the processes that shaped the world of the twenty-first century, much as prehistorians find social and symbolic factors as well as economic ones to explain the European Bronze Age.

My point of view is that of an archaeologist, seeing human actions as the most significant factor that has shaped the whole of the landscape across centuries or millennia. Landscape is a complex artifact from which we can learn about both the past and the present. I regard landscape as an idea rather than a thing, however—an idea constructed from a mixture of knowledge, interpretation, and perception. But knowledge is always partial, interpretation always provisional, and perceptions personal, qualified by experience or self-interest, memory or imagination. Attributing significance to cultural landscape is therefore not straightforward.

Managing Change in the Historic Environment

My premise here is that conservation should seek to manage change everywhere within the historic environment, as well as to protect the "best" parts. This is a particularly necessary perspective for the cultural landscape, which is a dynamic, living set of complex systems that must have room for change if part of its character is not to be lost (Fairclough, Lambrick, and McNab 1999). But managing change should also be the objective for conserving sites and monuments. Places protected as "monuments," set aside from everyday life and preserved for research, education, or tourism (for example, Guardianship Monuments in state ownership in England, which had their heyday in the early days of conservation), will always be a minority. The majority of the historic environment is in everyday use, and this means accepting that a consequence of continued use is continued change. Continued use of the historic environment might mean putting buildings to new uses, or changing urban areas through regeneration, or farming land in new ways and so creating "new" landscape.

This is not an argument that only economic values matter but the opposite. There are numerous ways to value the historic environment: amenity, aesthetics, environmental, academic, educational, and local. All these ways are based to a greater or lesser degree on nonmonetary calculations. The social, personal, environmental, emotional, or psychological benefits of caring for the historic environment are probably worth more to society than economic gains from replacing it. These thoughts were clarified in the early 1990s when English Heritage, the government agency in England charged with promoting understanding and conservation of the whole historic environment, published its views on sustainability and the historic environment (English Heritage 1997), and it has again been central to the recent review that produced Power of Place (Historic Environment Review 2000a).

Nor is accepting the need for change an argument that all or any change is acceptable. For the historic environment, sustainability means controlling change and choosing directions that capitalize most effectively on the inheritance from the past. In any decision about change and about the impact of the future on the remains of the past, therefore, we should be conscious of two separate questions: (1) how to reconcile minimizing loss with the needs of the present and (2) how to ensure that the balance we strike does not reduce too greatly our successors' options for understanding and enjoying their inheritance. What is enough to keep for our purposes? How much might the future need?

A central concept of sustainable development, therefore, is "enough-ness." We cannot pass on everything that we inherited completely unchanged, because "everything" encompasses our whole environment, which we need to use and adapt, and anyway we have some obligation to leave our own mark, to add to history. What is most important—and achievable—is that somehow we leave our successors with the ability to know their own past, to assess its significance for themselves, to decide for themselves how to live with its remains and what to pass on in their turn. This means leaving them enough of the historic environment, either unchanged or with reversible changes, to make their own choices.

Conservation is therefore about passing on options. We cannot know what the future will want to keep, but we can seek to pass on enough to allow future generations to make their own decisions, and to not close too many doors for them. As always, however, "enough" is hard to calculate, especially in relation to the historic environment, which is all-embracing, our whole habitat, the source of our identity. Can there ever be enough?

The reassessment of conservation theory that was prompted by new ideas on sustainability confirmed the need for two parallel approaches to determining enough-ness. There is a need to keep mechanisms of selective preservation, which characterized the early evolution of conservation in England, but these mechanisms need to work alongside a broader-based approach designed to manage change sustainably in every part of the historic environment.

The treatment of archaeological sites in England demonstrates these two approaches to conservation and their relationship. A selective protection system is well established—"scheduling," a legal designation deriving ultimately from the United Kingdom's first Ancient Monuments Act, enacted in 1882. It protects a minority of sites (less than 10 percent) where permanent preservation is considered feasible, largely arresting change in a representative sample of monuments that are judged to form a core of enough-ness, at least for academic and scientific purposes. In parallel, however, a wider, more flexible approach has been developing since the 1970s and 1980s as part of the spatial planning system; this approach was codified and made universal in 1990 in government instructions to local authorities known as Planning Policy Guidance (PPG) (DOE 1973, 1990). It allows for any archaeological remains to be taken into account in designing new developments, to achieve full preservation, modification, or excavation. This pioneering PPG pushed to the forefront of conservation the ambition of managing change everywhere.

Seeking to manage change throughout the historic environment has the advantage of drawing conservation into a much wider field. Selective designation protects relatively few monuments and has tended to limit conservation to a few specific fields such as monuments and buildings, or to small parts of the landscape but never the whole. Within these fields, conservation has been further restricted to a sample: the most admired designed gardens, the "best" architectural set pieces, the most visible archaeological sites (Fairclough 1999a).

On the other hand, trying to manage change everywhere without necessarily a presumption of preservation allows any aspect of the historic environment to be taken into account and everything inherited from the past to be given some level of consideration when change is planned. A wide variety of perspectives is needed (purely scientific or expert views are rarely enough), and one of conservation's future roles could be to facilitate the formulation and exchange of views on significance. This ought to lead to a more democratic, inclusive approach, promoting stronger common cultural ownership and protecting the locally valued throughout the wider cultural landscape.

The Impact of Sustainable Development on Conservation Theory: Ten Years since Rio

England

Many European governments have produced national strategies for sustainable development since Rio. The current U.K. Sustainable Development Strategy is called "A Better Quality of Life" because the focus of sustainability has shifted from the purely environmental to the social. It defines sustainable development as the combination of three mutually supporting factors: economic (development), social (communities), and environmental (managing impact on natural and cultural resources). Undue prominence may still be given to economic aims, but recognition of social and environmental aspects has gained ground, and cultural matters are coming to be recognized as fundamental.

The basic aim of sustainable development is to pass on a renewable system to the future. This concept works for global ecosystem issues, for which it was designed. The issues are different for the historic environment. The material, physical components of heritage are nonrenewable (a building or an archaeological site once lost is gone forever without the possibility of authentic replacement), and in this sense sustainability is not applicable.

When English Heritage started to think about sustainable development in 1992, there was still a widely held misconception that it was a "green" issue without relevance to heritage, because heritage is finite and nonrenewable. Looking hard at the applicability of sustainable development to the historic environment, however, drew thinking away from the physicality of the heritage, and its intrinsic or inherent values, toward people's relationship with it and toward how it is culturally defined and evaluated in multiple ways. At the same time, an emerging view of the historic environment began to recognize that it exists everywhere, not just at special places, and that it can be regarded in some respects as infinite and renewable. These shifts in thinking began to make the principles of sustainability more relevant, and two linked ways forward were identified.

The first way was one of scale, viewing the historic environment as a whole, not as separate sites, and preferably at a large scale, such as landscape or city. On that basis, managing change (balancing gains and losses) becomes practical. There is room for serious, constructive debate about which combination of elements, what overall character, to pass on to the future as a sort of cultural ecosystem.

The second was one of significance: here, the renewable system is regarded as our perception and evaluation of the historic environment rather than the material heritage itself. This also means that it is possible to treat the historic environment as a renewable resource. New heritage (i.e., late-twentieth-century heritage, new landscapes of intensive agriculture, the physical remains of postindustrialization, the archaeology of the motor car, cold war sites) is constantly being made or discovered. More important, "old" heritage is continually remade, changed, and modified, and its significance is reconstructed under the influence of new perspectives, new participants, and new politics.

Thinking at a landscape scale played a large part in the development of English Heritage's ideas about sustainability during the 1990s, but so did the issues of integrated management, spatial planning, quality of life, and landscape (Fairclough 1995). *Conservation Issues in Strategic Plans* (Countryside Commission, English Heritage, and English Nature 1993) and *Conservation Issues in Local Plans* (English Heritage, Countryside Commission, and English Nature 1996), for example, were two volumes of guidance for local planning authorities, produced jointly by England's conservation agencies. They promoted the integration of all aspects of conservation (e.g, archaeological, architectural, aesthetic, ecological) and the incorporation of conservation into all spatial planning policies, not merely as separate policies concerned with protection as an end in itself.

They were also among the first works to start defining what sustainable development means in practical terms for conservation. They explored concepts such as environmental capacity and thresholds, although in terms of an ultimately flawed attempt to use the metaphor of environmental capital by identifying "critical" and "constant" capital of all types. In use, "critical" rapidly came to mean merely nationally important sites, and "constant" came to be seen as disposable assets; introducing a third category, "tradeable," did not rescue the concept.

Debate has now moved on, largely through two projects—one developing a theory of sustainability that was of special relevance to cultural and historic resources and the other defining the concept of quality of life capital as a practical tool kit for identifying and evaluating environmental capital. English Heritage's Historic Landscape Characterisation program was developed in parallel and is described later.

Sustaining the Historic Environment (English Heritage 1997) was the product of the first of these two projects and of a more focused look at how sustainable development related to archaeology and the historic environment, particularly the landscape. Just as the general ideas on sustainable development were becoming more widely accepted, it highlighted for the heritage sector several issues that were central to achieving sustainable development:

- a concern for the present, not the past per se
- an emphasis on the role of people and participation in evaluation and decisions
- numerous ways of seeing multiple value and significance, including cultural (identity, distinctiveness, place), educational and academic (informational, evidential), economic, resource (environmental footprints), recreational (life, enjoyment), and aesthetic
- a focus on the value of the local and the commonplace as much as the exceptional
- the promotion of the idea of managing change everywhere

Its key principles—restated in the more recent *Power of Place* (Historic Environment Review 2000a)—were the need for

- increased understanding and awareness of the whole of the historic environment
- the need to take a long-term view of actions
- greater public involvement in environmental decision making
- awareness of different scales (at that time, critical, constant, tradeable, but also regional/local, landscape/place)
- recognition that where possible change should be reversible
- informed decisions, that is, a precautionary approach

Although issued as a discussion paper, *Sustaining the Historic Environment* generated substantial support and wide acceptance but little discussion, because it was treated from the first largely as a definitive policy statement to guide action (Fairclough 1999c). Its main proposals and views formed the basis for much of the thinking in *Power of Place* and thereafter in the government response, *The Historic Environment: A Force for the Future* (DCMS/DETR 2001).

The concept "quality of life capital" grew out of the early thinking on environmental capital, which despite its immaturity had laid the ground for a new methodology. This was loosely characterized under the slogan "What Matters and Why," another version of the enough-ness question (see Countryside Commission, English Nature, and English Heritage 1997). The new approach was based on the idea of attributes, or *affordances*. This approach looks less at the inherent qualities of a place or a thing than at the services, attributes, and values that it provides for people, thus taking into account a multiplicity of value systems. It was tested in a series of regional pilots by a variety of bodies at different scales and summarized in a detailed methodology. Two application guides (to help manage change on individual sites and prepare spatial plans) have been published under the title *Quality of Life Capital* (Countryside Agency et al. 2001) to emphasize the shift in focus toward the social and to connect to the U.K. Sustainable Development Strategy.

The *Power of Place* report brought all these ideas together in a highly focused look at the future of the historic environment. It was the report of a national review of all policies relating to the historic environment, carried out for the government during 2000 by English Heritage by a widely representative national steering group, five working groups, two consultations (Historic Environment Review 2000b), and extensive opinion polling (MORI 2000). The review was carried out for the heritage and related sectors, with representatives of property owners, developers, and business and community groups as well as conservationists.

The final report is a vision of the future of the historic environment based on recognizing its central contribution to society and the economy. Its starting point is evidence from extensive opinion surveys that most people care greatly about the historic environment. They regard it as an essential part of life and identity, crucial to quality of life and health. They wish to see it protected and used sustainably, for education, for tourism, and to improve the everyday setting of their lives. Many of *Power of Place*'s messages are about how to ensure broader popular and democratic inclusion in the decisions that dictate its care and use. It emphasizes that good understanding of the whole historic environment is needed if change is to be managed sustainably.

European Context

Parallel approaches exist across Europe. Two examples give a flavor of this wider background, before we look briefly at some pan-European frameworks.

In Scotland, a consultation report titled *Passed to the Future: Sustaining the Historic Environment* (Historic Scotland 2002) argued that sustainable use of the historic environment requires

- recognition of the value of the historic environment to society, not only for economic, educational, and quality of life reasons, but also for identity, sense of place, and local diversity/distinctiveness, and biodiversity;
- good stewardship (identifying the resource's *capacity for use*, ensuring that reuse, adaptation, and new design are of a *high quality*);
- working together (*participation*, maximizing everyone's contribution and ensuring democratic access to decision making); and
- assessing impact (knowing the long-term effect of decisions and avoiding change whose effects are unknown).

In the Netherlands, the Belvedere Memorandum examines the relationship of cultural heritage to spatial planning and promotes the idea of "conservation through development," that is, managing change (Netherlands State Government 1999). It recognizes the significance of cultural heritage at various levels: identity and sense of purpose, a source of information, ecological and economic importance, and as part of the defense (a "backlash") against globalization. It aims to ensure that cultural heritage is "consistently and coherently involved in the use of public space" by focusing on design and development, using cultural heritage as a source of inspiration for design, and integrating it with recreation, tourism, water management, and other factors in plans for new development (Hallewas 2002).

Of the many pan-European frameworks that exist, three examples should suffice. The first is the Council of Europe's Helsinki Declaration. It sets out a series of principles as common reference points and lists the attributes of the cultural heritage that could contribute to sustainable development and to economic wealth (Council of Europe 1996). It identifies the need for cross-sector strategies and collaboration; the interrelationship of the state, public authorities, and the voluntary sector; and the scientific and educational use of the cultural heritage.

The most recent Europe-wide statement on spatial planning and sustainability is contained in the European Union's *European Spatial Development Perspective (ESDP)* (European Union 2000). This is a "nonbinding framework for national and regional planning" designed to improve economic and social cohesion, sustainable development, and balanced competitiveness across Europe. It has three objectives: a balanced and polycentric urban system, parity of access to infrastructure and knowledge, and prudent management and development of the natural and cultural heritage. It tends, unfortunately, to view cultural heritage only in terms of management and protection, as self-centered rather than as an integral part of the other objectives, but this should improve as the *ESDP*'s ideas are put into practice.

The *ESDP* is already becoming the foundation of more detailed regional approaches. NorVision, covering the North Sea parts of Norway, Sweden, Denmark, Germany, the Netherlands, and the United Kingdom (NorVision 2000), presents itself as a regional specification for putting the *ESDP* into practice, identifying nine key themes, including the "controlled use" of valuable natural and cultural landscapes, not limited to those formally protected. The perspective is predominantly natural, however, seeking to establish the sustainable coexistence of nature conservation with human activities, as if the landscape were not already the product of such interaction.

Finally, the *European Landscape Convention* (Council of Europe 2000), published and opened for signature in Florence in October 2000 and not yet in force, is set firmly in the context of sustainable development. This new convention states clearly the need for better care of the landscape, based on its contribution to cultural diversity and an overriding emphasis on democratic participation. The convention acknowledges that the quality and diversity of European landscapes are a common resource of wide public interest, a basic component of European heritage, and favorable to economic activity and jobs, all claims that connect directly to the sustainability debate. It believes that proper care and appreciation of the landscape will create unity across Europe, safeguard our common heritage, consolidate European identity, form local cultures, and improve the quality of life for people everywhere (Déjeant-Pons 2002).

Most usefully, the convention defines landscape very simply: "an area, as perceived by people, whose character is the result of the action and interaction of natural and/or human factors." It emphasizes that landscape exists everywhere and that it covers the entire territory (natural, rural, urban and peri-urban, land, inland water, and marine areas and areas of special significance as well as those that are everyday, ordinary, or degraded). It refers not only to the so-called designed landscape, but to all features that, directly or indirectly, have been created by people's actions and decisions—in a word, the "cultural landscape." Finally, it calls on European states to study, understand, and assess their landscapes as a starting point for managing change.

Diversity of Meaning: More than One View of the Cultural Landscape

"Cultural landscape" is not a new term, but it still does not have a single meaning. Most definitions, however, include the concept of people and nature interacting (e.g., the Florence Convention; the World Heritage criteria; Bennett 1996; Droste, Plachter, and Rössler 1995; Hajós 1999), and the Florence definition is as good as any. Perhaps there is no need for definition to go any further; beyond that, there are simply different viewpoints and assumptions. As long as everyone's assumptions are clearly laid out, we can all work together.

As an archaeologist, I am convinced by training and philosophy that the landscape's most important aspect is the time-depth of human activity and above all the presence of the human past. Most other uses of the term seem to me to ignore the contribution of culture and time-depth to the landscape and the extent to which even events several thousand years old can still be read in the landscape. This seems especially so where the appearance of an area depends on a picturesque, apparently timeless (but usually quite recent), and preferably threatened (and thus not threatening) lifestyle. In describing such lifestyles, the word *traditional* is often used as a shortcut to a series of powerful but unhelpful myths that lie at the heart of the sentimental view of cultural landscape: harmony with nature, the noble savage (or at least the dignified peasant), even Edens (candidates for the World Heritage List). These myths romanticize nonmodern, usually rural lifestyles that are too often now almost entirely unsustainable; in doing this, they prevent real engagement with the cultural landscape as the historic dimension of the real world.

The sentimental view of cultural landscape can also exclude landscapes that have seen a great deal of change. They are seen as damaged, or as aberrations, because they do not show harmony. In reality (in my reality, anyway), such landscapes include some of the best examples of cultural landscapes, those that most clearly demonstrate human interaction with nature. It would seem that just enough cultural interaction creates "good" landscapes, worthy of the World Heritage List; too much produces landscapes waiting only to be redeveloped. This is another dimension of the enough-ness issue. When has enough change occurred to make a landscape unworthy of care? When has there been enough survival to create a landscape worth keeping?

The same problem arises in the evaluation of historic buildings if primacy is given to art historical values rather than to historic significance. "It is too altered to be listed" is sometimes heard in England about a building that has been changed from the architect's original intention even if the alterations reflect historic and social changes. This ignores the maxim that buildings are never finished, merely started. For buildings, moreover, it is sometimes possible to know the architect's intention; in contrast, there is rarely a knowable starting point for the landscape, and the search for the unspoiled seems even more futile.

This perspective has of course been presented here with some exaggeration but still short of caricature. It is an ahistorical perspective, and the study and conservation of cultural landscape needs a strong archaeological basis as a corrective to it. The use of archaeology—interpreted most broadly as a set of theory and methods for reading material culture, whether deposits, buildings, artifacts, or the landscape—is in any case essential because so much of the landscape's story was never documented in historical sources, even in "historic" periods. But it is also necessary because archaeologists bring to cultural landscape an understanding of time-depth and long-term processes. The cultural landscape is usually seen in terms of space and geography. But its principal dimensions are actually time and history, diversity (the young and the old, the grand and the ordinary, the widespread and the localized), and process (creation and change), all of which are the raw material of archaeological practice (Fairclough 1999b).

Theory into Practice: Historic Landscape Characterisation and Managing Change

Establishing Historic Landscape Characterisation in England

The need for archaeological perspectives on the landscape prompted the establishment by English Heritage of the Historic Landscape Characterisation (HLC) program. The ideas that underpinned this were developed in parallel with the work on sustainability and integration described above.

One of the first steps was a research program in 1993–94 to review the philosophy and theory of landscape conservation and current methods of studying historic landscape. It proposed a methodology of assessment and characterization at county scale, borrowing some techniques from landscape architects (Countryside Commission 1993). Its conclusions, and a description of the first years of implementation, were published as *Yesterday's World, Tomorrow's Landscape,* a title chosen to emphasize that landscape conservation is concerned with managing change and looking forward (Fairclough, Lambrick, and McNab 1999).

This project was supported by English Heritage's simultaneous collaboration with the Countryside Commission, the national agency responsible at that time for landscape preservation. We helped the Countryside Commission to write *Views from the Past,* their statement on the historic dimension of the landscape (Countryside Commission 1994, 1996). We were also involved with the Countryside Commission's Countryside Character Map project and English Nature's Natural Areas equivalent. This produced a national map as the basis for starting to take decisions about the direction of future change. It divided England into 159 discrete areas (Countryside Agency 1999; Countryside Commission 1998), each characterized at the national scale in terms of scenic, natural, and historic attributes. Further work is now adding a more detailed layer, with more than 2,100 subareas, sharing about 75 types, moving closer to the level of detail that HLC uses.

Successful integration, however, requires each component to be firmly grounded before it can be integrated with others. In addition to joint work, therefore, English Heritage carried out its own separate work on landscape, as it had on sustainability, and for the same reasons. This separate work produced an atlas with a national perspective similar to the Countryside Character Map, and created Historic Landscape Characterisation to be carried out at the county level.

The *Atlas* includes a "character area"–based assessment of the whole country, using the pattern of historic settlement (Roberts and Wrathmell 2000). Although based on mid-nineteenth-century maps and census data, the patterns revealed in the *Atlas* (three large provinces with twenty-eight subprovinces) are proving to be of very early origin, and recognizable in the landscape's overall pattern for more than one thousand years. The work formed part of English Heritage's Monuments Protection Programme, which carries out national thematic evaluations of archaeology and the historic environment as the basis for managing change or designation. The *Atlas* therefore has a number of benefits: it is a serious research tool (a companion synoptic volume has since been published;

Roberts and Wrathnell 2002), a supplement to the Countryside Character Map, a context for designation, and a framework for understanding county-scale Historic Landscape Characterisation.

HLC is a national program established between 1994 and 1999, following the *Yesterday's World, Tomorrow's Landscape* project and *Views from the Past*. It is still in progress but is approaching a halfway point (see Fig. 1); it may be completed by 2008. HLC maps are made at the county level—areas small enough to keep a reasonably detailed level of work, yet large enough to have a big picture and to keep a landscape, not a site, perspective. They fit into the higher-level frameworks mentioned earlier (the Countryside Character Map, the English Heritage Settlement Atlas, and the European Landscape Convention) and in turn provide frameworks for local studies or archaeological and architectural site data.

Figure 1
Progress with national program of county-based HLC projects as of December 2002. Drawn by Vince Griffin, English Heritage.

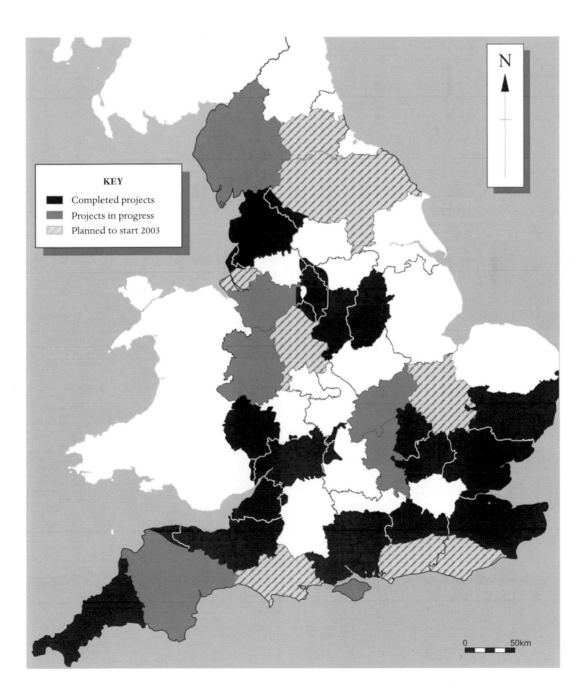

HLC creates for the first time in England a detailed view of the archaeological, historic, and cultural interest of all of a county's landscape (see Fig. 2, Color Plate 1). It is a new, albeit first-draft, understanding of the archaeological and historic aspects of all present-day landscape. The maps also have the benefit of emphasizing the landscape of the past few centuries that are too often overlooked or dismissed. HLC maps will also become benchmarks for measuring future change, as they are topical snapshots of the landscape's character and our reaction to it.

Like the *Atlas,* HLC serves many purposes (see Fairclough 1999d:pt. 2; Fairclough 2002a; Fairclough, Lambrick, and Hopkins 2002; Herring 1998; and individual HLC project reports). Each county-based project is carried out for English Heritage by local government archaeological services as part of their Sites and Monuments Records (SMRs), an example of the national-local partnerships that underpin the successes of the

Figure 2

Lancashire HLC: Geographic Information System printout using a "Broad Types" classification, an entry level to the GIS. Produced by Joy Ede and John Darlington; English Heritage/Lancashire County Council. *(See also Color Plate 1.)*

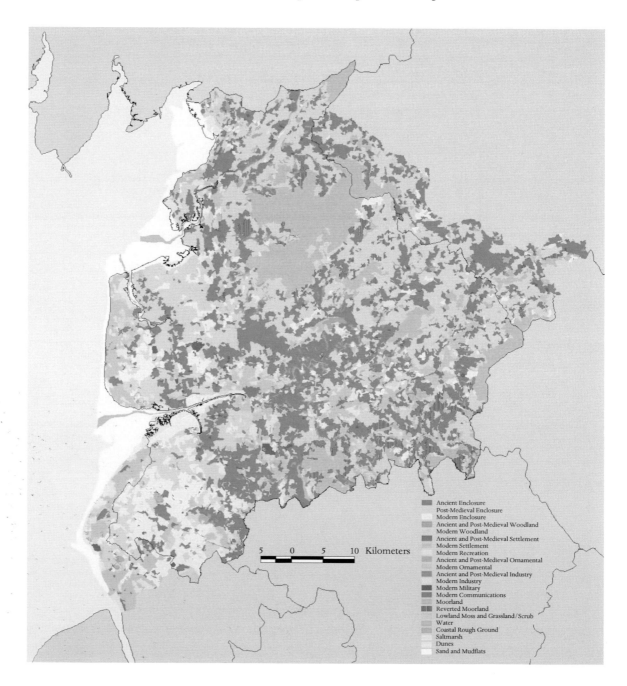

British system. With other layers of the SMRs, HLC is therefore a central component of historic environment conservation and spatial planning. It creates a freestanding landscape assessment that is focused exclusively on the archaeological and historic aspects of landscape. It does this, however, in a way that for the first time allows the historic and archaeological appreciation of the landscape to be properly integrated with other scenic assessments to create practical landscape assessments and action plans (e.g., Lancashire's Landscape Strategy [Lancashire County Council 2001]).

Historic Landscape Characterisation in Europe

The European Landscape Convention encourages other countries to develop ways of understanding and managing their cultural landscape (Fairclough and Rippon 2002:chaps. 2, 3). There is also a ten-country European Union–funded Culture 2000 program—European Pathways to the Cultural Landscape (EPCL)—that is carrying out twelve projects to explore ways to understand the cultural landscape in different national contexts, as well as try to introduce more people to it through both real or virtual "pathways" (see Fairclough and Rippon 2002:chaps. 12, 16, 19). A few examples of how other European countries are dealing with the cultural landscape follow.

In Denmark, *valuable cultural environments*, that is, geographically delineated areas that reflect essential traces of the development of society, such as whole villages, towns, or harbors, or individual elements, such as buildings, hedges, or roads, are being defined by charting attributes such as time, landform, and theme (e.g., agriculture) to identify characteristic or rare examples of each combination (DFNA 2002; Stoumann 2002). The Belvedere Memorandum in the Netherlands also incorporates assessment at landscape scale to identify special areas (75 areas and 105 towns) of high value, against a background of a precautionary "base cultural value." It combines values based on archaeology, historical geography, and historic buildings (van Beusekom 2002; Deeben et al. 1997; Hallewas 2002).

Lists of special areas have also been compiled for Wales: thirty-six "outstanding" and twenty-two "special" areas, supported by written and photographic characterizations (Cadw, Countryside Council for Wales, and ICOMOS-UK 1998, 2001). But attention is now turning to "associative landscape," that is, landscape insofar as it evokes or articulates memory, imagination, belonging, and alienation (Gwyn 2002). In Wales, this is closely linked to national identity, with being Welsh seen within a wider British identity and connected to the relationship of place and community in the Welsh imagination: strong emotional and personal ties to historic traditions such as "chapel" (nonconforming religions), coal and steel, hill farming, or the Welsh language.

For Ireland, the Archaeological Landscape Project (ALP) compiled a preliminary National Inventory of Archaeological Landscapes, containing 223 areas, which it recommended should be protected as if they were monuments (Cooney, Condit, and Byrnes 2002). ALP also tested English-style characterization (following its use for the Irish Heritage Council in County Clare [Environmental Resource Management and ERA-Maptec

2000]) and concluded that a national program of HLC would be needed to support the inventory (Heritage Council 2001). In parallel, less historically inspired programs of landscape assessment, based on aesthetics and ecology, are also being carried out, as in England (DOELG 2000).

In Scotland, finally, a centralized program of Historic Land-Use Assessment is under way, mapping land use in a way derived from the pioneering Cornwall project in England. It focuses on current land cover more than on historic process and adds an overlying map of "relict landscape areas" where the density of visible surviving archaeological sites is highest, thus bringing into a single GIS database some of the different aspects of an English SMR (Dixon and Hingley 2002; Dyson-Bruce et al. 1999; Macinnes 2002).

England's HLC

Premises and Scope

The HLC program in England is based on a series of simple premises, which together add up to a strong new approach that is fundamental to managing change in the cultural landscape.

(a) *Historic landscape character exists in the here and now, and everywhere.* HLC is conservation led, concerned with understanding the present-day landscape's historic character to help us manage change. It deals with the landscape that exists around us today, seeking to identify and evaluate the historic character of that landscape, whatever its date. It seeks to do this everywhere, creating geographically comprehensive if sometimes superficial maps rather than detailed work on only a few parishes (Fairclough 1999a).

(b) *Historic landscape character is important for local as well as national values.* The localness of historic landscape character is often one of its primary attributes (Fairclough forthcoming). Local diversity is treated as an issue of national importance, especially in the context of sustainability and public participation, but landscape character in itself is a product of place. National comparisons are of limited use, hence the English policy of not producing a register of special areas of historic landscape.

(c) *Historic landscape character is defined by the interaction through time of people and their environment and is produced by process and change in the past.* What distinguishes HLC from other forms of landscape assessment is its recognition of the centrality to landscape character of time-depth and of cultural and historical processes and the extent to which change rather than continuity marks the English landscape (whatever else it is, it is not timeless!). Its acceptance that change is sewn into the very fabric of the cultural landscape makes it easier to embrace the concept of managing change (Fairclough 1999b).

(d) *Historic landscape character is created by perception and understanding.* HLC recognizes that "landscape" is first and foremost
an idea. Its components are all too real: material things such
as hedges or buildings, walls or earthworks that can be damaged or destroyed and which need looking after. Landscape
itself is primarily a construct, however, an idea that binds
those physical components into something greater than their
parts. It is doubly "cultural": made in the past by people
through culture and created in the present day from cultural
attitudes. Landscape only exists once someone has visualized
or conceptualized it, and therefore HLC maps are not objective data but a portrayal of a particular perspective, a matter
of interpretations rather than record (Fairclough 1998).

(e) *Historic landscape character is dynamic and living.* If landscape is
only an idea, this does not exonerate us from the need to care
for it, but that care needs to acknowledge change. Much of
HLC concerns living patterns, for example, of land cover or
woodland, and these are seminatural: they are culturally
modified, yet alive. Unmanaged hedges will become rows of
trees; uncoppiced woodland will grow into forest; ungrazed
moor, heath, and pastureland will become scrubland and eventually woodland. Conservation needs to take account of
process if it is to be successful, and HLC is a guide to past and
present processes (Fairclough 1994).

(f) *Historic landscape character provides an accessible forum for democratic participation in managing change.* Different people have
different perceptions and responses, which highlights the need
for participation and for acknowledging the multiplicity of
ways of appreciating landscape. We all have our own cultural
landscape, in our minds or memories, and therefore everyone
has a way into the debate. To manage change effectively, we
must find ways to take account of these different views.

The scope of cultural landscape that the HLC program adopts is
diverse and inclusive. The various facets of "historic landscape character" can
be summarized as follows, from the most physical to the most intangible:

- *The broad historic dimension of the current landscape,* using area,
  not point, data. This is a generalized understanding of the patterns of features such as hedges, walls, quarries, mines, roads,
  tracks, and canals; more broadly still, the character and distribution of settlement itself and the pattern of land use, fields, and
  land cover.
- *Evidence for how people changed the environment throughout the past.*
  These are the processes underlying material remains that
  have created the palimpsest of the cultural landscape. Major
  processes taken into account include exploitation of the land
  for food from animals and plants, the winning of raw materials

(wood, stone, minerals), woodland clearance, habitat creation, and patterns of enclosure and ownership.

- *Spatial and territorial patterning.* Nonhistoric landscape assessment is topographically determined, defining discrete areas such as valleys or uplands. Most land use and activity in the past, however, required communities to have access to a wide range of resources—woodland, grazing, arable, or fishing—spread across the geographic grain of the landscape. Access to them could be by seasonal migration or through cross-grain territories at various scales, such as parishes that extend from coast to interior across a range of zones, or from local high pasture to river meadow; in some areas, the pattern exists at micro-scale in each parish.
- *How people appreciate the cultural landscape.* There are many ways of seeing landscape—as primary evidence for understanding our world and its past, as the distinctive character of places, through associations (literary or mythological), aesthetic appreciation, love of "nature" and ecological value, sense of belonging (and alienation?), and memory, personal and social. All these different ways need somehow to be captured by HLC.

Of all these components, the least work has been achieved on the last. It is the next new frontier of theoretical development, so far difficult and labor intensive, with few developed methodologies. It does, however, form one of the more experimental threads of the Culture 2000 European Pathways to the Cultural Landscape program. The English project in this program, Bowland and the Lune Valley, will give it particular attention. Operating in the context of a completed HLC map, it will experiment with learning how best to establish the views on the cultural landscape that are held by local residents and by the adjacent urban population of Lancaster, for whom the area is their landscape hinterland, in which they are not quite resident but more than visitors and tourists.

Method and Uses
The HLC method itself is fundamentally simple (for a more detailed summary, see Fairclough 1999d:pt. 1; Fairclough 2002a). The map of a county is divided into areas of land of different size, their size arising from the grain of the landscape itself. Sometimes (usually in very diverse fine-grained landscapes) the areas are small, perhaps a few fields sharing a particular pattern, or a twentieth-century military airfield. Usually, they are quite large, as befits the scale of the whole project at county level. Each separate area or land parcel is defined by its main, generalized landscape attribute, such as unenclosed land, enclosed land of various types, urban land, woodland, or industrially affected areas. Each area might contain a diversity that is only broadly summarized by its main type, so that at all times the maps view landscape at a suitable level of generalization. It is landscape character, not individual sites, no matter how large, that is taken into account.

The HLC databases are part of Sites and Monument Records, the basic tool of archaeological resource management in Britain. HLC therefore sits alongside parallel and linked databases, records, and maps of other aspects of the historic environment such as archaeological and architectural urban surveys, records of archaeological sites and buildings, historic mapping, ecological and land use data, place-names, and air photograph evidence for crop marks and other buried archaeology. They are thus plugged into spatial planning and agri-environmental structures and to other conservation activities—integration in action.

The projects create computerized "maps" in GIS that hold and present information and ideas at many levels. These maps are highly flexible in use, in part because they are based on GIS, but principally because of the philosophy behind them (see Fig. 3, Color Plate 2). They aim at being territorially comprehensive, and they have an area-based structured recording of visible attributes of the landscape and their interpretation in terms of date, function, origin, or evolution that encourages questions and research (see Fig. 4, Color Plate 3). The GIS is not one fixed map but the raw material for

Figure 3

Lancashire HLC measuring landscape-scale change after comparison with nineteenth-century historic maps. Produced by Joy Ede and John Darlington; English Heritage/ Lancashire County Council.
(See also Color Plate 2.)

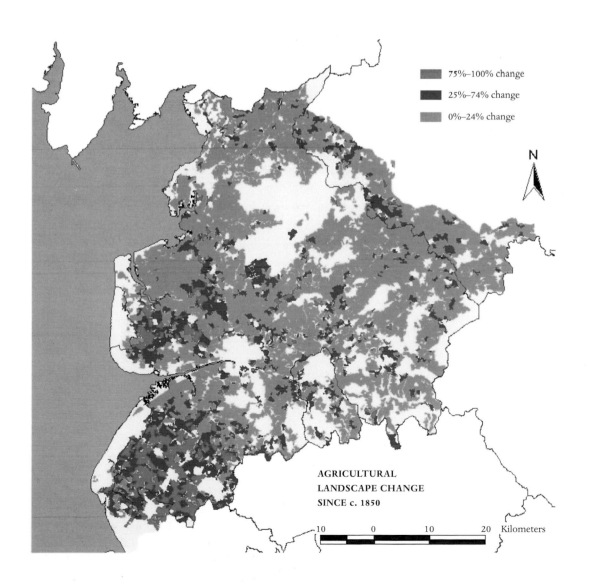

75%–100% change

25%–74% change

0%–24% change

N

AGRICULTURAL
LANDSCAPE CHANGE
SINCE c. 1850

10   0   10   20   Kilometers

Figure 4

Hampshire historic landscape types. Produced
by Peter Atkinson after George Lambrick;
English Heritage, Hampshire County Council,
Oxford Archaeological Unit.

(See also Color Plate 3.)

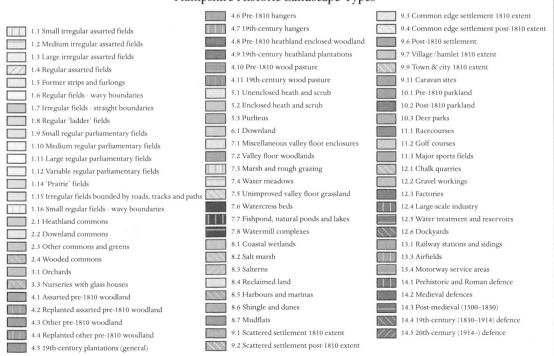

Hampshire Historic Landscape Types

- 1.1 Small irregular assarted fields
- 1.2 Medium irregular assarted fields
- 1.3 Large irregular assarted fields
- 1.4 Regular assarted fields
- 1.5 Former strips and furlongs
- 1.6 Regular fields - wavy boundaries
- 1.7 Irregular fields - straight boundaries
- 1.8 Regular 'ladder' fields
- 1.9 Small regular parliamentary fields
- 1.10 Medium regular parliamentary fields
- 1.11 Large regular parliamentary fields
- 1.12 Variable regular parliamentary fields
- 1.14 'Prairie' fields
- 1.15 Irregular fields bounded by roads, tracks and paths
- 1.16 Small regular fields - wavy boundaries
- 2.1 Heathland commons
- 2.2 Downland commons
- 2.3 Other commons and greens
- 2.4 Wooded commons
- 3.1 Orchards
- 3.3 Nurseries with glass houses
- 4.1 Assarted pre-1810 woodland
- 4.2 Replanted assarted pre-1810 woodland
- 4.3 Other pre-1810 woodland
- 4.4 Replanted other pre-1810 woodland
- 4.5 19th-century plantations (general)

- 4.6 Pre-1810 hangers
- 4.7 19th-century hangers
- 4.8 Pre-1810 heathland enclosed woodland
- 4.9 19th-century heathland plantations
- 4.10 Pre-1810 wood pasture
- 4.11 19th-century wood pasture
- 5.1 Unenclosed heath and scrub
- 5.2 Enclosed heath and scrub
- 5.3 Purlieus
- 6.1 Downland
- 7.1 Miscellaneous valley floor enclosures
- 7.2 Valley floor woodlands
- 7.3 Marsh and rough grazing
- 7.4 Water meadows
- 7.5 Unimproved valley floor grassland
- 7.6 Watercress beds
- 7.7 Fishpond, natural ponds and lakes
- 7.8 Watermill complexes
- 8.1 Coastal wetlands
- 8.2 Salt marsh
- 8.3 Salterns
- 8.4 Reclaimed land
- 8.5 Harbours and marinas
- 8.6 Shingle and dunes
- 8.7 Mudflats
- 9.1 Scattered settlement 1810 extent
- 9.2 Scattered settlement post-1810 extent

- 9.3 Common edge settlement 1810 extent
- 9.4 Common edge settlement post-1810 extent
- 9.6 Post-1810 settlement
- 9.7 Village/hamlet 1810 extent
- 9.9 Town & city 1810 extent
- 9.11 Caravan sites
- 10.1 Pre-1810 parkland
- 10.2 Post-1810 parkland
- 10.3 Deer parks
- 11.1 Racecourses
- 11.2 Golf courses
- 11.3 Major sports fields
- 12.1 Chalk quarries
- 12.2 Gravel workings
- 12.3 Factories
- 12.4 Large-scale industry
- 12.5 Water treatment and reservoirs
- 12.6 Dockyards
- 13.1 Railway stations and sidings
- 13.3 Airfields
- 13.4 Motorway service areas
- 14.1 Prehistoric and Roman defence
- 14.2 Medieval defences
- 14.3 Post-medieval (1500–1830)
- 14.4 19th-century (1830–1914) defence
- 14.5 20th-century (1914–) defence

almost infinite numbers of maps, drawing different sets of information and interpretation from the data set in response to specific questions, such as a need to compare different areas or to describe a particular area. It can be used to discover and demonstrate time-depth, to examine past and possible future degrees and types of change, or to question the current state of knowledge. It can be easily combined with other data and amalgamated or simplified according to need, and it is easily updated with new data, new understandings, conflicting theories and ideas, or changing interpretations.

The method is still evolving. The first project in Cornwall was carried out in 1993–94 on paper maps without GIS; its classification was simple (approximately eighteen types at first) (Herring 1998). More recent projects, those in Lancashire (Darlington 2002) and Herefordshire, are more sophisticated, especially because they use GIS. This allows them to record the attributes that lead to an interpretation rather than only the interpretation itself. It is possible to attribute subsidiary types to an area, or to identify earlier episodes of landscape character. Data can be attached to each area, for example, to record the information sources used, the degree of confidence with which interpretation has been made, the assumptions made, or any ancillary information such as relevant place-names. This is more flexible and transparent, allowing interpretation and the creation of models but retaining the ability to rework them.

Finally, the foregoing should have made evident how HLC does not create a single story of the landscape's history, or a single map of any interpretation. Instead, it creates a resource—a set of interpretations and ideas—for creating a wide variety of narratives or an almost infinite number of maps and analyses and for answering many different questions, both research based and conservation led. It also has potential to bring together from their different backgrounds all the people with an interest in landscape because it uses language that is easily understood by landscape architects, ecologists, or planners. This is an important reason why the HLC maps are daily helping to inform planning decisions affecting archaeology and the landscape, to understand SMR data and the distribution of surviving sites, and to target new research into areas where it is most needed.

The cultural landscape is more readily accessible to everyone than are individual buildings or archaeological sites. It can be appreciated in such a wide range of different ways, from the archaeological to the aesthetic, or from the purely personal to the collective historical, that everyone can participate in at least one way. We all have our own landscape, if not on our doorsteps, then at least where we take holidays, where we grew up, or in our memories or imaginations. This shared inheritance helps all people to engage with the processes of identifying significance and taking decisions on managing change.

By providing a platform for future work that can be updated and revised, the HLC maps offer the potential for public participation. Once available on the Web or in public libraries or schools, it should be possible for residents and frequent visitors to contribute their own views. There could be systems for them to make changes, to add their own perspectives, and gradually to build up a genuinely participatory HLC map alongside the archaeologists' expert viewpoint. This will help to embed a culture of managing change responsibly, from a position of historic understanding, into the decision-making process: a goal of sustainable development.

Conclusion

The Historic Landscape Characterisation program in England was established to provide understanding of the cultural landscape and to raise awareness of its richness, so as to extend effective protection and management from individual sites to the wider landscape. As such, it summarizes many of the themes of this chapter. It brings together the arguments for attempting to manage change broadly across the whole historic environment and for adopting the principles of sustainability.

Helping to manage change is one of HLC's main objectives. It achieves this by providing the information without which conservation cannot be successful, by augmenting and supporting existing SMR and other data, by creating new information about the landscape, and especially by providing improved appreciation of the historic dimension of the landscape against which to set current needs. It also contributes to integration of cultural interests with other types of environmental care, so that all aspects of the landscape and the environment can be considered together, supporting rather than conflicting with each other.

The principal arena for using HLC is the spatial planning system: the preparation of development plans and the exercise of local development control through the control of planning permission. But it also affects other areas: hedgerow protection orders, landscape strategies designed to enhance the countryside, the agri-environmental programs that are gradually shifting the European Union's Common Agricultural Policy from supply-led farm support to delivering environmental benefits through incentives to farmers. All these are areas of managing change that require knowledge and understanding to ensure that informed decisions are taken (Fairclough and Rippon 2002:203–6).

HLC, and its increasing use, is thus becoming a main delivery mechanism for conservation and managing change in the historic environment. It provides new information for heritage management to guide landscape and farming policies, and it creates common ground for people to join the debate about the landscape's future. It will help us to find out how to pass on a landscape that is historic and rooted in culture and how to leave enough to allow our successors to make their own decisions about the landscape they wish to live with. HLC, or similar ways of understanding and managing the cultural landscape, should therefore be a key component of sustainable development. The spread of the idea beyond England suggests that it will become one of the driving forces of the European Landscape Convention.

Acknowledgments

Proper, comprehensive acknowledgments would be longer than this chapter, because all the work I have described has been produced collectively by an army of colleagues, friends, and partners, from those in English Heritage and the Countryside Commission to partners from many European countries and all the project officers who have carried out Historic Landscape Characterisation projects. Many are mentioned in the references, but most are anonymous. At the very real risk of being invidious, I would, however, like to single out a few long-term colleagues and collaborators who have been involved throughout most of the various work programs described: David Brook, Kate Clark, Mike Coupe, Jan-Kees Hagers, Richard Kelly, George Lambrick, Richard Lloyd, Leslie Macinnes, Liz Page, Carol Somper, David Stocker, and Carys Swanwick. To all these and more, I must acknowledge an enormous amount of help, advice (not always heeded, of course), and support.

References

Bennett, G. 1996. *Cultural Landscape: The Conservation Challenge in a Changing Europe*. London: Institute for European Environmental Policy.

van Beusekom, E. 2002. Historic landscapes in the Netherlands. *In Europe's Cultural Landscape: Archaeologists and the Management of Change*, ed. G. J. Fairclough and S. J. Rippon, 49–54. EAC Occasional Paper No. 2. Brussels and London: Europae Archaeologiae Consilium and English Heritage.

Cadw, Countryside Council for Wales, and ICOMOS-UK. 1998. *Register of Landscapes of Outstanding Historic Interest in Wales*. Cardiff: Cadw.

Cadw, Countryside Council for Wales, and ICOMOS-UK. 2001. *Register of Landscapes of Special Historic Interest in Wales*. Cardiff: Cadw.

Cooney, G., T. Condit, and E. Byrnes. 2002. The Archaeological Landscape Project: An approach to cultural landscapes in Ireland. In *Europe's Cultural Landscape: Archaeologists and the Management of Change*, ed. G. J. Fairclough and S. J. Rippon, 39–48. EAC Occasional Paper No. 2. Brussels and London: Europae Archaeologiae Consilium and English Heritage.

Council of Europe. 1996. *Declaration on the Political Dimension of Cultural Heritage Conservation in Europe*. MAC-4(96) 1 rev. Helsinki: Council of Europe.

Council of Europe. 2000. *European Landscape Convention*. European Treaty Series No. 176. Florence: Council of Europe.

Countryside Agency. 1999. Countryside Character volumes: vol. 4, *East Midlands* (CA10); vol. 5, *West Midlands* (CA11); vol. 6, *The East* (CA12); vol. 7, *South East* (CA13); vol. 8, *South West* (CA14). Cheltenham: Countryside Agency.

Countryside Agency, English Heritage, English Nature, and the Environment Agency. 2001. *Quality of Life Capital: Managing Environmental, Social and Economic Benefits*. Cheltenham: Countryside Agency.

Countryside Commission. 1993. *Landscape Assessment Guidance*, CCP423. Cheltenham: Countryside Commission.

Countryside Commission. 1994. *Views from the Past: Historic Landscape Character in the English Countryside*. Consultation report. Cheltenham: Countryside Commission.

Countryside Commission. 1996. *Views from the Past: Historic Landscape Character in the English Countryside*. CCW4. Cheltenham: Countryside Commission.

Countryside Commission. 1998. Countryside Character volumes: vol. 1, *North East* (CCP535); vol. 2, *North West* (CCP536); vol. 3, *Yorkshire and the Humber* (CCP536). Cheltenham: Countryside Commission.

Countryside Commission, English Heritage, and English Nature. 1993. *Conservation Issues in Strategic Plans*. CCP420. Cheltenham: Countryside Commission.

Countryside Commission, English Nature, and English Heritage. 1997. *What Matters and Why: Environmental Capital, a New Approach*. Cheltenham: Countryside Commission.

Danish Forest and Nature Agency (DFNA). 2002. *CHIP–Cultural Heritage in Planning: Identifying Valuable Cultural Environments through Planning.* Copenhagen: Ministry of Environment and Energy.

Darlington, J. 2002. Mapping Lancashire's historic landscape: The Lancashire Historic Landscape Characterisation programme. In *Europe's Cultural Landscape: Archaeologists and the Management of Change,* ed. G. J. Fairclough and S. J. Rippon, 97–105. EAC Occasional Paper No. 2. Brussels and London: Europae Archaeologiae Consilium and English Heritage.

Deeben, J., D. P. Hallewas, J. Kolen, and R. Wiemer. 1997. Beyond the crystal ball: Predictive modelling as a tool in archaeological heritage management and occupation history. In *Archaeological Heritage Management in the Netherlands: Fifty Years of State Service for Archaeological Investigations,* ed. W. J. H. Willems, H. Kars, and D. P. Hallewas, 76–118. Assen on Amersfoort: Van Gorcum fur Rijkdienst voor het Oudneidkundig Bodermonderzoek (ROB).

Déjeant-Pons, M. 2002. The European Landscape Convention, Florence. In *Europe's Cultural Landscape: Archaeologists and the Management of Change,* ed. G. J. Fairclough and S. J. Rippon, 13–24. EAC Occasional Paper No. 2. Brussels and London: Europae Archaeologiae Consilium and English Heritage.

Department for Culture, Media and Sport/Department of Transport, Local Government and the Regions (DCMS/DETR). 2001. *The Historic Environment: A Force for the Future.* PP378. London: HMSO. www.culture.gov.uk/heritage.

Department of the Environment (DOE). 1973. *Planning Circular 23/77: Historic Buildings and Conservation Areas.* London: HMSO.

Department of the Environment (DOE). 1990. *Planning Policy Guidance Note 16: Archaeology and Planning.* London: HMSO.

Department of the Environment and Local Government (Ireland) (DOELG). 2000. *Landscape and Landscape Areas: Consultation Draft and Guidelines for Planning Authorities.* Dublin: DOELG.

Dixon, P., and R. Hingley. 2002. Historic land-use assessment in Scotland. In *Europe's Cultural Landscape: Archaeologists and the Management of Change,* ed. G. J. Fairclough and S. J. Rippon, 85–88. EAC Occasional Paper No. 2. Brussels and London: Europae Archaeologiae Consilium and English Heritage.

Droste, B. von, H. Plachter, and M. Rössler, eds. 1995. *Cultural Landscapes of Universal Value: Components of a Global Strategy.* Jena: Gustav Fischer-Verlag.

Dyson-Bruce, L., P. Dixon, R. Hingley, and J. Stevenson. 1999. *Historic Land-Use Assessment (HLA): Development and Potential of a Technique for Assessing Historic Landuse Patterns. Report of the Pilot Project 1996-1998.* Edinburgh: Historic Scotland and the Royal Commission on the Ancient and Historical Monuments of Scotland.

English Heritage. 1997. *Sustaining the Historic Environment.* London: English Heritage.

English Heritage, Countryside Commission, and English Nature. 1996. *Conservation Issues in Local Plans.* London: English Heritage.

Environmental Resource Management and ERA-Maptec, Ltd. 2000. Pilot study on landscape characterisation in County Clare. Prepared for the Heritage Council, Oxford/Dublin.

European Union. 2000. *European Spatial Development Perspective.* Potsdam: European Union.

Fairclough, G. J. 1994. Landscapes from the past—Only human nature. In *The Ecology and Management of Cultural Landscapes—The Proceedings of an International Association of Landscape Ecology (UK) Conference at Cheltenham, April 1993,* ed. P. Selman, 64–72. Landscape Issues, vol. 11, no. 1. Cheltenham: Cheltenham and Gloucester College of Higher Education.

Fairclough, G. J. 1995. The sum of all its parts: An overview of the politics of integrated management in England. In *Managing Ancient Monuments: An Integrated Approach*, ed. I. W. Brown and A. R. Berry, 17–28. Mold: Association of County Archaeology Officers/Clwyd County Council.

Fairclough, G. J. 1998. Assessment and characterisation: English Heritage's historic landscape policy. In *Landscapes—Perception, Recognition and Management: Reconciling the Impossible?* ed. M. Jones and I. D. Rotherham, 43–51. Proceedings of a conference at Sheffield, 1996. Landscape Archaeology and Ecology, vol. 3. Sheffield: Wildtrack Publishing for the Landscape Conservation Forum and Sheffield Hallam University.

Fairclough, G. J. 1999a. Protecting the cultural landscape: National designations and local character. In *Managing the Historic Rural Environment*, ed. J. Grenville, 27–39. London: Routledge and English Heritage.

Fairclough, G. J. 1999b. Protecting time and space: Understanding historic landscape for conservation in England. In *The Archaeology and Anthropology of Landscape: Shaping Your Landscape*, ed. P. J. Ucko and R. Layton, 119–34. One World Archaeology, vol. 30. London: Routledge.

Fairclough, G. J. 1999c. The S-word: Sustaining conservation. In *Conservation Plans in Action: Proceedings of the Oxford Conference*, ed. K. Clark, 127–31. London: English Heritage.

Fairclough, G. J., ed. 1999d. *Historic Landscape Characterisation*. Papers presented at an English Heritage seminar held at the Society of Antiquaries, December 11, 1998. London: English Heritage.

Fairclough, G. J. 2002a. Cultural landscape, computers and characterisation. In *2002: Archaeological Informatics: Pushing the Envelope*, ed. G. Burenhult, 277–94. Computer Applications and Quantitative Methods in Archaeology, Proceedings of the 29th Conference, Gotland, April 2001. BAR Series 1016. Oxford: Archaeopress.

Fairclough, G. J. 2002b. Cultural landscape and spatial planning: England's Historic Landscape Characterisation Programme. In *Heritage of the North Sea: Conservation and Interpretation*, ed. L. M. Green and P. T. Bidwell, 123–49. Papers presented at the Historic Environment of the North Sea InterReg II Conference, March 29–31, 2001, South Shields. Shaftesbury: Donhead.

Fairclough, G. J. Forthcoming. Place and locality: A non-monumental heritage? In *Proceedings of the Interpreting Historic Places Conference, York, 3-7 September 1997*.

Fairclough, G. J., G. Lambrick, and D. Hopkins. 2002. Historic Landscape Characterisation in England and a Hampshire case study. In *Europe's Cultural Landscape: Archaeologists and the Management of Change*, ed. G. J. Fairclough and S. J. Rippon, 69–83. EAC Occasional Paper No. 2. Brussels and London: Europae Archaeologiae Consilium and English Heritage.

Fairclough, G. J., G. Lambrick, and A. McNab. 1999. *Yesterday's World, Tomorrow's Landscape*. The English Heritage Historic Landscape Project, 1992–94. London: English Heritage.

Fairclough, G. J., and S. J. Rippon, eds. 2002. *Europe's Cultural Landscape: Archaeologists and the Management of Change*. EAC Occasional Paper No. 2. Brussels and London: Europae Archaeologiae Consilium and English Heritage.

Gwyn, D. 2002. Associative landscape in a Welsh context. In *Europe's Cultural Landscape: Archaeologists and the Management of Change*, ed. G. J. Fairclough and S. J. Rippon, 187–92. EAC Occasional Paper No. 2. Brussels and London: Europae Archaeologiae Consilium and English Heritage.

Hajós, G., ed. 1999. *Denkmal—Ensemble—Kulturlandschaft: Am Beispiel Wachau. Beiträge Internationales Symposion vom 12. bis 15. Oktober 1998 Dürnstein (Österreich)*. Wien: Verlag Berger.

Hallewas, D. P. 2002. The Belvedere Project: An integrated approach in the Netherlands. In *Europe's Cultural Landscape: Archaeologists and the Management of Change*, ed. G. J. Fairclough and S. J. Rippon, 55–59. EAC Occasional Paper No. 2. Brussels and London: Europae Archaeologiae Consilium and English Heritage.

Heritage Council. 2001. *Towards Integrated Policies for Ireland's Landscape*. Kilkenny: Heritage Council.

Herring, P. 1998. *Cornwall's Historic Landscape: Presenting a Method of Historic Landscape Character Assessment*. Truro: Cornwall Archaeology Unit and English Heritage, Cornwall County Council.

Historic Environment Review. 2000a. *Power of Place: A Future for the Historic Environment*. London: English Heritage.

Historic Environment Review. 2000b. *Viewpoint: Consultation Papers for the Review of Policies Relating to the Historic Environment*. London: English Heritage.

Historic Scotland. 2002. *Passed to the Future: Sustaining the Historic Environment*. Edinburgh: Historic Scotland.

Lancashire County Council. 2001. *A Landscape Strategy for Lancashire*. Preston: Lancaster County Council.

Macinnes, L. 2002. Examples of current national approaches—Scotland. *In Europe's Cultural Landscape: Archaeologists and the Management of Change*, ed. G. J. Fairclough and S. J. Rippon, 171–74. EAC Occasional Paper No. 2. Brussels and London: Europae Archaeologiae Consilium and English Heritage.

Market Opinion Research International (MORI). 2000. *Attitudes Towards the Heritage: Research Conducted for English Heritage*. London: MORI.

Netherlands State Government. 1999. *The Belvedere Memorandum: A Policy Document Examining the Relationship between Cultural History and Spatial Planning* (Belvedere—Beleidsnota over de relatie cultuurhistorie en ruimtelijke inrichting). The Hague.

NorVision. 2000. *NorVision, a Spatial Perspective for the North Sea Region*. Essen: NorVision Working Group.

Roberts, B. K., and S. Wrathmell. 2000. *An Atlas of Rural Settlement in England*. London: English Heritage.

Roberts, B. K., and S. Wrathmell. 2002. *Region and Place: A Study of English Rural Settlement*. London: English Heritage.

Stoumann, I. 2002. Archaeology and the cultural environment: An example from the Danish Wadden Sea region. In *Europe's Cultural Landscape: Archaeologists and the Management of Change*, ed. G. J. Fairclough and S. J. Rippon, 61–68. EAC Occasional Paper No. 2. Brussels and London: Europae Archaeologiae Consilium and English Heritage.

Social Sustainability: People, History, and Values

Setha M. Low

MY INTEREST IN SOCIAL SUSTAINABILITY GROWS out of personal as well as professional reflections on the meaning of the built environment for defining who we are—as individuals and as groups. To discuss these concerns, however, I need to shift the unit of analysis from considerations of economics and cultural landscapes to individual histories, needs, and values and focus on how we can sustain the social relations and meanings that make up our complex life-world. I begin with my own experiences and research.

As I drive Interstate 10 from Palm Springs to West Los Angeles, my personal history passes by inscribed in places, institutions, and cultural markers. I am reminded of where I went to college, where I spent my summers as a child, and where I got my first job. These physical reminders provide a sense of place attachment, continuity, and connectedness that we are rarely aware of but that play a significant role in our psychological development as individuals and in our "place identity" or "cultural identity" as families or ethnic and cultural groups (Low and Altman 1992).[1]

But what happens when your places are not marked, or even more to the point, when your personal or cultural history is erased—removed by physical destruction and omitted from historical texts? The redevelopment of Paris by Baron Haussmann and removal of buildings around Notre Dame in the nineteenth century are a classic example of the erasure of a working-class and poor people's history (Halloran 1998). In the United States we have been more subtle. For instance, the contextually complex, residential streets of Bunker Hill were lost in the modernist redevelopment of downtown Los Angeles (Louksitou-Sideris and Dansbury 1995–96), and Robert Moses obliterated entire working-class neighborhoods to make way for the Cross-Bronx Expressway in New York City.

At Independence National Historical Park in Philadelphia, there is no record of the people who built the buildings (African Americans), or financed the Revolution (Jewish Americans), or fed the soldiers (women, mothers and wives). The processes of historic preservation, planning and development, and park interpretation re-created the colonial period as a white, male space. Even the documentation of lost buildings and physical context is missing from the histories of minority peoples during colonial times.

African Americans in Philadelphia, though, are fighting to reclaim their history by supporting research and setting up archives to ensure that their history and culturally significant sites are included. The African American community in New York was successful in contesting the federal government's claims to the African American Burying Ground, demanding its commemoration and preservation, but was less successful in preserving the Audubon Ballroom, where Malcolm X was shot. Thus even as histories are erased, they are re-searched and rediscovered so that they can be commemorated.

Ellis Island, only four hundred meters from the New Jersey shore, is inaccessible to the residents of surrounding neighborhoods. Their lack of economic resources makes the cost of the ferry ride prohibitive, especially for large family outings. Residents want a bridge from Ellis Island to Liberty State Park to provide free access for their community, but historic preservationists argue that a bridge will destroy visitors' experience of arriving by water. Conflicting values derived from distinct social needs and assumptions often produce these kinds of conservation and heritage site problems but can be resolved through a better understanding of those values and their meanings for local populations. Here I address the problem of how to incorporate conflicting cultural values and diverse cultural histories at heritage sites to enhance their social sustainability.

Definitions

What do we mean by "social sustainability"? Following Throsby (1995), sustainability refers to the evolutionary or lasting qualities of the phenomena, avoidance of short-term or temporary solutions, and a concern with the self-generating or self-perpetuating characteristics of a system.[2] Drawing a parallel with natural ecosystems that support and maintain the "natural balance," "cultural ecosystems" support and maintain cultural life and human civilization (Throsby 1999). Sustainable development is the preservation and enhancement of the environment through the maintenance of natural ecosystems, whereas culturally sustainable development refers to the preservation of arts and society's attitudes, practices, and beliefs.

Social sustainability is a subset of cultural sustainability; it includes the maintenance and preservation of social relations and meanings that reinforce cultural systems. Specifically, it refers to maintaining and enhancing the diverse histories, values, and relationships of contemporary populations. To understand social sustainability—at the level of individuals and groups—I need to expand Throsby's analysis by adding three critical dimensions:

1. Cultural ecosystems are located in time and space: for a cultural ecosystem to be maintained or conserved, its place(s) must be preserved (Low 1987). Cultural conservation and sustainability require place preservation. This rather obvious point is crucial when dealing with the material environment and issues of cultural representation at heritage sites.

2. Anthropologists employ a variety of theories of how cultural ecosystems work in particular places over time. For example, anthropologists have studied the ecological dynamics of natural systems to understand sociopolitical changes in the cultural ecosystems of farmers and have

developed cultural evolutionary schemes to predict settlement patterns and sociocultural development in the third world. Many of these cultural ecology theories were subject to historical critiques; nonetheless, the dynamic and predictive aspects of cultural ecosystem models are useful when examining social change at a particular site.

The case of the historic Parque Central in San José, Costa Rica, illustrates this point. Until 1992, Parque Central was a well-established, spatially organized, cultural ecosystem made up of shoeshine men on the northeast corner (Fig.1), pensioners on the southwest corner (Fig. 2), vendors and religious practitioners on the northwest corner (Fig. 3), and prostitutes and workmen on the center inner circle. The established cultural ecosystem, however, was disrupted in 1993 when the municipality closed the park and redesigned the historic space (Fig. 4) to remove users perceived as unattractive to tourists and the middle class (Low 2000).

The redesign destroyed the "natural balance." A new social group, a gang of young men, took over the public space, creating an even more dangerous and undesirable environment, and young Nicaraguans, rather than Costa Ricans, became the main inhabitants on Sunday. This case illustrates the fragility of existing cultural ecosystems (and its diverse niches); when the sociospatial niches (places) are destroyed, the system may not be able to maintain itself.

Figure 1
Shoeshine men in Parque Central. Photo by Setha M. Low.

Figure 2
Pensioners sitting at the southwest corner of Parque Central. Photo by Setha M. Low.

Figure 3
Healers' corner, Parque Central. Photo by Setha M. Low.

Figure 4
The refurnished kiosk in Parque Central. Photo by Setha M. Low.

3

4

1

2

3. The third important dimension is cultural diversity. Biodiversity, so critical to the physical environment as a genetic repository and pool of adaptive evolutionary strategies, has its social counterpart in cultural diversity. Cultural diversity became a "politically correct" catchphrase during the 1980s in the United States, but it has not been addressed in planning and design—much less sustainable development—practice. While sustainable development includes maintaining cultural diversity as a conceptual goal, there is little agreement, much less research, on what it means. But cultural diversity provides a way to evaluate cultural and social sustainability.

For example, I have been studying patterns of cultural use in large, urban parks and heritage sites over the past ten years. Based on this research, the Public Space Research Group has developed a series of principles that encourage, support, and maintain cultural diversity—and, I would argue, social sustainability (Low et al. 2002). These principles are similar to William H. Whyte's rules for small urban spaces that promote their social viability, but in this case, the rules promote and/or maintain cultural diversity. Among their directives are the following:

- If people are not represented in historical national parks and monuments and, more important, if their histories are erased, they will not use the park.
- Access is as much about economics and cultural patterns of park use as circulation and transportation. Thus income and visitation patterns must be taken into consideration when providing access for all social groups.
- The social interaction of diverse groups can be maintained and enhanced by providing safe, spatially adequate "territories" for everyone within the larger space of the overall site.
- Accommodating the differences in the ways social class and ethnic groups use and value public sites is essential to making decisions that result in sustaining cultural and social diversity.
- Contemporary historic preservation should not concentrate on restoring the scenic features without also restoring the facilities and diversions that attract people to the park.
- Symbolic ways of communicating cultural meaning are an important dimension of place attachment that can be fostered to promote cultural diversity.
- A large site can be designed and managed to offer spaces that foster local neighborhood community life and activity and at the same time provide special spaces and activities to attract culturally diverse users from a broader geographic area.

These social sustainability principles for urban parks and heritage sites are just a beginning. More research is required to understand the importance and difficulties of maintaining cultural diversity. But at the very least, they demonstrate how cultural diversity can be an essential component of evaluating the success of a cultural ecosystem. Cultural diversity is one observable outcome of the continuity of human groups in culturally significant places—an important aspect of social sustainability.

This modified cultural ecosystem–diversity model provides an effective theoretical basis for defining social sustainability. *But social sustainability encompasses more than understanding cultural ecosystems and diversity. It implies a moral and political stance vis-à-vis sociocultural systems— maintaining them, supporting them, and, in some cases, improving them.* And it is in this sense that a new series of questions must be asked. Is social sustainability applicable to all populations? We have been assuming that human ecosystems do not compete with each other, but of course they do. A successful cultural system can overrun another. Is this what we mean by sustainability, natural selection of cultural ecosystems and the survival of the fittest based on an evolutionary or a sociobiological model? Or should we be protecting weaker groups, systems, and urban niches from stronger ones? And who is "we"? These are moral and political questions that must be addressed in our discussions of application and practice. For the moment, though, I will assume that "we" refers to conservation practitioners and social scientists who are involved in site analysis and that our goal is to sustain cultural groups on or near a heritage site and for whom the site is significant.

Ultimately, we need to address issues of social sustainability at various scales: the local, the regional, and the global. Social sustainability at the local scale has been illustrated by the examples I have presented so far, that is, understanding the cultural dynamics of a place so that specific individuals and their histories and values are sustained at or near the heritage site, across generations, over time. At the regional scale, social sustainability might be better conceptualized through a regional plan that supports not only individuals but also neighborhoods, communities, churches, associations, and the institutional infrastructure necessary for the survival of cultural values and places of larger groups throughout history. Dolores Hayden's *Power of Place* (1995) provides a vision of documenting and commemorating cultural histories of minorities and women that go beyond the local and sustain larger elements of society. Social sustainability at the global scale moves closer to where we began, with David Throsby's "sustainable development" based on intergenerational, and, I would add, cultural, equity and environmental justice.

But other work covers this ground. Instead I would like to offer a research strategy, Rapid Ethnographic Assessment Procedures (REAPs), for incorporating diverse cultural histories and values and enhancing social sustainability at the local scale. I present two cases, Independence National Historical Park and Ellis Island, as examples of how REAPs help us to understand the histories, values, and relationships on a site, a first step toward enhancing their social sustainability.

Rapid Ethnographic Assessment Procedures

Background

The intent of a Rapid Ethnographic Assessment Procedure is to provide ethnographic information on local populations in order to "evaluate alternatives and assess planning impacts on ethnographic resources and associated user groups" (National Park Service 2000:196). Ethnography is concerned with the people associated with parks, with their cultural systems or ways of life, and with the related sites, structures, material features, and natural resources. Cultural and ethnic systems include expressive elements that celebrate or record significant events, and many carry considerable symbolic and emotional importance for local cultural groups (National Park Service 2000:165).

The National Park Service (NPS) first employed ethnographic research in connection with western Native American communities having long-standing associations with certain parklands. These lands—natural resources and, in the case of objects and structures, cultural resources— are required by Native Americans or other local communities for their continued cultural identity and survival. The NPS calls these lands "ethnographic resources," and the peoples associated with them "traditionally," "park-associated" peoples (Crespi 1987). In providing systematic data on local lifeways, applied ethnographic research is intended to enhance the relationships between park management and local communities whose histories and associations with park cultural resources are unknown or poorly understood (Bean and Vane 1987; Crespi 1987; Joseph 1997). In many newer national parks, the NPS shares jurisdiction with other federal agencies, state and local governments, and Indian nations or other culturally distinctive communities. The resulting complexity of planning tasks makes ethnographic research with affected communities especially helpful (Mitchell 1987).

The literature points to several kinds of benefits from ethnographic research. One is in the area of conflict management, for example, where local communities anticipate adverse impacts from new park or heritage site designations or changes to existing parks. Wolf (1987) describes the contribution made by ethnographic research to community relations in the difficult process of establishing a National Historic Park around sites in Atlanta associated with the life of Martin Luther King, Jr. Ethnographic knowledge helped management to identify opportunities for compromise and potential mitigating measures (Wolf 1987). The process of ethnographic research with culturally distinctive communities affected by construction projects can give a certain credibility to agency decision making (Liebow 1987).

Community empowerment is another benefit in that relationships established create a dialogue between officials and local neighborhood and cultural groups who would not otherwise have a voice in the planning process. Joseph (1997) stresses the collaborative nature of the applied ethnographic research done by the NPS, wherein ordinary citizens and community leaders participate alongside elected officials, park managers, and the researchers. I have suggested that most preservation problems in cultural landscapes, especially vandalism, underutilization, and neglect, could be prevented with more dialogue between the community and the governmental agency (Low 1987).

A third important benefit of ethnographic research is that it presents and represents the cultural heritage of local communities within the overall programming of site resources. Ethnographic information is useful in presentation, particularly for heritage sites such as Minuteman, in Massachusetts, that include existing communities within their borders. Minuteman has endeavored to restore and preserve farming as a traditional cultural practice within the historic environment the park preserves and interprets. Information that may be uncovered only through ethnography, such as the gendered division of labor on family farms, may be crucial to the continued effective management of a generations-old practice (Joseph 1997). Where the presentation of historic objects is concerned, ethnographic information, gained from living members of the associated cultural group, can reveal uses and meanings not apparent in the objects themselves (Brugge 1987).

"Most cultural landscapes are identified solely in terms of their historical rather than contemporary importance to the community" (Low 1987:31), privileging historical meanings over those of the geographically and/or culturally associated communities. This oversight often promotes friction and local disagreements that can be solved through the knowledge produced by a REAP. Social sustainability of these sites cannot be maintained without the cooperation of local populations, which means supporting their needs and values while at the same time preserving the historical qualities of the heritage site.

Methodology

In a REAP, a number of methods are selected to produce different types of data from diverse sources that can be triangulated to provide a comprehensive analysis of the site. A brief description of each method is presented below. See Table 1 for a summary of the product and outcome of each.

1. *Historical and Archival Documents.* The collection of historical documents and review of relevant archives, newspapers, and magazines begins the REAP process. At historically significant sites, this process may be quite extensive, especially if secondary sources do not exist. This method of data collection is very important, as it is through a thorough understanding of the history of the site that areas of cooperation and conflict often become clear and identifiable.

2. *Physical Traces Mapping.* Physical traces maps record the presence of liquor bottles, needles, trash, clothing, erosion of planting, and other traces of human activities. These maps are completed based on data collected early in the morning at each site. Records of physical evidence of human activity and presence provide indirect clues as to what goes on at these sites during the night. Physical traces mapping assumes that there is a base map of resources and basic features available that can be

Table 1
REAP Methodology

Method	Data	Product	What Can Be Learned
Historical and archival documents	Newspaper clippings, collection of books and articles, reading notes	History of the site's relationship to the surrounding communities	Provides historical context for current study and planning process
Physical traces mapping	Collected trash, patterns of erosion	Description of nighttime activities on site	Identifies evening activities not observed
Behavioral maps	Time-space maps of sites	Description of daily activities on sites	Identifies cultural activities on site
Transect walks	Transcribed interviews and consultant's map of site	Description of site from community member's point of view	Community-centered understanding of the site; local meaning
Individual interviews	Interview sheets	Description of responses of cultural groups	Community responses and interest in site
Expert interviews	Transcription of in-depth interviews	Description of responses of local institutions and community leaders	Community leaders' interest in site planning process
Impromptu group interviews	Transcription of meeting	Description of group perspective, educational value	Group consensus of issues and problems
Focus groups	Tape recording and transcription of discussion	Description of issues that emerge in small-group discussion	Elicits conflicts and disagreement within cultural group
Participant observation	Field notes	Sociocultural description of the context	Provides context for study and identifies community concerns

used to locate the physical traces. Otherwise, part of the task is to create such a map, both for the physical traces and for the behavioral maps. At many archaeological sites a base map might not be available, adding another step to the research process.

3. *Behavioral Maps.* Behavioral maps record people and their activities located in time and space. These maps arrange data in a way that permits planning and design analyses of the site and are very useful in developing familiarity with the everyday activities at the site and its problems. They are most effectively used in limited park areas with a variety of social and economic uses where the researcher can return repeatedly to the various social spaces during the day.

4. *Transect Walks.* A transect walk is a record of what a community consultant describes and comments on during a guided walk of the site. The idea is to include one or two community

members in the research team, to learn about the site from their point of view. In most REAPs local consultants work with the researcher as collaborators. In the transect walk, however, this is especially important in that the method is dependent on the quality of the relationship between the collaborator and the researcher.

5. *Individual Interviews.* Individual interviews are collected from the identified populations. The sampling strategy, interview schedule, and number of interviews vary from site to site. In most cases on-site users and residents who live near the site are interviewed, but in specific situations interviews might be collected more broadly.

6. *Expert Interviews.* Expert interviews are collected from those people identified as having special expertise to comment on the area and its residents and users, such as the head of the vendors' association, neighborhood association presidents, the head of the planning board, teachers in local schools, ministers of local churches, principals of local schools, and representatives from local parks and institutions.

7. *Impromptu Group Interviews.* Impromptu group interviews are conducted where people gather outside public places or at special meetings set up with church or school groups. The goal of group interviews (as opposed to individual interviews or focus groups) is to collect data in a group context as well as to provide an educational opportunity for the community. Impromptu group interviews are open-ended and experimental and include any community members who are interested in joining the discussion group.

8. *Focus Groups.* Focus groups are set up with those people who are important in terms of understanding the park site and local population. As opposed to the large, open group interviews, the focus groups consist of six to ten individuals selected to represent especially vulnerable populations, such as schoolchildren, seniors, and the physically challenged. The discussions are conducted in the language of the group directed by a facilitator and are tape recorded.

9. *Participant Observation.* The researchers maintain field journals that record their observations and impressions of everyday life in the park. They also keep records of their experiences as they interact with users and communities. Participant observation is a valuable adjunct to the behavioral maps and interviews. It provides contextual information and data that can be compared to what is seen and said to enable accurate data interpretation.

10. *Analysis.* Interview data are organized by coding all responses and then content analyzed by cultural-ethnic group and study question. Transect walks, tours, and interviews are used to produce cultural resource maps for each group. Focus groups determine the extent of cultural knowledge in the community

and identify the areas of conflict and disagreement within the community. Mapping, transect walks, individual and expert interviews, and focus groups provide independent bodies of data that can be compared and contrasted, thus improving the validity and reliability of data collected from a relatively small sample. As in all ethnographic research, interviews, observation, and field notes, as well as knowledge of the cultural group patterns and local politics, are used to help interpret the data collected.

A number of procedures are used to analyze the data. First, the resource maps are produced by an overlay method that combines the behavioral maps, physical traces, and participant observation notes. These maps are descriptive in that they summarize activities and disruptions on site. Second, a research meeting is held in which each participant summarizes what they have found in their interviews. These are general observations that guide the research team (or researcher) as they begin to develop more precise coding strategies. This synthetic stage provides a place to start thinking about what has been found. The "general summaries" are used to explore theoretical approaches and prioritize the coding procedure.

Third, each generalization is broken down into a set of codes that can be used to analyze the field notes. Once this is completed, the interview questions are reviewed and a similar coding scheme is developed. The interview coding relies on the findings of the maps, the field notes, and the structure of the questions themselves. This is the lengthy part of the analysis process and requires discussion between the research team and the client and, in some cases, individual stakeholders. Some coding schemes may require multidimensional scaling and a quantitative analysis, although qualitative content analysis is usually adequate in a REAP. Because a REAP is a "rapid" procedure, there are usually fewer than one hundred fifty interviews, and therefore they can be analyzed by hand. The advantage of a qualitative analysis procedure is that the data are not abstracted from their context and therefore retain their validity and detail. Fourth, the various analyses are triangulated, and common elements, patterns of behaviors, and areas of conflict and differences, both in the nature of the data and in the group themselves, are identified.

Rapid Ethnographic Assessment Procedures for Heritage Conservation Sites

Two National Park Service projects, one at Independence National Historical Park, focusing on the importance of ethnicity and cultural representation in park use, and the other at Ellis Island, evaluating access alternatives, are discussed here. The issues involved—identifying the stakeholders, community, and local users, eliciting their cultural values, understanding the meanings that the site holds for various groups, and giving voice to their concerns and perspectives—are similar to those considered by a conservation professional whose task is to evaluate a site for its social sustainability.

Independence National Historical Park: Ethnicity, Use, and Cultural Representation

In 1994 Independence National Historical Park began developing a general management plan that would set forth basic management philosophy and provide strategies for addressing issues and objectives over the next ten to fifteen years. The planning process included extensive public participation, including a series of public meetings, televised town meetings, community tours, and planning workshops. As part of this community outreach effort, the park wanted to work cooperatively with local ethnic communities to find ways to interpret their diverse cultural heritages in the park's portrayal of the American experience. The study, therefore, was designed to provide a general overview of park-associated ethnic groups, including an analysis of their values and the identification of cultural and natural resources used by and/or culturally meaningful to the various groups.

The research team spent considerable time interviewing cultural experts and surveying the neighborhoods located near Independence National Historical Park. Based on these interviews and observations, four local neighborhoods were selected for study: Southwark for African Americans, Little Saigon for Asians and Asian Americans, the Italian Market area for Italian Americans, and Norris Square for Latinos. These neighborhoods were selected based on the following criteria: (1) they were within walking distance of the park (excluding Norris Square); (2) they had visible spatial and social integrity; and (3) there were culturally targeted stores, restaurants, religious organizations, and social services available to residents, reinforcing their cultural identity. The Jewish community could not be identified with a spatial community in the downtown area; therefore, members of both Conservative and Orthodox synagogues in the Society Hill area were interviewed as a "community of interest" rather than as a physically integrated area. In thirty-six days of fieldwork, 135 people were consulted in the form of individual and expert interviews, transect walks, and focus groups. Table 2 presents the product and outcome of each method used.

The data were coded and analyzed by cultural group and study question. All places in and around the park having personal and cultural associations for our research participants were recorded on cultural resource maps. One map was prepared for each cultural group.

Relevant Findings: Cultural Representation

Many participants were concerned with issues of cultural representation. Some assimilated Italian Americans and Jews were ambivalent about presenting themselves as distinct from other Americans. African Americans, on the other hand, saw a lack of material and cultural representation in the park's historical interpretation. For some, the park represented the uneven distribution of public goods: "So much for them [tourists, white people] and so little for us [African Americans, working-class neighborhood residents]." Asian Americans and Latinos favored a curatorial approach less focused on national independence and integrating their immigration stories

Method	Data	Duration	Product	What Can Be Learned
Historical and archival documents	Newspaper clippings, collection of books and articles, reading notes	7 days	History of site's relationship to surrounding communities	Provides historical context for current study and planning process
Behavioral maps	Time-space maps of sites	2 days	Description of daily activities on site	Identifies cultural activities on site
Transect walks	Transcribed interviews and consultant's map of site, special places, special events, and culturally significant areas	6 days	Description of site from community member's point of view; problem with using tour guides—ample data but seemed rote	Community-centered understanding of site; local meaning; identification of sacred places
Individual interviews	Interview sheets in English, Spanish, Vietnamese, or Chinese with map	12 days	Description of responses of cultural groups in informal settings	Community responses and interest in the park
Expert interviews	In-depth interview transcriptions	10 days	Description of responses of local institutions and community leaders	Community leaders' interest in the park planning process
Formal-informal discussions; participant observation	Interview sheets	20 days	Description of context and history of project; description of park needs	Provides context for study and identifies NPS and community concerns
Focus groups	Field notes, tape recorded in English, Spanish, and Vietnamese; used facilitator and translator	6 days	Description of issues that emerge in small-group discussion (difficult to organize, conduct, and transcribe)	Enables understanding of conflicts and disagreement within cultural group

Table 2
REAP Methodology at Independence National Historical Park

and colonial struggles into a more generalized representation of liberty and freedom within the American experience. Italian Americans, too, were interested in a more inclusive representation—not ending park interpretation in 1782 or 1800 but continuing to the present.

Three of the cultural groups—African Americans, Latinos, and Jews—mentioned places they would like to see commemorated or markers they would like to see installed to bring attention to their cultural presence within the park boundaries. Many participants—particularly Latinos, African Americans, and Asians—saw the need for more programming for children and activities for families. Unlike the visual, pictorial experience the tourist seeks, residents in general were interested in the park's recreational potential, its sociable open spaces where one can get food, relax, and sit on the grass, or as a place for civic and cultural celebrations. These residents wanted the park to be a more relaxed, fun, lively place. As a group, Latinos made the most use of the park for recreational purposes in their leisure time. Latinos were particularly interested in developing the recreational potential of the park, but their sentiments were echoed by at least a few consultants in each of the other ethnic groups.

Relevant Findings: Cultural Values

The REAP demonstrated that the park holds multiple values for Philadelphians that are often overlooked because of management's emphasis on accommodating visitors. "Visitors" was a problematic term, as residents who use the park do not see themselves as visitors. Treating everyone as a visitor (read "tourist") neglects an important sense of territoriality. The resident incorporates the park into her home territory; the visitor knows she is a visitor. To the resident, the park is symbolically and functionally part of the larger landscape of the city and the neighborhood. The resident likes being surrounded by familiar sights and places, follows her own rhythm in moving around the city, and enjoys a proprietary right of access. Those sensibilities are offended by crowds of tourists, by the denial of free access to historic sites (that is, when not part of a tour), and perhaps by an emphasis on official interpretations. The more the park sets its landmarks off from the surrounding city, reducing everyday contact with residents, the more the objects and places lose their meaning for residents.

The REAP of Independence National Historical Park is an example of issues of ethnicity and culture corresponding with either use or nonuse. Identifying relevant cultural-ethnic groups as constituencies that live in the local neighborhood, or that traditionally have a relationship to the park, and then learning about those groups and neighborhoods through the REAP methods provides a quick but complete snapshot of the community and its diverse values, meanings, and sense of cultural representation. Further, this REAP was able to distinguish between conflicting visitor and resident values and suggest possible solutions. The space the park occupies—who gets to use it and whose identity is reflected in it—is as symbolic for local people as Independence Hall and the Liberty Bell are for tourists (Taplin, Scheld, and Low 2002).

Ellis Island Access Alternatives: Conflicting Cultural Values

The research goal was to provide commentary from an ethnographic perspective on four alternative scenarios (bridge, subsidized ferry, elevated rail, and tunnel) proposed in *A Progress Report: Ellis Island Bridge and Access Alternatives*. For the purposes of this project, the culturally appropriate populations included the local users of Battery Park and Liberty State Park; local providers of services at Battery Park and Liberty State Park, including vendors and small-scale tourist services; residents of the Jersey City neighborhoods adjacent to Liberty State Park; special populations such as children, the elderly, and the physically challenged; and "traditional cultural groups," those people whose families entered through Ellis Island or who are themselves immigrants with identities and aspirations connected symbolically to Ellis Island.

The research focused on constituency groups; further into the project, however, when constituency analysis did not provide statistically significant clustering of similar people and points of view, a values orientation–based analysis was incorporated. The constituency groups provided a guide to sampling the users and residents on the three sites— Battery Park, Liberty State Park, and the Jersey City neighborhoods surrounding Liberty State Park (Lafayette, Van Vorst, and Paulus Hook)— who were consulted concerning their perceptions of possible positive or negative impacts of each of the proposed access alternatives. Their attitudes and concerns were collected through a series of REAP data collection methods including behavioral maps, transect walks, individual interviews, expert interviews, impromptu group interviews, and focus groups completed at the various field sites (see Table 3). A total of 318 people were consulted: 117 through individual interviews in the two parks, 113 through impromptu group interviews in neighborhood gathering places, and 88 in focus groups both in the parks and in neighborhood churches and institutions.

The data were analyzed by coding all responses from the interviews and focus groups and then compared by constituency group. Constituency groups were defined as groups of people who share cultural beliefs and values and who are likely to be affected by the proposed access alternatives in a similar way. Correlational, content, and value orientation analyses were used to present the various positions held by consultants across the subgroups studied in this project.

Relevant Findings: Interests and Attitudes

In Battery Park, the people who were the most concerned about the negative impact of a bridge were the service managers, city employees, park employees, ferry representative, can collector, and tour bus driver, that is, those constituencies with a vested interest in the success and profitability of Battery Park. The greatest differences in attitudes about the proposed

Table 3
REAP Methodology for Ellis Island Access
Alternative Project

Methods	Data	Duration	Product	What Can Be Learned
Physical traces mapping	Map of trash and clothing left in parks	1 day	Description of physical condition of site	Identifies night activities that would be affected by proposed bridge and alternatives
Behavioral maps	Time-space maps of site, field notes	2 days	Description of daily activities on site	Identifies daily activities that would be affected by proposed bridge and alternatives
Transect walks	Transcribed interviews and consultant's map of site, field notes	4 days	Description of site from community member's point of view	Community-centered understanding of site; local meaning
Individual interviews	Interview sheets, field notes	10 days	Description of responses of the constituency groups	Community and user responses to proposed bridge and alternatives
Expert interviews	In-depth interview transcriptions	5 days	Description of positions of local institutions and community leaders	Community leaders' responses to proposed bridge and alternatives
Group interviews	Field notes, video or tape recorded	5 days	Description of various community groups and their responses to the bridge and alternatives	Involves neighborhood and church groups in planning process; provides for public discussion of issues in local context
Focus groups	Field notes, video or tape recorded	2 days	Description of issues that emerge in small-group discussion	Enables development of a typology of responses and in-depth discussion of alternatives

bridge were found between people who were there for recreation versus those who were working in Battery Park—the former were more positive, the latter more negative—and between people who were immigrants and those who were native born—the immigrants were more positive, the native born more negative. Overall, Battery Park users were most concerned about the economic consequences of the proposed access alternatives, but there were a number of people who were concerned about access to Ellis Island or who questioned the social priorities of the bridge alternative.

In Liberty State Park, constituency groups were not predictive of attitudes toward the alternatives, with the one notable exception of such vested interests as Liberty State Park officials and workers, who were overwhelmingly against the proposed bridge. The active recreation users, such as walkers and cyclists, were more in favor of the bridge than were the passive user groups and organized group leaders. There was also a sharp distinction between Latino and non-Latino consultants: the Latino consultants were very positive about the access alternatives compared to non-Latino groups. The same differences in attitude between user type (work-related use versus recreational use) and place of origin (immigrant versus native born) found in Battery Park were found in Liberty State Park. The two most frequently cited value orientations were health and recreation and park quality—quite a contrast from the economic findings in Battery Park—followed by aesthetic concerns and concerns about improved access.

The residents of the various neighborhoods surrounding Liberty State Park were generally in favor of the proposed bridge and less interested in the other alternatives, yet each neighborhood had a slightly different perspective on the issue. Paulus Hook residents had very mixed opinions about the proposed bridge and were concerned about potential problems, such as increased traffic or limited parking. Van Vorst residents were more positive and considered the proposed bridge a way to increase democratic access to Ellis Island. They saw the recreational benefits of the bridge as improving their neighborhood. Lafayette residents were the most positive about the proposed bridge because it would allow them to visit Ellis Island without paying the ferry fare that was perceived as too high for families and groups of children to afford in this low-income area. They, too, saw the bridge as an amenity that would add to the beauty and recreational potential of Liberty State Park and their local community.

Relevant Findings: Value Orientations

Table 4 presents the value orientations compared across the parks and neighborhoods. What is clear from this comparison is that each area has slightly different priorities and concerns. Battery Park workers and users are not at all concerned about the cost of the ferry or the bridge but instead are concerned about the possible economic consequences of the proposed access alternatives. Liberty State Park workers and users, on the other hand, are concerned about the health and recreation advantages and park quality disadvantages of the access alternatives. The residents of Lafayette, Van Vorst, and Paulus Hook are most concerned with the cost

Table 4

Value Orientations by Site in Ellis Island Access Alternative Project

Value Orientation	Battery Park	Liberty State Park	Surrounding Neighborhoods	Total
Cost	0	7	35	42
Access	13	8	20	41
Park quality	6	11	20	37
Economic	23	7	6	36
Health and recreation	9	11	9	29
Choice	9	7	5	21
Aesthetic	6	8	6	20
Social priorities	10	7	2	19
Political	8	5	3	16
Education	4	3	8	15
Personal	8	3	1	12
Safety and comfort	4	5	3	12
New technology	5	5	0	10
Ecological	2	3	4	9
No impact	9	0	0	9
Community quality	0	0	7	7

of the ferry or proposed access alternative. Cost, access, park quality, and economics were the most frequently mentioned concerns for all groups. Table 4 is useful for understanding the variation among these populations and can be referred to as a way to judge how often a concern was expressed by consultants in this study.

Conclusion

The practice of historic preservation and restoration can disrupt a local community's sense of place attachment and disturb expressions of cultural identity for local populations. New ethnic and immigrant groups can be excluded from a site, because of a lack of sensitivity to cultural values, nonverbal cues from architecture and furnishings, and symbols of cultural representation. Cultural diversity and indigenous cultural ecosystems are difficult to sustain, especially within the constraints of creating, managing, or maintaining a heritage site. Creative forms of cultural representation and a deeper understanding of cultural values are fundamental to cooperative, ongoing use and maintenance by contemporary groups.

Social sustainability, as a subset of cultural sustainability, is dependent on the maintenance of the existing cultural ecosystem and cultural diversity but can be more easily studied at the site level. REAPs can be used to elicit the histories, values, and relationships of local populations who are often overlooked at heritage sites. Understanding these populations' social relations and meanings enhances our ability to promote social sustainability. Resolving value conflicts and developing more inclusive cultural representations are just two of many possible solutions for promoting more successful local identification with the site.

Acknowledgments

I would like to thank the members of the Public Space Research Group—Dana Taplin, Suzanne Scheld, Tracy Fisher, and Kate Brower—for their participation in these research projects. I have gained insight from their discussions, publications, and analyses. Maria Luisa Achino-Loeb and Joel Lefkowitz discussed the concept of sustainability with me; the conclusions, however, are my own.

Notes

1   Anthropologists spend much of their lives arguing about the categories "ethnicity" and "culture." "Ethnicity" is a slippery term that evokes different meanings when used by the informant as an identity marker (e.g., I am ethnically Jewish, or I am a WASP) and when used as an analytic category by an anthropologist or census taker (e.g., The informant appears to be Asian American or an African American). "Culture" is equally problematic. The term "culture" (lowercase *c*) often refers to local traditions or practices that might define an ethnic group, whereas "Culture" (capital *C*) refers to an analytic category with overarching meanings. Further, ethnicity and culture covary with nationality and other political designations. Here I use "ethnic group" and "cultural group" interchangeably and do not try to untangle the multiple intellectual histories of the terms. I prefer "cultural group" as it is clearer in terms of the traditions and histories that I am discussing. On the other hand, Italian Americans and Puerto Ricans can be considered ethnic groups, since ethnicity is colloquially understood as biological or derived from immigrant group status in the United States, and culture usually refers to the arts.

2   Throsby (1999) examines sustainability in the context of the environment, linking the term "sustainable" with the word "development." *Sustainable development* marries the ideas of sustainable *economic* development with *ecological* sustainability, "meaning the preservation and enhancement of a range of environmental values through the maintenance of ecosystems in the natural world" (Throsby 1999:15). Throsby employs the concepts of distributive justice and intergenerational equity to evaluate fairness in the distribution of welfare, utility, or resources over time.

References

Bean, L. J., and S. B. Vane. 1987. Ethnography and the NPS: Opportunities and obligations. *CRM Bulletin* 10(1):36–44.

Beebe, J. 1995. Basic concepts and techniques of rapid appraisal. *Human Organization* 54:42–51.

Brugge, D. M. 1987. Cultural use and meaning of artifacts. *CRM Bulletin* 10(1):14–16.

Crespi, M. 1987. Ethnography and the NPS: A growing partnership. *CRM Bulletin* 10(1):1–4.

Ervin, A. M. 1997. Trying the impossible: Relatively "rapid" methods in a city-wide needs assessment. *Human Organization* 56:379–87.

Halloran, M. 1998. *Boston's "Changeful Times": The Origins of Preservation and Planning in America.* Baltimore: Johns Hopkins University Press.

Hayden, D. 1995. *The Power of Place*. Cambridge, Mass.: MIT Press.

Joseph, R. 1997. Cranberry bogs to parks: Ethnography and women's history. *CRM Bulletin* 20:20–24.

Liebow, E. 1987. Social impact assessment. *CRM Bulletin* 10(1):23–26.

Louksitou-Sideris, A., and G. Dansbury. 1995–96. Lost streets of Bunker Hill. *California History* 74(4):394–407, 448–49.

Low, S. M. 1987. A cultural landscapes mandate for action. *CRM Bulletin* 10(1):30–33.

Low, S. M. 2000. *On the Plaza: The Politics of Public Space and Culture*. Austin: University of Texas Press.

Low, S. M., and I. Altman. 1992. *Place Attachment*. New York: Plenum.

Low, S. M., D. Taplin, S. Scheld, and T. Fisher. 2002. Recapturing erased histories: Ethnicity, design and cultural representation. *Journal of Architectural and Planning Research* 19(4):282–99.

Mitchell, J. 1987. Planning at Canyon de Chelly National Monument. *CRM Bulletin* 10(1):27–29.

National Park Service. 2000. Applied Ethnography Program. NPS Web site http://www.cr.nps.gov/aad/appeth.htm.

Taplin, D., S. Scheld, and S. Low. 2002. REAP in urban parks: A case study of Independence National Historical Park. *Human Organization* 61(1):80–93.

Throsby, D. 1995. Culture, economics, and sustainability. *Journal of Cultural Economics* 19:199–206.

Throsby, D. 1999. Cultural capital. *Journal of Cultural Economics* 23:3–12.

Wolf, J. C. 1987. Martin Luther King, Jr. *CRM Bulletin* 10(1):12–13.

Sustainability and the City

M. Christine Boyer

"HISTORY" HAS BEEN THE MANNER in which modern societies organize change. Historians look back at the traces of the past still pertinent to the present and attempt to preserve traditions, to sustain them as a living force buttressed against change. But change is inevitable, ever accelerating, and the gap inevitably widens between history and the recollection of facts—or memory. Limiting this discussion to the conservation of the built environment, I want to argue that the concept of sustainable cities relies on how this gap between history and memory is negotiated—in a static didactic manner or as an open-ended process of improvisation. But first we need to explore the tension between history and memory that issues of preservation and conservation always create.

Maurice Halbwachs taught that collective memory or the act of recollection depends on social frameworks such as families, religions, or myths and places such as houses or cities, landmarks or monuments.[1] These frameworks are containers for thoughts, or stored memories; hence they facilitate recollection, or remembering. But how are these frameworks constructed, how do they come to reflect *collectively* shared concepts or perceptions? And if the framework is architectural, how do bricks and mortar generate memories, tell stories, and relate to myths? These are questions to which the advocates of collective memory seldom reply.

Halbwachs's tension between history and memory allows that memory is alive, in permanent evolution and change, whereas history is a reconstruction, always problematic and incomplete. Furthermore, memory, since it is a mental act, is individual and personal, whereas the framework in which memory is stored is socially constructed, shared by a group or a collective. But what is the link between the individual memory and the collective history? How do we move from one to the other? Here again, under analysis, the answers appear to be missing. Thus history and memory are problematic terms and the link between individual or collective recall seldom specified.

David Lowenthal exploits this problem, claiming that history and conservation of the built environment—or what he calls heritage—are two completely different operations.[2] The fabrication of "history," he asserts, is heritage's virtue, not its vice, for heritage willfully exaggerates and omits, frankly invents and forgets, and thrives on memory gaps and ignorance. We should accept that "fiction is not the opposite of fact but its comple- ment, giving our lives a more lasting shape."[3] History, Lowenthal argues, seeks to tell the truth and relies heavily on evidence and critical accuracy. It tries to reduce the very bias, errors, and irrationalities on which heritage thrives. History, moreover, assumes it speaks in a universal language, open to all, whereas heritage is never universally true, often speaking only to a select group and their falsified legacies.

Lowenthal develops a list of ways in which heritage alters the past: (1) it upgrades, making the past appear better than it was; (2) it updates, restoring only from the perspective and interests of the present; (3) it jumbles different time periods and incongruous events, presenting them all together; (4) it selectively forgets what may appear too negative or too incomprehensible; (5) it contrives genealogies, erecting fictitious lin- eages; and (6) it claims precedence as a virtue, for possession of a tradition is good enough. At the end of this list he offers an aside: "(These modes of contrivance, have much in common with cinema, through which many if not most people derive compelling notions of the past)."[4]

Just as heritage thrives on creating "artifice" and "fictionalizing" the past—or so Lowenthal assumes—the public is thrilled to consume these fictions and delusions. Apparently "LITE" history, like the American beer, is easy to consume and less harmful than the unadulterated product. Lowenthal closes his argument by claiming, "As a living force the past is ever remade. . . . Only a heritage reanimated stays relevant." And: "To reshape is as vital as to preserve [and, we might add, to fabricate]."[5]

While accepting that societies constantly change, reshape, and animate the social frameworks in which memories are stored, exploiting the difference between history and memory, in the manner suggested by Lowenthal, playing topsy-turvy with "authenticity" and turning "fabrica- tion" into a virtue does not address the issues of sustainability. It conflates the container of memory with the memories the container engenders, and this is where the issue of sustainability lies. While the construction of the container may be specific to time and place, constantly reconstructing its framework, memory should not be tampered with so lightly if the her- itage industry is to avoid the manipulations of advertisements, ideologies, religions, and nations.

To be clear about this difference, we need to be more specific about the type of memory containers we create and how they affect recol- lection and recall. Thus we must address the issue of how the collective memory of a city is constructed and shared. We need to question whether a city's topological forms and its architectural expressions can be common ground for open-ended reverie and inventive thinking.

Frances Yates, in *The Art of Memory*, argues that memory work involves a mental stroll through the rooms of a house or the sites of a city, using the icons stored in this imaginary container as prompts to uncover associated ideas. This is a method that facilitates the repetition of previously stored material in an essentially static manner.[6] But Mary Carruthers, in *The Craft of Thought*, disagrees and argues that the aim is to offer a thinker the means to invent material on the spot. In other words, the art of memory is a device for discovering something new.[7] She agrees that architecture provides the major metaphor for memory locations but insists this is also a trope for invention, for composing and fabrication and not just storage. She notes that the Latin word *inventio* provides the root for both *inventory* and *invention*. Having an inventory of stored images arranged in an ordered fashion is essential for any inventive thinking. But the association of images with specific contents is done in an open-ended manner through analogy, transference, and metaphor and thus allows for creative inventions.[8]

In an analogical manner, I would argue that the issue of sustainability with respect to the conservation of the built environment lies with Carruthers's, not Yates's, approach to the art of memory. The sites and images of a city and the tourist routes that engender remembering ought to be associated with invention in the sense of "discovery" or creative thinking, not merely the reiteration of previously stored material. What is important is the memory work, not the site, the latter only giving clues to the process of thinking that should follow.

To highlight the difference in this mode of remembering from the static account of collective memory, Carruthers draws on the example of the Vietnam Veterans Memorial in Washington, D.C.[9] It has become a pilgrimage site for a diverse set of individuals or groups—those who fought the war and believed in its justness, those who fought the war but did not believe it was just, and those who opposed it and remain convinced of its illegality and immorality. Yet the bare names of those Americans who died in Vietnam that are inscribed in stone on the wall have become the generators of millions of memories for the various people who visit the site. There is nothing meaningful about these names, yet the wall invites storytelling, and it is those stories that make the experience memorable. In a shared activity of recollecting stories, the various groups come together to reflect on the experience of the war. Some bring memory tokens to leave at the site, others take photographs or rubbings of particular names. These acts enable each individual to draw on this material, to translate it into their own stories, and turn it into new memories. It is the monument itself that sustains this open-ended inventive thinking about the Vietnam War.

How do we apply this open-ended inventive thinking to historic sites and images of the city? How do we turn them into frameworks for sustaining memories?

Let me turn to New York City for examples of how "history" and "memory" have been treated in the past three decades. I will look at how the image of the city has been played with in three projects in which the urge to conserve the built environment and images of the city have played a considerable role: South Street Seaport, where it was assumed that the images of the city being manipulated were authentic and that the process of urban design and historic preservation were antidevelopment; Battery Park City, in which nostalgia for older images of the city came to the fore and blended with policies of urban design and real estate development; and Times Square Now! where there is a free-for-all competition for signage, lighting, and advertisement that creates a ludic playground with no pretension of authenticity and where historic preservation now aids development.

South Street Seaport

South Street Seaport, just a ten-minute walk from City Hall in lower Manhattan, was a typical waterfront restructuring game in the 1960s. The last vestiges of New York's mercantile history—an eleven-block area of four- and five-story late-eighteenth- and nineteenth-century commercial structures—seemed imperiled by a 1960s Wall Street building boom and the relocation of Fulton Market, which had held to the site since 1822. From an urban redevelopment point of view, the area contained only shabby structures, dilapidated piers jutting out into the East River, marginal enterprises, and residential squatters. It was entitled in those years to be officially designated a "slum." Since the financial district was overcrowded and running out of space, the Lower Manhattan Plan of 1966 proposed that office and luxury residential towers be built on landfill extended out to the pier lining the entire waterfront from the Brooklyn Bridge on the East River to Battery Park on the Hudson River.

But there were other hopes for the waterfront as well, for some thought that as shipping activity was declining, it was a splendid time to recapture its glory through a maritime museum. And the Friends of South Street Seaport proposed to establish a living outdoor museum that would re-create the ambience of a "street of ships" out of four blocks of the old mercantile district along the East River, with the old counting house of Schermerhorn Row as its centerpiece (Fig. 1). So began a long negotiating scheme in which parcels of land were traded back and forth between a number of players while various economic downturns and a glut in office real estate development pushed the redevelopment off until the late 1970s.

In 1977 South Street Seaport was designated a Historic District, but now the meaning of "preservation" was stretched beyond preserving the rich history of New York's nineteenth-century maritime development to a new goal, the creation of a twenty-four-hour-a-day tourist attraction accompanied by residential and commercial development. In 1979 the Rouse Company joined the city, the Seaport Museum, and the Urban Development Corporation in a plan to turn South Street Seaport into a festival marketplace on the model of Boston's Faneuil Hall and Baltimore's Harborplace. Transfer of development rights were experimented with for the first time in New York City to create an

Figure 1
South Street Seaport. Contested blocks for preservation and transfer of development rights, circa 1976.

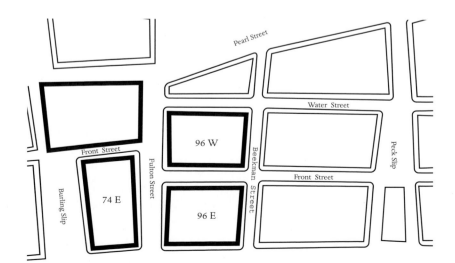

enlarged development district surrounding the famed historic structures of Schermerhorn Row. The city allowed the development rights of these structures to be transferred to nonhistoric westward blocks adjacent to the Row where they would allow a super-high tower to be erected.

The Titanic Memorial Lighthouse guarded the entry to this highly theatrical and illusionistic space. Having crossed this border, the tactile qualities of granite, brick, and stone spelled out a hurly-burly atmosphere while the tin shed–like structure opened to the street lent itself to old marketing techniques. Fronting on the river, on Pier 17, a newly constructed market hall offered a new public gathering place, and throughout the district, design controls dictated logos, outdoor signage, historic markers, and posters in order to underscore its maritime theme. Lest the visitor to the Seaport should wander just a few blocks away from this historic tableau, Richard Haas's trompe l'oeil wall mural entitled *Arcade* outlining Schermerhorn Row (Fig. 2) and the Brooklyn Bridge relayed the work of the artifice and returned the point of perspective back to the centered tableau.

Since conservation of the built environment is gradual and piecemeal, it usually takes a backseat as development forces rise. By the time South Street Seaport officially opened in 1983, three quarters of its museum exhibition space had been reassigned to Cannon's Walk, an interior arcade of shops. Cultural resuscitation stalled while redevelopment gained an advantage.

What a difference fifteen years can make! Today it is difficult to find the original city tableau that had been carefully put in place. Instead, commercial space has been stockpiled until Fulton Market was emptied and Pier 17 was taken over by chain stores. The nautical fish themes have been erased without as much as a smelly trace. South Street Seaport has become a ghost town waiting until it can be turned into a

Figure 2
South Street Seaport. Richard Haas trompe l'oeil wall mural, winter 1993. Photo by M. Christine Boyer.

twenty-four-hour shopping mall for lower Manhattan residential spaces that are beginning to sprout. The jargon of authenticity of place was not a commercial success.

Battery Park City

On the other side of lower Manhattan, another isolated city tableau, Battery Park City, arose. On ninety-two acres of landfill at the southern tip of Manhattan, this idealized New York neighborhood was put into place during the 1980s (Figs. 3 and 4). As one writer noted, "If this newest part of Manhattan . . . were a movie set, New Yorkers would laugh at its impossible concentration of city landmarks."[10] Here one can find the look of prewar apartment houses combined with the views and atmosphere of Brooklyn Heights and the reproduction of Central Park lampposts and benches, the inspiration drawn from the private enclave of Gramercy Park as well as the great landscape inheritance of Olmsted's Central Park. All were collected here in miniaturized form.

This "urban dream" was based on a 1979 master plan that embodied design guidelines specifying architectural elements and styles borrowed from the city's best residential sections such as Fifth Avenue, Central Park West, and Riverside Drive. It was informed as well by Manhattan's grid street pattern and the subtler effects of its lighting, signage, and colors. The authors of the master plan decided, and most New Yorkers agreed, that there was nothing wrong with Manhattan as it appeared and that "most of the attempts by [modernist] architects and planners to rethink the basic shape of the city have resulted in disaster."[11]

Although, being built on new landfill, Battery Park City did not depend on or borrow from the instinct of historic preservation, the organizing principles of this collection of architectural and urban forms was a backward-binding nostalgia that longed to repossess and return to New York's 1920s commercial heyday. Fifty acres were dedicated to public space, be they vest-pocket parks between skyscraper towers, indoor atriums and palm trees, festival marketplaces, or waterfront promenades accompanied by an active program of public art and electric lighting displays (Fig. 5).

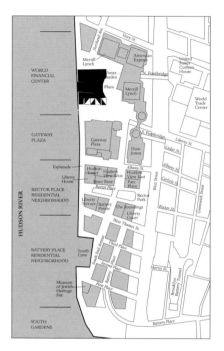

Figure 3
Battery Park City Plan, circa 1988

Figure 4
Battery Park City, 1975–85, Cesar Pelli architect. © Peter Aaron/Esto.

South Cove, a seashell-shaped park, played on a variety of child-hood experiences, from its wooden boardwalks to its lookout towers in the shape of the Statue of Liberty's crown, its bowed bridge, and its semicircular jetty juxtaposed against a rocky coastal garden of beach grass, wild roses, and sumacs. This tableau tried to reestablish New York's heritage as a river town. To the north, the nearly two-mile-long promenade ends in Hudson River Park, whose eight acres of rolling fields and meadows were inspired by the nineteenth-century landscape architects Olmsted and Vaux.

Battery Park City taught New Yorkers how to feel, not think, about the past, how to overcome the sense of failure and crisis that modernism provided and that the near-bankruptcy of the city's fiscal crisis in the mid-1970s symbolized. It was a cleverly designed artifice whose architectural devices were intended to steep the viewer in nostalgic images drawn from its heroic past, and it appears to have been successful. It is a particular historic text that borrows the techniques of persuasion and propaganda from the world of advertising. For Battery Park City, in the end, was the creation of image builders who, to quote their prose, saw the place as "More New York, New York."

Not surprisingly, to announce the opening of the World Financial Center in fall 1988, a series of photo-essays, or "City Tales,"

Figure 5
Battery Park City, Winter Garden facade, circa 1995. Photo by M. Christine Boyer.

were commissioned by the advertising, design, and marketing group Drenttel Doyle Partners. The firm asked the poet Dana Goia and writers such as Jamaica Kincaid and Mark O'Donnell to describe what they like about New York. They could choose their own topics, which ranged from eavesdropping on New Yorkers' conversations to praising all-night Korean grocery stands to experiencing arrivals and departures through Grand Central Station to studying New Yorkers' unusual employment. Thus the fabricated and simulated artifice of Battery Park City, instead of producing architecture for spectators, in the end created spectators, through its elaborate advertising campaign, for its architecture.

Times Square Now!

Now once again the city spectator wanting to view the city tableaus of Manhattan must jump-cut northward to Times Square, where another artifice is playfully at work. But we must also remember that as we move from South Street Seaport to Battery Park City and on to Times Square, we have jumped decades as well, from the 1970s to the 1980s and now to the 1990s and the twenty-first century. Whether for financial or nostalgic purposes, the instrumental discourse and regulating codes of zoning ordinances, urban design procedures, and signage requirements began in the mid-1980s to prescribe and mediate the artifice remaking Times Square.

Although the zipper on the Times Square building still flashed out the news as an electronic device of some kind has done since the early twentieth century, the Great White Way—as the bowtie area formed by the confluence of Broadway, Seventh Avenue, and Forty-second Street was commonly known—was a thing of the past. And in 1982 the artist Jenny Holzer's "Truisms," contrived proclamations and posed clichés, moved across the Spectacolor Board in Times Square proclaiming "PRIVATE PROPERTY CREATED CRIME" and "YOUR OLDEST FEARS ARE THE WORST ONES," proving prophetic about the fragility of the place.

By the end of the 1980s, one could count at least nine new hotel and office towers sprouting above Forty-third Street along the Broadway spine and another seven or so office towers on the midblocks east of Seventh Avenue. All of these have turned Times Square into a mundane corporate office park, without major public acknowledgment or protest. The legal and conservation battle during the 1980s was myopically focused on the massive four-tower redevelopment project, or Times Square Center, proposed for the south end of the square.

On the other hand, those who waged a battle to preserve the traditions of the Great White Way were seduced by the false allure that accompanies the creation of every nostalgic theme park. Hoping to fix its image, lest developers sweep it away, they established design codes and regulations for signs, lights, and setbacks that configured the look of the place. A decreed amount of "lutses" (light units in Times Square) (Fig. 6, Color Plate 4) began to adorn the facade of every new hotel and office tower that dots the area, because by 1987 neon signage was required by law. And a nostalgic themed street, 42nd Street Now!—with an assemblage of astonishing imagescapes—was put into place (Fig. 7).

Figure 6
"Lutses" in Times Square. The Virgin Store, circa 1998. Photo by M. Christine Boyer. *(See also Color Plate 4.)*

Once upon a time, Times Square–Forty-second Street was a place where prostitutes, pimps, and hucksters rubbed shoulders with out-of-town conventioneers, theater audiences, corporate executive secretaries, tourists, and families. But now Times Square's vice zone, which reached its zenith in the 1970s when more than one hundred X-rated adult bookstores, peep shows, and topless clubs concentrated there, has been broken up by a 1995 zoning ordinance that allows only eight such establishments to remain. Evidently eight is the number that offers some "authentic" allure without tipping the scale of morality.

But spiraling real estate prices and exorbitant rents have done more damage to the old Times Square than any zoning regulation or design guideline ever could have wrought. The last pieces of this remodeled media center are currently falling into place. Sixteen years ago, when the city and state decided to clean up Times Square, they offered developers of the four giant office towers located at the heart of the X and known as

Figure 7
Times Square–42nd Street sites. From Executive Summary "42nd Street Now!" 1993. © Robert A. M. Stern Architects.

Times Square Center—a center designed several times by the architectural team of Philip Johnson and John Burgee in the early 1980s— unbelievably large tax abatements if they would turn Times Square into a new headquarters for financial corporations. The collapse of New York's real estate market in the 1980s and an array of lawsuits put an end to that dream. Meanwhile, the public and the architects were given time to rethink the importance of Times Square as the crossroads where consumers and producers of popular culture inevitably meet. And historic preservationists had time to fight for many of the remaining Broadway theaters in the Times Square area.

Hopes for a new financial district to rival Wall Street gave way to a new reality that Times Square–Forty-second Street would soon become the media center of the world. As the idea developed, the four giant towers have been replaced piecemeal: the fifty-one-story tower housing Condé Nast Publications—the publisher of the *New Yorker, Vogue,* and *Vanity Fair,* among other noteworthy magazines—lies on the northeast corner of Broadway and Times Square. Across from this site on the west side of the Square, Reuters news and information services erected a thirty-story headquarters. Two more towers will be built on the south side of Forty-second Street, east and west of Seventh Avenue, whose tenants are likely to be Disney and Home Box Office.

Following the special zoning requirements, the Condé Nast structure contains a ten-story cylinder cantilevered over the northwest corner and outfitted with an eight-story digital billboard—the Nasdaq sign whose brilliance is amazing. This technologically advanced wraparound sign can display more than 16.7 million distinct colors, making advertisements, stock information, and motion pictures dance before the spectator's eyes. On the southwestern end of the Condé Nast building, adorning the curved edge of its lower facade, a metal grid permits a mixture of advertising gimmicks including video and electronic screens. Four huge billboard panels looming out over the cityscape form a crown, adorned with satellite dishes, radio antennae, and other high-technology equipment. The design for the new thirty-story Reuters building proposed similar gestures, such as a fourth-floor newsroom visible from the street and a news zipper extending down to the sidewalk, all of which were intended to make the pedestrian aware that media art is the required adornment for all commercial architecture in Times Square.

Some believe the revival of Times Square–Forty-second Street began in 1993 when Disney decided to make a modest investment in what was then considered a dead and dreary center of Manhattan by agreeing to renovate the New Amsterdam Theater on Forty-second Street and open a Disney Store. The city was more than willing to offer this entertainment giant both subsidies and guarantees that it would not risk its brand name, feeling secure that Disney would lure others in its powerful wake. Almost a decade later, the entire thirteen acres of Times Square–Forty-second Street contain the hottest real estate in the world.

The overall cleanup of Times Square–Forty-second Street generated spin-off effects enlarging its theatrical tableaus: the Stardust Dine-O-Mat on Forty-third Street appeared to be a 1940s blue-plate restaurant with waitresses attired as if they were one of the Andrews Sisters; a Hansen's Times Square Brewery Restaurant and a Ferrara's delicatessen, a virtual reality emporium called Cinema Ride, and a dozen or so other "themed" places carried out their play on history. By the twenty-first century, however, these themed restaurants and simulated rides appeared to be on the decline. Meanwhile, media power developed its full strength, and it is hard to compete with global giants. Besides the Disney Company, Warner Brothers, the Virgin Megastore, Live Entertainment of Toronto, and AMC, there are a range of television studios along Broadway and Seventh Avenue, such as MTV's glass-walled music studios, ABC-TV's *Good Morning America*, and the Nasdaq studio. AMC even moved an old burlesque house on the south side of Forty-second Street, the landmark Empire Theater, 170 feet down the street to make room for entrances to Madame Tussaud's Wax Museum and a twenty-five-screen movie theater complex.

None of the acts in this revival show, however, has been accomplished without a great deal of anxiety and fear that the area has been mauled, sanitized, Disneyfied—in other words, fallen into the disreputable position of having been fully fabricated in the sense that Lowenthal described.[12] Hence the conservation of Times Square arouses a general fear that no one will ever experience in this commodified place the unique reality of New York. Some blame Mickey Mouse as the virtuoso in charge of a marketing show that offers token images of the city laced with saccharine cheer in preference to the dirty real thing. Others fear the burning heat of a cultural meltdown when popular art and the mainstream commandeer the show. They maintain a snobbish contempt for Disney, Warner Brothers, and the Ford Motor Company, all of whom are making their architectural debut on the reinvigorated stage of Times Square. Others believe that seedy old Times Square was utterly authentic, ablaze with stroboscopic liveliness and vibrating energy sustaining a tempo of desire both pleasurable and degenerate. They wish that Disney could be banished to the South Bronx, to an invisible rather than an animated presence. Still others point out that the advertising war of signs taking place around the Square has raised the entry stakes to billions of dollars in the competition to obtain mediaspace in this preeminently televisual place. At such a level, it is guaranteed that only mega-corporations can play in the real estate game. In other words, architectural critics and connoisseurs of high art are appalled by what they see in the Square.

Conclusion

These three examples of what can be called physical frameworks for collective memory have been influenced by three different approaches to history: one based on authenticity, the other steeped in nostalgia, and the third celebrating the spectacle. But what does this tell us about sustainability—or the creation of an open-ended process of inventive memory?

In the search for authenticity, South Street Seaport sharpened the tension between history and memory, constructing a static container that failed to create rapport with the past. Perhaps the search for authenticity is merely an apology for past traditions that need to be resuscitated, brought back to life and given a useless meaning in the present. Like any museum collection, the open-air museum of South Street Seaport collected whatever from wherever that had a nautical theme—boats, lighthouses, materials, logos—but they appeared out of context and resisted demands for change and improvisation.

The nostalgic gestures of Battery Park City, on the other hand, constructed a didactic container, blatantly fabricating its framework. Slightly more successful as a memory container than South Street Seaport, Battery Park puts the artifice of construction on display. In this sense it makes use of most of the ways that Lowenthal claims heritage alters the past: by upgrading, updating, jumbling times and places together, selectively forgetting, erecting fictitious lineages. But all these uses of "history" nevertheless focus their attention on the re-creation of a heroic New York—celebrating the city as the leader of global capitalism. The architects and urban designer bent the framework to conform to this conception. Modern architecture and planning were banished, megastructures were out, and fabricated historicized backdrops were the consoling theme.

The spectacle of Times Square erects a different framework that mixes together authentic, nostalgic, and commercial instincts. It is multivocal, moving across the layered substrata in different directions, reaching out to various versions of what is Times Square. This framework tries to animate the private worlds in which memory is formed in an open-ended manner, aware of a plurality of pasts and the different temporal rhythms of change. It sets up an animated play as a series of Times Squares. The list includes

- a blatantly commercialized space, the quintessential element of the spectacle;
- a luminous space, where the fiery reds of the neon signs form a major element of the spectacle;
- a historic space, whose major success is the reinvigoration of seven Forty-second Street theaters;
- a space of nostalgia, enhanced by the theme-park effects of 42nd Street Now!
- a space for public art, sometimes willfully critical, and for commercial art, with the full power of competitive publicity ornamenting the walls; and
- a media space, not only where the conglomerates gather, but also where the latest electronic wizardry is on full display.

It is debatable whether Times Square achieves the sustainability I claim it has or whether its driving force is merely distraction displayed in public space. Herbert Muschamp, current architectural critic of the *New York Times*, is wary about the success of Times Square. While he notes that it is great to see that people have been drawn back to the place, he adds,

> [T]he cost of drawing them there could be substantial. In media terms, Times Square represents the blurring of the boundary between advertising and editorial, and the resulting distortions of truth. In architectural terms, it represents a blurring of the boundary between art and commerce, and a

sacrifice of the idea that architecture is also a medium for conveying truths about the urban condition. Truth in architecture is not the same as accuracy in news reporting. It is not an objective truth. But the idea that architecture and real estate are the same thing is one of the grander deceptions New York practices upon itself.[13]

By mentioning "truth" four times. modified by "distortions" and "deceptions," Muschamp takes us back to the problematic duality explored at the beginning of this chapter—the "sustainability" of urban frameworks as a work of history or fabrication. He assumes that Times Square once contained a unique, even authentic experience and makes an appeal implicitly to history as the stable source from which contemporary representations should draw. Hence the duality reappears: history, embedded in editorials and architecture, seeks to tell the truth, relying heavily on evidence and critical accuracy; fabrication distorts, tells lies, and deceives.

Like Lowenthal who raised fabrication as a virtue, Muschamp, in his reliance on history, erased the necessary distinction between the container of memory and the engendering of memory. Architecture and urban space can only be the framework that excites a remembering mind and allows each individual to draw from his or her own memories, critical thoughts, and perceptions of place. If architecture and urban space hold the pretension to be an accurate teller of tales, or offer an authentic experience of place, they become static containers under the guise of didactic or truthful intentions. And they are bound to fail.

But if the spatial framework allows each individual to assemble his or her own stories, composing something new out of the experience, then Times Square becomes a "sustainable" place. Seeing urban space as a framework that sets up a constant play between past and present architectural forms, establishing ambivalent open-ended conundrums and analogies, makes it impossible to assigned fixed meanings. This is the variability and spontaneity of any cityscape at its most dense, a series of images that explode in multiple directions.

Notes

1 M. Halbwachs, *The Collective Memory* (New York: HarperColophon, 1950).

2 D. Lowenthal, "Fabricating Heritage," *History & Memory* 10, no. 1 (spring 1998):5–24.

3 Lowenthal, "Fabricating Heritage," 18.

4 Lowenthal, "Fabricating Heritage," 12.

5 Lowenthal, "Fabricating Heritage," 19.

6 F. Yates, *The Art of Memory* (Chicago: University of Chicago Press, 1966).

7 M. Carruthers, *The Craft of Thought: Meditation, Rhetoric, and the Making of Images* (Cambridge: Cambridge University Press, 1998).

8 Carruthers, *The Craft of Thought,* 11.

9 Carruthers, *The Craft of Thought,* 35–40.

10 M. de Courcy Hinds, "Shaping Landfill into a Neighborhood," *New York Times,* March 23, 1986, sec. 8, p. 1.

11 P. Goldberger, "Battery Park City as a Triumph of Urban Design," *New York Times,* August 31, 1986, p. H1.

12 A sampling of criticism can be taken from M. Berman, "Times Square, Times Square," *Village Voice,* July 18, 1995, pp. 23–26.

13 H. Muschamp, "A Tower That Flaunts Its Contradictions," *New York Times,* September 26, 1999, p. 43.

Sustainability and Buildings: Sustainable Solutions to Decay and Infestation in Timber

Brian Ridout

THE *QUEEN CHARLOTTE*, a first-rate English warship of one hundred guns, was launched at Deptford in 1810 and rotted so quickly that it was necessary to rebuild her before she could be commissioned for sea (Ramsbottom 1937). The Royal Navy's ships had always suffered from decay, but the severity of the new problem attracted the attention of newspapers, and "dry rot" became a popular topic for speculation (Ridout 2000). It soon became apparent that the damage would also occur in buildings, for example, where kitchen floor joists were embedded in damp earth (Lingard 1819), and many people sought an explanation (e.g., George 1829; Wade 1815). Bowden (1815), of the Navy Office, eventually concluded that the use of unseasoned imported softwoods in a dank environment was a major cause of the difficulties with ships. Oak, the traditional construction timber, had become almost impossible to obtain in sufficient quantity to support the navy by the end of the eighteenth century (Greenhalgh Albion 1926), and it was supplemented with large quantities of softwood, predominantly from northern Europe. Johnson (1795) similarly considered that the change from oak to softwood and the latter's use in situations in which it would remain damp were the causes of dry rot in buildings.

The problem with warships had its roots in earlier centuries, when monarchs, deaf to the entreaties of their naval advisers, sold oak forests to iron- and glassworkers in order to swell the royal coffers (Ramsbottom 1937). Unfortunately, oak suitable for the huge curved timbers of warships was needed in enormous quantities, took centuries to grow, and was not a sustainable resource when felled indiscriminately. The *Temeraire*, for example, a warship built in 1798 from oak felled in the Hainault forest, required two thousand mature trees for its construction (Ramsbottom 1937). Availability was assisted somewhat by the importation of European oak, but escalating prices also reduced affordability for building works, and softwoods with a poorer natural durability became the usual construction timber in England from about 1750 onward.

Although the softwoods used in England during the eighteenth and nineteenth centuries did not have the durability of oak, they were not generally perishable timbers. The navy's problems were largely resolved by the use of iron hulls, and it was realized that dry rot in buildings could be avoided by keeping the timber dry. Decay fungi were therefore a significant problem only where there was poor maintenance, or where unusual circumstances allowed the wood to remain wet for prolonged periods. An example of the latter would be speculative construction that progressed as and when money was available (Britton 1875). Wood-boring insects could not cause much damage either, because they could only attack sapwood, and this formed only a small proportion of the wide, mature pine tree trunks that were converted into building timbers. Commercial equilibrium had been restored, but it was not going to last because wild forests were finite, and by the end of the nineteenth century the problem of a nonsustainable resource had reemerged, driving down still further the natural durability of the timber.

By the beginning of the twentieth century large structural sizes of softwood had become difficult to obtain in England, and the use of wood for these large components had given way to reinforced concrete or steel (Bateson 1948). Natural forests had become depleted or more difficult to exploit, and timber was obtained increasingly from regenerated forests or plantations. This trend was to accelerate. Vast quantities of softwoods were used as trench and mine props during the 1914–18 war (Stobart 1927), and this led to a serious timber shortage after the war. Nevertheless, large quantities of European timber were imported into England during the interwar years to meet the demand for low-cost housing. This timber was of such poor quality that sometimes fungus had to be brushed from stacks before it could be distributed from the timber yard (Dewar 1933).

The search for a sustainable timber resource has inevitably led from the ancient wild forests of Europe to managed woodlands, in which economic considerations require that the trees be encouraged to reach a marketable size in the shortest time. The timber need not have the poor durability described by Dewar (1933), but neither does it have the durability of its wild grown equivalent. This is not just a European problem; it is occurring in many other parts of the world. If we are going to seek sustainable solutions to decay problems in building timbers, then we must first consider why a change in the way a tree is grown might change the properties of the timber we obtain from it.

Sapwood and Heartwood

European redwood trees (*Pinus sylvestris*) from natural forests tended to be about two hundred years old when felled (Fig. 1), while plantation *P. sylvestris* is generally grown on a far shorter crop rotation. Stands are now thinned to increase the growth rate by reducing competition from adjacent trees, and trees are grown on good soils, where possible, to increase crop viability. Uusvaara (1974) quantified this somewhat by stating that pine enters a diameter class meeting saw log requirements in southern Finland at a minimum height of 18 feet (5.5 m) and a top diameter of 5.5 inches (140 mm). He found that 9 percent of trees would reach the minimum saw log size on poor soil (*Vaccinium*-type vegetation) and 40 percent on better-quality soils (*Myrtillus* and *Oxalis-Myrtillus*–type vegetation) after a growth period of thirty to thirty-five years.

Figure 1
Five-hundred-year-old European redwood
(*Pinus sylvestris*) in the Kenozero National
Park in northwest Russia. The redwood trees
used for buildings in the United Kingdom
were generally 200 to 300 years old when
felled, and the wood had good natural durability. Photo by Brian Ridout.

The minimum growth period for *P. sylvestris* to reach a marketable size in the United Kingdom tends to be about fifty-five years, producing trees with a diameter of about 200 millimeters (breast height). It is difficult to obtain larger-dimension softwood timbers in England. A tree grows from its apex, and as it increases in height, it increases in width. The increase in width takes place in a narrow band of tissue, the cambium, which is situated just under the bark. The cambium produces both inner bark (phloem) cells and outer wood (xylem) cells. The outer wood is called the sapwood.

The sapwood zone of the tree is the only part of the woody stem that contains living material. Active conduction takes place in the sapwood, and, because it is saturated with sap, air is excluded. This provides the tree with an outer barrier that protects against many pathogens. When the tree is felled the sapwood dries through levels where an assemblage of decay organisms can invade, and the active role it played in the living tree means that the sapwood has a higher nutrient content than the rest of the trunk. Sapwood of any timber species is therefore vulnerable to decay.

Heartwood is formed around the pith of the living tree when the innermost sapwood cells die. The removal of nutrients and the deposition of a range of organic substances, some of which may have biocidal properties, accompany this change. It is these organic substances (grouped under the broad term "extractives") that give the heartwood whatever natural durability it is destined to acquire.

The age at which the change from the ultimately perishable sapwood to the more durable heartwood commences is variable. Bruun and Willberg (1964) showed that it commenced after thirty to forty years in Finnish pine, but this was influenced by north-south geographic variations. Uusvaara (1974) found in his plantation study that the change commenced after twenty years. Uusvaara summarizes as follows: "As the amount of heartwood seems to be associated simultaneously with age, growth rate and site type, wood with a particularly low heartwood percentage will be obtained from young fast growing pine plantations" (p. 84). And he concludes: "The average percentage of heartwood in plantation grown pine is only a half of the percentage in stems of natural origin" (p. 88).

Natural durability is dependent on heartwood content (Fig. 2), but even when heartwood is present, there is another potential complication.

Figure 2
Joint cut in a 200-year-old log of European
redwood in the Kenozero National Park. Note
the minimal outer sapwood zone and the
close, evenly spaced growth rings in the heartwood. Photo by Brian Ridout.

Juvenile Wood

The first few growth rings nearest to the pith in any tree constitute the juvenile core, which may be sapwood or heartwood. This immature wood differs from adult wood in several ways, but of most concern for structural purposes are cell wall differences. The thickest layer of the cell wall contains microfibrils of cellulose (rather like reinforcing bars in concrete), which, in adult wood, are oriented nearly parallel to the longitudinal axis of the tree. This means that longitudinal shrinkage of adult timber is minimal. Microfibrils in juvenile wood are shorter and at significantly larger angles to the axis, so that longitudinal shrinkage is more pronounced, and a solid wood product may deform lengthways during unrestricted drying if excess juvenile wood is present. The large fiber angle also means that the wood is weaker than normal wood of the same density and may break under load with a brash type of tension failure (Krahmer 1986).

The duration of the juvenile period is probably highly variable and may differ according to the characteristic studied (Zobel and Sprague 1998). Generally, it is assumed to extend for the first ten to twenty years of growth. All trees have a juvenile core, but the wider growth rings produced by thinning the plantation to create growing space, and/or the narrower bole diameter produced by early felling, greatly increase the amount of juvenile material present in converted timber (Fig. 3). Ramsay Smith and Briggs (1986) provide the data presented in Table 1. Their findings are in accordance with those of Elliot (1970), who reviewed the literature and showed that dense growing of pine, which slowed the growth rate, also reduced the volume of juvenile wood.

Table 1
Changes in percent of juvenile wood present at different growth rates/tree age at felling for Douglas fir, assuming a twenty-year juvenile period.

Age of Tree When Felled	Rate of Growth (rings/25mm)	Width of Juvenile Core (mm)	Percent of Juvenile Wood in Trunk
540	30	25	5
72	4	125	25
36	2	250	60

Figure 3
Stack of plantation-grown redwood in a U.K. woodyard. The stack is composed mostly of juvenile wood and sapwood with blue-stain fungus. This wood has very little natural durability. Photo by Brian Ridout.

It is apparent from the discussion so far that the trees that reach the minimum age for saw logs of thirty to thirty-five years in Finland (Uusvaara 1974) would consist entirely of sapwood and juvenile wood. The data provided by Ramsay Smith and Briggs (1986; see Table 1) also suggest that an economically viable crop rotation period with other timbers is likely to produce a high percentage of juvenile wood. The question, for our purposes here, is what effect this has on durability, a subject that has not been well researched in recent years.

The Durability of Juvenile Wood

Rennerfelt (1947) studied the resistance to decay of blocks of European redwood (*P. sylvestris*) that were inoculated with a range of fungi and stored for four months in Kolle flasks. These blocks were taken from outer heartwood and inner heartwood, and resistance to decay was quantified by percent weight loss. Some of Rennerfelt's results are shown in Table 2. These data suggest that fungi vary in their ability to decay mature heartwood (outer heartwood) and that it can be significantly resistant to attack by some species. *Serpula lacrymans*, for example, generally produces a weight loss in the inner heartwood that is a high percentage of that produced in the sapwood, while the outer heartwood seems to be fairly resistant to attack. Inner and outer heartwood weight losses only coincide when the tree is so young that there is probably no mature heartwood present.

The natural durability of wood seems to be associated with its extractive content. Rudman and Da Costa (1959) demonstrated this many

Table 2
Percent weight loss of pine samples after four months' exposure to decay fungi (data from Rennerfelt 1947).

a. *Coniphora puteana* (wet rot)

Age of Tree	Sapwood	Outer Heartwood	Inner Heartwood
269	35.5	2.3	39.3
230	38.7	16.1	39.5
213	32.2	4.3	21.6
193	39.3	23.9	32.8
85	29.4	19.3	31.8
34	35.9	19.2	32.5

b. *Lentinus lepideus* (wet rot)

Age of Tree	Sapwood	Outer Heartwood	Inner Heartwood
259	40.0	24.0	35.4
230	44.0	38.3	43.3
213	35.8	25.0	32.7
193	45.4	36.8	41.7
85	33.5	20.6	28.2
34	50.7	46.0	45.0

Table 2   cont.

c. Serpula lacrymans (dry rot)

Age of Tree	Sapwood	Outer Heartwood	Inner Heartwood
269	38.5	0	29.1
230	42.8	0.7	35.6
213	43.8	0.8	20.0
193	55.8	1.1	1.7
85	33.5	1.2	–
34	42.7	16.3	17.6

years ago, when they tested the decay resistance of teak to two decay fungi. They found that resistance did not begin until between five and ten growth rings from the pith had been formed and that resistance to decay in all the timber was drastically reduced if the extractives were removed by solvent treatment. These extractives were then added to sawdust from mountain ash, and the resistance of that normally susceptible species was found to be significantly enhanced in most of the samples. Variation in extractive content between trees was sometimes considerable and appeared to be genetically rather than environmentally controlled.

The extractives that confer decay resistance in western red cedar (*Thuja plicata*) have been investigated and found to be mostly thujaplicins and thujic acid. Nault (1988) studied extractives from six healthy old trees (260–710 years old) and ten healthy second-growth trees (42–77 years old). He found that extractives increased from the pith to the outer heartwood and decreased in the sapwood. Older wood had more extractives than younger ones. He concluded, "Products made from the wood of younger trees, with reduced amounts of thujaplicins, will be less resistant to decay than those made from older trees" (p. 78).

Rennerfelt (1945) showed that two phenolic compounds (pinosylvin and pinosylvin monomethyl ether) found in the heartwood of European redwood (*P. sylvestris*) were highly toxic to fungi. Browning (1963) considered that these compounds (stilbenes) are responsible for the durability of *P. sylvestris* heartwood, while, more recently, Celimine et al. (1999) showed that the stilbenes contributed to wood decay resistance against brown rot fungi but were ineffective against white rot fungi. Their results depended, however, on the test method used.

Rennerfelt (1947) considered that the difference he had found between the durability of inner and outer heartwood (see Table 2) was caused by the distribution of the stilbenes. It would seem either that the stilbenes were not so plentiful in the inner heartwood (juvenile wood) or that inner heartwood contained a higher percentage of the ether Rennerfelt had found less efficient as a fungicide than pinosylvin. These suppositions are supported by the results of Erdtman, Frank, and Lindstedt (1951), which demonstrated that the mature heartwood from 252 Swedish pine trees (from all over Sweden) averaged 0.96 percent of the stilbenes, while the core averaged 0.77 percent. Erdtman and Misiorny (1952) then analyzed twenty trees from three stands for the stilbenes and obtained an average of 1.4 percent (of air, dry weight) from the outer heartwood and 0.75 percent from the cores. Further analysis showed that about 28 percent of the stilbenes from mature heartwood and 18 percent from the core wood was pinosylvin.

These results would seem to explain Rennerfelt's observations, but the work needs to be repeated using modern analytic techniques. The distribution of stilbenes, for example, is in agreement with Bergström et al. (1999) who also showed that pinosylvin levels declined from the outer heartwood toward the core, but their measurements were taken over a distance of only a few millimeters.

Celimine et al. (1999) complicated the situation by suggesting that the most important effect of stilbenes might be to exclude free water from the timber and thus make it less available to fungi. The distribution of stilbenes across the trunk, as reported by Rennerfelt and his Swedish colleagues, should therefore tend to make the juvenile wood wetter than the mature heartwood, and this has been demonstrated by Zobel and Sprague (1998). The latter authors also state that the moisture distribution may reverse when mature heartwood is formed, and the juvenile wood becomes flooded with resins and polyphenols. They believe that this flooding ultimately makes the juvenile wood more resistant than mature heartwood to decay. This view contradicts the data presented in Table 2 and is certainly not universally true, because Zabel and Morrell (1992) provide several references to demonstrate that resistance to decay usually increases from the core to the heartwood–sapwood boundary in a variety of tree species.

Sustainability and Durability: A Difficult Combination

The continuing and sustainable use of timber as a construction material requires that it be grown as a commercially viable crop. This usually means that it is grown on the shortest practical rotation; ancillary products, for example, thinnings removed to encourage growth, must be salable, and the final product has to be appropriate for a range of end uses. Moore (2000) informed us that 55 percent of the wood cut throughout the world is used as an energy source, 30 percent is used for pulp, and only 15 percent is used as solid wood for construction. The share of this market used by building conservation must be very small, and we cannot expect forestry practices to change generally to meet our requirements for durable timber.

The timber produced by modern forestry practices, particularly if it is softwood, may be very different from the material used historically in the buildings we wish to conserve. Sapwood has no durability, but Desch and Dinwoodie (1981) reported that modern softwood logs might have 25 to 30 percent sapwood when they were taken to the sawmills, while Linscott (1970) found that seventy-eight lengths of imported rough-sawn European redwood, obtained from timber merchants in Sussex, contained more sapwood than heartwood. Sapwood averaged 66.3 percent of the surface area and 52.5 percent of the volume, but in some pieces these figures were as high as 88 percent and 90 percent, respectively.

The decay resistance of juvenile wood seems to vary considerably, but there is evidence to suggest that resistance may be poor, at least until mature heartwood production is firmly established. Unfortunately, juvenile wood accounts for the remainder of many commercial logs if the sapwood is discounted.

Lack of durability is not perceived to be a problem for most solid wood end uses because the reduced level of natural decay inhibitors means that the wood will (in most cases) readily accept pressure impregnation with fungicides. Falk (1997), for example, quoted an annual figure for copper-chromium-arsenic (CCA) treated timber production in the United States of 8 million metric tons. This additional process adds to the cost of the product, however, and may ultimately produce a disposal problem if a structure is demolished. Falk (1997) estimated that there were more than 85 million metric tons of CCA-treated timber in service, and McQueen and Stevens (1998) calculated that the quantity of this timber removed from service would rise to over 430 million cubic feet by the year 2004. Most uses had a perceived design life of about twenty years. Pretreatment may be essential if perishable timber is going to be used in a hazardous environment, but it cannot be viewed as a permanent solution. Chemical treatments may just change the sequence of organisms that invade, and most treatments will fail eventually if the environment favors decay.

If we, who are concerned with historic buildings, cannot influence the way in which building timbers are generally produced, we can at least enhance their conservation by an awareness of timber quality. It is certainly still possible to obtain durable timber for repairs from trees that have grown for several centuries, but this is not a sustainable resource. Forest regeneration will not produce a "like for like" replacement wood unless the forests are left for generations in the future to exploit. We must therefore perceive individual building components as having a potential value equal to the rest of the building, even if visitors do not see them.

There is still much that can be achieved. We should be aware that most timber decay organisms require excess moisture and that they may be avoided by good maintenance. If decay organisms are present, then we may advocate a policy of minimum intervention (Ridout 2000) and conserve as much of the original material as possible.

In some high hazard environments (e.g., timbers embedded in permanently damp walls, or sites where there are subterranean termites) the use of timber with a durability equivalent to the original may be the only authentic and permanent repair option. This timber may be reused from another less fortunate building. This procedure has a historical precedent. Our predecessors would not have discarded good building timbers that could be salvaged from unwanted or decrepit buildings. Unfortunately, many people believe that this form of repairs will distort the historical record or introduce decay organisms into the building. The first problem can be overcome by marking or recording the repairs, and the second possibility may be evaluated by acquiring a sound knowledge of decay mechanisms. A more significant objection might be the risk of damage to woodworking tools caused by nails or other inclusions in the timber. Not a sustainable resource perhaps, but large quantities of usable historical timbers are discarded every year because their quality is unrecognized.

Another option, which might be practical in some situations, would be to set aside land containing growing conservation-quality trees. The woodland might not be commercially viable for timber production, but it might have amenity, scientific, or some other value that will justify its existence.

Whatever the situation, sustainable solutions must commence with a clear understanding of the problem, or the deterioration will reoccur. There is little to be gained by squandering precious resources on the symptoms when the underlying causes remain. This moral, and the general problem of natural durability, may now be summarized by a case study.

The Imperial City of Hue: A Case Study

In 1993 the Imperial City of Hue in Vietnam was declared a World Heritage Site. History has not been kind to Vietnam, and the temples and mausoleums were in a poor state of repair. The primary problem seemed to be a variety of subterranean termites. In 1995 UNESCO signed a partnership agreement with a major pesticide manufacturer in order to preserve and promote the world's historic treasures, and the termites at Hue were considered a suitable case for treatment. The task was not a simple one. The treatment philosophy was to treat ground and walls, existing timbers, and new timbers. This philosophy is well established for many types of decay organisms and in many countries. It is based on the idea that if an organism eats wood and the building is made from wood, then the organism will eat the building.

The chemical formulations used were efficient insecticides based around an insect nerve poison, but coordination of the treatments with the restoration program was difficult, the lingering smell of the insecticides was unpleasant, and treatment was abandoned after the first temple had been dismantled and reerected. A different approach to treatment had to be found, and we were asked to investigate the problem.

Treatments that use large volumes of biocides are becoming increasingly unpopular because of perceived or actual risks to human health and the environment. This change in attitudes has provoked the development of an approach referred to as Integrated Pest Management, or IPM. An IPM system seeks to control a pest organism by understanding and manipulating the various parameters that allow the pest species to flourish (Ridout 2001a, 2001b; Simmonds, Belmain, and Blaney 2001). It aims to develop methodologies that are practical, effective, economical, and protective to both human health and the environment. Pesticides may be required, but their use is limited, and they are targeted. This approach was developed for agricultural pests, but it also works well with timber-destroying organisms.

Our starting point for the Imperial City of Hue was the observation that although the buildings were constructed from wood, many of them were one hundred to two hundred years old. If the termites could destroy the timbers, then the original buildings would have been lost many years ago. Clearly, the two major timber species from which the buildings were constructed, *Erythrophloeum fordii* and *Hopea pierrei*, must be immune from termite attack unless something happens to change the properties of the wood (Fig. 4). The comprehensive treatment of all timbers with chemicals will therefore serve no useful purpose.

Wood durability depends on wood chemistry and perhaps on wood density. Both *Erythrophloeum* and *Hopea* are loosely termed "ironwoods" because of their hardness, and *Hopea*, at least, has a chemistry that makes the wood unavailable to most wood-destroying organisms. Loss of durability will occur if a fungus or progression of fungi can invade the wood and modify the chemistry (Ridout and Ridout 2001). Most woods will have some progression of organisms that will eventually attack and modify them if they stay wet enough for long enough, and investigations with other types of wood have shown that even a low level of fungus attack will radically alter wood chemistry (Esser and Tas 2002). Termites, which attack *Erythrophloeum* and *Hopea*, must therefore be seen as secondary wood-destroying organisms and fungi as the primary problem (Fig. 5). If we

Figure 4
Ironwood (*Erythrophloeum fordii*) columns in a temple in Hue, Vietnam. This timber is immune to termite attack, and the insects can attack only the ends of the timber where there has been water penetration and the wood chemistry has been modified by fungi. The fungus is the primary colonizer; the termites are a secondary problem. Photo by Brian Ridout.

Figure 5
Post and rafter junction decayed by the wet rot fungus *Phellinus senex*. The ironwood is now suitable for the termites to colonize. Photo by Brian Ridout.

can stop the building timbers from being decayed by fungi, then termites will not attack most of them. The key to termite control in the Imperial City is therefore to keep the buildings dry.

All wood decay fungi, including *Phellinus senex* (the main problem species in the Imperial City), require a plentiful supply of water, and the history of Vietnam throughout most of the twentieth century has not been conducive to good building maintenance. Many historical buildings have severe building faults and extensive decay by fungi and colonies of termites.

An accurate diagnosis of the problem allows the limited resources available to be targeted effectively. Manpower to undertake effective maintenance should be easier to obtain than massive amounts of insecticides, and the environmental impact is diminished.

A further important advantage of careful problem assessment is that the retention of original timbers may be maximized. This is clearly goods news for building conservation, but less obvious is the fact that naturally durable timber is becoming increasingly difficult to obtain. Logging concessions in Vietnam have been sold to foreign companies, and the conservation authorities cannot afford to buy the timber. This means that the timber for repairs must be illegally acquired from clandestine logging activities in Laos or some other species of wood must be used. The temple of Thaito Mie in Hue, for example, was reconstructed in 1971 using timber that ultimately proved to have poor durability (Fig. 6). This was done because the traditional construction timbers were unavailable, but the result has been the destruction of the principal pillars by *Coptotermes formosanus*, one of the world's most destructive termites (Fig. 7). The change in timber durability has changed the status of the termites from secondary to primary pest and added a major complication to conservation.

Figure 6
Traditional ironwoods are now very difficult to obtain. The temple of Thaito Mie in Hue was reconstructed using an unknown but readily available local timber. Photo by Brian Ridout.

Figure 7
The timber had poor natural durability, and now termites are the primary colonizers. Photo by Brian Ridout.

PART THREE

Practicing Sustainability: Case Studies

Toward a Sustainable Management Plan:
The Case of Stonehenge and Avebury

David Batchelor

STONEHENGE AND AVEBURY ARE TWO of the most famous and important prehistoric sites in Europe and indeed the world, but while many people are familiar with the two main monuments, the impressive archaeological landscapes in which they sit are less well known. The two land parcels of Stonehenge and Avebury were together inscribed a World Heritage Site (Site C373: Stonehenge, Avebury, and associated sites) in 1986. The two areas, comprising more than 4,500 hectares, are about thirty kilometers apart. There are numerous other prehistoric structures, including many for ceremonial and funerary uses, the great majority of which were built between four thousand and six thousand years ago. Many of these survive as significant landscape features today, and they are interrelated one to another and also with the host landscape. What we see today are relict cultural landscapes, which even in their eroded state remain as a testament to the skills and efforts of the peoples who built and used them. Managing these landscapes often involves reconciling the sometimes conflicting interests of landowners, visitors, and the monuments themselves. Developing a management plan begins to establish the principles of sustainability in the local, regional, national, and international contexts.

Beginning with the Stonehenge area, we find arguably the most famous stone circle in the world, but we also find many other monuments. For example, another massive henge was constructed at Durrington Walls between 2800 and 2200 B.C. It is almost 500 meters in diameter and comprises a huge earthen bank and ditch, now partly infilled. To the southwest of Durrington Walls stood a smaller henge, known as Woodhenge, which enclosed concentric rings of postholes. An enigmatic monument, known as the Stonehenge Cursus, can be found to the north of Stonehenge. This elongated enclosure, 100 to 150 meters wide, runs for 2.8 kilometers. Its purpose is not well understood, although it appears to be connected to funerary monuments and may have had a ceremonial function relating to the dead. Again, it is constructed from earth and chalk quarried from external flanking ditches.

Perhaps some of the most impressive earthen structures in the Stonehenge area are the round barrow cemeteries that date to the early

Bronze Age. At this time, individual burials started to take place; the rich graves contained inhumations and cremations and were covered with large circular mounds of chalk and earth that were quarried from surrounding circular ditches. There are many linear cemeteries, each containing large numbers of barrows, which are situated carefully within the Stonehenge landscape on true ridge lines or false horizons when viewed from the center, so they are visible both from Stonehenge itself and from other key parts of the area. Barrow groups such as the Normanton Down Group to the south of Stonehenge contain a huge variety of round barrow types, including disc, bell, bowl, and pond barrows. Each barrow has a central primary inhumation, usually cut below the contemporary land surface, with the mound constructed over it. Into this mound and the surrounding ditch are often cut secondary burials, which may be inhumation or cremation burials.

Stonehenge itself is famous for its stone circle surrounding the Trilithons (Fig. 1). This circle sits within an earthen henge and is approached by a processional route defined by two earthen banks and ditches, known as The Avenue, which runs for 2.5 kilometers between Stonehenge and the River Avon. The first monument at Stonehenge was the earthen bank and enclosure ditch, approximately 100 meters in diameter, which has been dated to circa 2950 B.C. Within this enclosure were dug some fifty-six pits known as the Aubrey Holes, which may have held timber uprights. This enclosure, which may have its origins as a causewayed camp, has its principal entrance at the northeast, with a number of secondary entrances elsewhere on the circuit.

A second main phase spans between 2900 and 2500 B.C., when a timber setting, or multiple settings, was built within the henge and cremation burials were inserted into the now-empty Aubrey Holes and the ditch, which was filling up. The final phase encompassing the construction of the stone circle started circa 2400 B.C., when bluestone from the Presceli Mountains in Wales, more than 200 kilometers away, was transported to form part of a structure not seen today. Subsequently, enormous blocks of sarsen were

Figure 1
The stone circle of Stonehenge, showing the condition of the stones.
© Crown copyright. NMR.

dragged from the Avebury area of the Marlborough Downs, worked at Stonehenge to form the shapes we see today, and used to build the outer stone circle and inner horseshoe of five Trilithons. A Trilithon comprises two large uprights with a cross lintel and has come to epitomize the site. Throughout its long life Stonehenge retained its principal entrance in the northeast, which aligns with the midsummer sunrise and up to which The Avenue comes. The horseshoe setting of the inner five Trilithons is arranged around this midsummer axis, with the open end toward the sunrise (the northeast) and the largest and most delicately shaped Trilithon closing the end and forming a focus on the central point. The stones went through a number of relatively minor reorderings until about 1600 B.C., when the site was abandoned. It is the intricate working of the stone and the use of sophisticated structural engineering and architectural techniques that sets Stonehenge apart and makes it unique among contemporary structures.

The archaeology of the Avebury area, while similar to Stonehenge in many ways, has its own distinct character and palimpsest of monuments. It contains without doubt the most visually impressive earth structure in the United Kingdom, Silbury Hill. This enormous and extraordinary mound, which has been described as the largest man-made mound in Europe, is more than 40 meters high. It is surrounded by a large quarry ditch, which due to the level of the water table has yet to be fully excavated.

The Windmill Hill Causewayed Enclosure is one of the earliest monuments built in the area and comprises a roughly circular enclosure formed of three concentric rings of banks and ditches, which are pierced at regular intervals by causeways. It was in use between 3000 and 2500 B.C. and measures about 300 by 400 meters at its widest point. There are numerous other monuments in the Avebury area that date to this general period and would have been in use during the Neolithic period and the early Bronze Age. These include other stone circles, long barrows, and round barrows, although the Avebury area has fewer barrow cemeteries than does Stonehenge.

The West Kennet Long Barrow is a particularly impressive monument built primarily of chalk rubble but which also has a stone facade. It is a tomb that comprises a long linear mound with stone burial chambers at the eastern end. The material for the mound was quarried from two flanking ditches. At 100 meters, it is the second longest such tomb in Britain; it is also one of the best preserved. Local sarsen stone was used to make the five burial chambers, the connecting passageway, and the facade. This tomb was used over a long period; it was constructed in 3700 B.C., the early Neolithic, and sealed by a huge portal stone in about 2000 B.C., during the Beaker period.

Avebury Henge comprises a roughly circular enclosure defined by an enormous bank and ditch approximately 350 meters in diameter, with the ditch on the inside of the enclosure (Fig. 2). The enclosure is cut by four entrances, which are still in use today with modern roads running through them. These entrances align approximately with the cardinal points of the compass. Within the enclosure, there were originally three stone circles, the largest one near the edge of the ditch and two smaller

ones situated toward the north and south. The stone circle is the largest in
the United Kingdom and, unlike Stonehenge, is composed of unworked
sarsen. The monument was built sometime between 2600 and 2100 B.C.
Phases of its construction are recognized structurally but are of unknown
date. Two ceremonial stone avenues lead to the monument, one of which
links the henge with another Neolithic monument, about 2.3 kilometers
away, known as The Sanctuary.

As in the case of Stonehenge, it is not the individual monuments
themselves, impressive though they are, that make these areas special. It is
the fact that we can recognize spatial planning and a set of interrelation-
ships (cosmology) that have evolved and developed over a considerable
period, in both cases in excess of one thousand years. Before looking at
the current situation at the two sites, it will be helpful to provide some
context relating to the legislative background and also to the World
Heritage Convention.

United Kingdom Legislation

The United Kingdom has a highly evolved and relatively comprehensive
system of land use planning and environmental conservation. This has
developed over time and has been somewhat piecemeal, but it provides a
significant degree of protection to natural and cultural sites through designation of valued conservation features and areas via archaeological or
historic building legislation and through structural and local plans and
policies and subsequent development control, via planning legislation.

The land use planning system in the United Kingdom is hierarchi-
cal in nature, with broad policy set nationally and more detailed planning
and control carried out at the regional or local level. Therefore, for the
World Heritage Sites, there are a number of policies that have an impact
on the activities within these areas but are not exclusive to them. However,
it is important to note that in the United Kingdom a World Heritage Site
does not receive any special or additional statutory controls. Recently, this
policy framework has taken on board commitments made by the U.K. government under international treaties, such as the RAMSAR convention on

wetlands and the Valletta Convention, and also has reflected the legislation deriving from the European Commission. In addition to the statutory controls afforded by the planning system, there are numerous ways in which this may be influenced by nonstatutory means, such as management plans for properties prepared by landowners.

UNESCO Guidance

Under the current wording of the World Heritage Convention (WHC), there is little or no direct reference to the principles of sustainability. However, the convention was ratified in 1972, when the concepts of sustainability had not been well defined. Nevertheless, sustainability is implicit in the convention and is encompassed in the overriding aim to protect and conserve cultural and natural heritage of "outstanding universal value" for future generations. The current World Heritage Site operational guidelines in effect expand guidance on how to apply the WHC at a site-based scale. They are being updated and rewritten at present, and I am assured they will fully encompass the principles of sustainability.

World Heritage Site Management Plans

It is against this backdrop that English Heritage together with partners such as the National Trust have set about developing World Heritage Site (WHS) management plans for all of the U.K. mainland sites, including Stonehenge and Avebury. These follow and indeed build on the existing World Heritage Center guidance and on current best practice for site management such as that developed in Australia by James Semple Kerr. It was decided that there would be separate management plans for Stonehenge and Avebury. These plans are seen as setting the framework for a more sustainable management regime, and it is the associated WHS implementation plans that are then seen as the main driver for sustainable management. We published the Avebury WHS management plan in 1998 and the Stonehenge plan two years later.

To achieve the production of these plans, we recognized that partnerships were necessary. We involved as many individuals and organizations as possible in a variety of ways and ensured that the general public had the chance to comment at many stages during the development of the plan. For instance, forty individuals and organizations were represented on the Stonehenge Management Plan group and several working parties reported to this group. After much consultation and work a draft was prepared and circulated to four hundred individuals and organizations locally, nationally, and internationally. In addition, thirteen thousand consultation leaflets were produced and distributed to all households in the area, bringing to their attention the availability of the consultation draft. Public meetings backed these up; regular briefings were held for both the general public and special interest groups as well as the press. The responses from the consultations were then considered, and where appropriate, changes were made in the drafting of the report.

On publication of the plans, this network metamorphosed into one that is now overseeing the implementation process and reviewing the priorities in these programs. English Heritage has made copies of the management plans for Avebury (Pomeroy 1998) and Stonehenge (English Heritage 2000) widely available by various means, including placing .PDF copies on the Internet and printing CD-ROM versions.

UNESCO set down a framework of four principal topics that need to be addressed in management plans; these are then further subdivided into chapter titles. The framework for Stonehenge follows.

(1) *Description and Significance of the WHS*
- Locational Information
- Significance of the WHS
- Existing Character of the WHS
- Current Management
- Planning and Policy Framework

(2) *Evaluation of Key Management Issues*
- Context
- Landscape Setting of Archaeological Features and Their Management
- Public Access and Sustainability
- Opportunities and Constraints on Future Management

(3) *Management Objectives*
- Vision for the Future
- Overall Long-Term Objectives
- Statutory and Policy Objectives
- Sustainable Landscape, Nature and Heritage Conservation Objectives
- Sustainable Tourism and Visitor Management Objectives
- Sustainable Traffic and Transportation Objectives
- Research Objective

(4) *Implementing the Plan*
- Mechanisms for Implementation
- Programme of Action
- Monitoring and Review

It will have been noted that sustainability is used in some of the chapter headings for the plan. I now wish to consider how we have begun to take on board the principles of sustainability in the preparation and implementation of the WHS plan. However, we have confined ourselves to those elements where influence can be brought to bear, and it must be recognized that there are larger and longer-term sustainability agendas that can and should have an influence as well, for example, the European Community's Common Agricultural Policy or even the Kyoto Accord.

To my mind there are five key elements to understanding and developing a sustainable management regime for a cultural landscape:

- *Inventory and Documentation*, including historical, administrative, and physical elements
- *Analysis*, leading to the assessment of the current condition and cultural, economic, and social significance

- *Research*, underpinning the whole process and leading to preparation and testing of management, conservation, and interpretation strategies
- *Understanding*, consultation and partnership with individuals and organizations to develop a consensus
- *Monitoring and review*, monitoring of the elements comprising the management plan and review of the applicability of current and new approaches

I have shown these in a linear form. However, there are a series of intermeshing cycles that take place for different aspects of the landscape being studied so as to generate a truly dynamic system. These cycles are seen as both multidisciplinary and interdisciplinary, and they are not confined to one professional group's interests or one particular aspect of management. It is only when one begins to develop holistic methods for understanding and managing the landscapes that one can begin to approach sustainability in a sensible and constructive way.

Inventory and Documentation

In a landscape as diverse as that found at Stonehenge or Avebury it is necessary to create an inventory, or series of linked inventories, which allow documentation of the differing components that constitute the landscape. These inventories should include not just the cultural and physical elements but also administrative, historic documentation, demographic, economic, and managerial aspects. Where possible all of these individual factors should be given a time-depth factor, because it is important to understand how we come to have what we are looking to manage and sustain into the future. For instance, it is important to understand how past farming practices may have affected the landscape not just in obvious and apparent ways such as visible crops and hedge and field boundaries but also in less visible ways such as water extraction, use of chemical fertilizers, or drainage of land.

Analysis

It is not enough to know what is where and who owns it. Analyzing what has led to today's landscape allows an appreciation of how we have what we have. It also leads directly into the need for further research and so begins a cycle leading to greater understanding of the resource and factors influencing it. I will draw on a few examples to illustrate these points.

Condition surveys of the cultural resource should be undertaken not only to monitor the current situation but also to provide a baseline of information against which subsequent surveys can be measured. This allows both overall and individual trends to be measured and then assessed. For instance, burrowing animals, in particular, rabbits and sometimes badgers, often try to take up residence in archaeological features, the softer excavated mound material being easier to dig into than virgin ground. Not only is this unsightly, it may lead to the loss of archaeological evidence, and it can and does produce health and safety problems for visitors. Site conditions need to be monitored continuously, as there is a balance to be struck between the potential for damage and danger, on the one hand, and the need to keep the grass cropped to maintain the established ecological system, on the other.

However, no matter how well managed and documented the site is, there is always the potential for the unexpected. For example, in late May 2000 a shaft appeared in the top of Silbury Hill. This was unexpected, as the top of the mound had been excavated as recently as the 1960s, and it appeared stable then and subsequently. What had happened was that a shaft dug at the end of the eighteenth century, which must have only had the upper few meters backfilled, had finally, after more than two hundred years, collapsed into the void below. The eighteenth-century excavations had been known and documented, but the fact that the shaft had not been backfilled completely had been forgotten in recent decades. The value of historical information such as photographs or drawings and paintings can be very useful in understanding the history of the site. Often these media give another dimension to the understanding of the past that is not present in the "official" record, whether this be owners' names on a map or clothes worn at the time.

Research

Both practical and theoretical research have a role in developing the frameworks on which the understanding and interpretation of a site can be hung. It is also important to recognize that research can lead to further research. English Heritage has been actively supporting the creation of archaeological research frameworks for both Avebury and Stonehenge. So far, only the Avebury framework has been published (AA&HRG 2001). These frameworks fit within the wider initiative that English Heritage is promoting to create regional research frameworks covering the whole of the country (Olivier 1996).

When the ditch at Avebury was excavated in the 1920s it showed its enormous physical size and associated structures and demonstrated how much they have been eroded or diminished over the passage of time. It was examples like this and many others in the United Kingdom that led the British Academy to establish the Experimental Earthworks Research Committee in the 1950s (Bell, Fowler, and Hillson 1996). The committee comprised a multidisciplinary team of scientists who drew up the plans for this project and executed it. The project came into being because, although we could see what had happened on a macro scale, that is, the ditch had been infilled, we had no real understanding of the processes that led to it or the time scales in which it happened.

The experimental earthwork site was situated on Overton Down, just to the east of what was to become twenty-six years later the eastern boundary of the Avebury World Heritage Site. It consisted of a length of ditch and accompanying rampart constructed to a set of consistent parameters. A number of measuring methods were built in, along with material to represent the archaeological material one finds in excavated sections. The earthwork was then sectioned at 2-, 4-, 8-, 16-, and 32-year intervals and will be sectioned again on its 64th and 128th birthdays in 2024 and 2088. To make a long story very short, the data from this experiment have been extremely important not only in archaeological but also in managerial terms.

Research needs to encompass more than just the cultural remains, and there needs to be an understanding of other factors such as transport infrastructure. Significant monuments at both World Heritage Sites are affected by roads, especially at Stonehenge, where a principal trunk road, the A303, is in need of upgrading to dual carriageway, and this road and a smaller one conspire to cut off the stones from the surrounding landscape.

Similarly, there has to be recognition of the needs and wishes of the hundreds of thousands of visitors to the sites every year. Tourism is a major industry in the United Kingdom, worth in excess of £25 billion to the economy, and sites such as Stonehenge and Avebury attract a high proportion of overseas visitors. At Stonehenge, overseas visitors constitute about 50 percent of the total. Not only do they bring income to the sites, but they also bring income into the shops, restaurants, and hotels and guesthouses in the locality. They require site information as well as infrastructure, such as parking and toilet facilities.

Last but by no means least, I have to mention agriculture, often seen as the enemy of landscape studies. We have to be more sophisticated and recognize that agriculture has played a significant part in the formation of the landscape we see today. Indeed, there is evidence of farming in this part of England for at least five thousand years. However, we also need to recognize that since World War II the United Kingdom has allowed agriculture to override many environmental and cultural concerns in its drive for self-sufficiency, in effect, an unsustainable regime. One of the effects of this on the visible cultural remains has been "ghetto" conservation, such as barrows fenced off from cultivation with no physical access and no proactive management of the enclosed areas. This can lead to animal infestation and scrub regrowth. However, this situation is beginning to change; we are seeing a more encompassing approach and an appreciation of the other elements that make up the countryside by all concerned with its management and future. In developing replacement management regimes that favor a particular aspect of the landscape, various factors—cultural, economic, social, and environmental—need to be taken into account.

One way of expressing these apparently conflicting factors is through "limits of acceptable change" modeling in which differing weight can be given to individual factors while maintaining those elements that are seen as significant. I do not propose to describe this methodology here; however, it is worth noting that the application of a Geographic Information System (GIS) allows for the relatively easy comparison of data and the use of these data within complex models (e.g., LAC models).

Geographic Information Systems

We have developed a GIS for the World Heritage Site composed of separate parts for Avebury and Stonehenge. Both parts of the GIS are compatible; that is, they are built to the same standards and are internally consistent. That not all of the data are represented in both parts of the GIS reflects the different histories and character of the sites.

A Geographic Information System, as its name implies, is a system that manages and stores information in a geographic way so as to enable analysis and understanding of the resources being studied. This is not a new concept, as manual methods for deriving such information have existed for many centuries. The increasing complexity of modern towns, in particular, led to the development of computer-based systems in the late 1960s. Initially, these were both locally based and data-oriented systems. In the past ten to fifteen years they have undergone a revolution, becoming more process oriented. To enable this to happen, the scale has increased, and the inclusion of data sets such as rainfall, temperature, and soils geology, together with demographic and economic data, allowed for complex analyses.

We are all familiar with maps, such as those covering landownership, land use, and landscape character, that are geographic or mapped representations of significant elements within the areas being studied. They may also be combined to form compilations with elements such as landscape character and archaeology. However, they share the disadvantage of all physical maps in that they are static and represent a single view, not only in terms of the elements displayed, but also in terms of the display itself, for example, scale and colors. The use of a GIS allows one to put these elements or data into a dynamic environment.

I do not propose to enter into a description of either GIS or the way in which we have put it to use for Stonehenge and Avebury, as this has been published elsewhere (see Batchelor 1997). However, in this discussion of sustainable management it is worth drawing out a few points from the time we have spent constructing and implementing the GIS. One of the most useful and beneficial outcomes of its implementation has been the way in which it has defused many situations that in the past resulted in impasse or worse. That the data used in the GIS still have all their original characteristics has helped to engender a feeling of "buying in" to the GIS. Ownership of individual sets of data can still be claimed by both individuals and groups, and this can then be combined in a way that is replicable and transparent. This has in effect eliminated the possibility, whether deliberate or not, of transposition of the data and removed the basis for claims of misrepresentation. This has not been the sole catalyst for our use of GIS; nor would I assert that it has been successful in all cases. However, it is significant that disputes about location and interpretation of data have decreased considerably since the GIS has been used.

Conclusion

I hope I have given an indication of how we are beginning—and I stress beginning—to put sustainability on the agenda at the World Heritage Site at Stonehenge and Avebury. We have come a long way fairly rapidly, in common with many cultural resource managers, in grappling with the wider implications of sustainability. However, we know that we have a long way to go. One thing I have drawn from this process is the need to set achievable goals that encompass both the short- and the long-term vision. It is necessary for staff morale and well-being to ensure that achievable targets are set and measured. That we have established a framework within which these can be developed and progressed collectively is a major factor ensuring that sustainability remains on everyone's agenda into the future.

From the work at Stonehenge and Avebury it is becoming apparent that applying sustainability in a cultural landscape management context is not so much the application of a methodology. Rather, it is the creation of a thought process both at the individual and the collective level. Initially, therefore, the effort and resources need to be directed toward creating this environment. Over time it should become intuitive. Then I think we can begin to move forward.

Many others have said that within a sustainable management cycle one needs to be able to take on board the more personal and somewhat ephemeral aspects of the landscape, whether this be sense of place, emotion, or perceptions. We are aware of the need to develop common languages and ways of expressing these at Stonehenge and Avebury—after all, the sites attract this type of thinking. However, it is only now that we have got the more physical components of the landscape aligned that we can begin to think about ways to express the less tangible, although in some ways more important, aspects. A word of caution: we must be slightly wary, as by their very nature these aspects are subject to change and therefore potentially unstable.

Recently, and quite correctly, the Taliban regime in Afghanistan came in for worldwide criticism for destroying the statues of Buddha. Similar destruction has occurred historically in Europe and elsewhere in the world. Taking an example from Avebury, many of the stones depicted in early drawings and maps were buried by farmers, or worse still, deliberately destroyed by Christian community leaders during the eighteenth and nineteenth centuries. In dealing with perceptions of monuments such as these, it is important that we take into consideration a multiplicity of views and do not allow one view to override others.

Acknowledgments

As is the case with many projects of this type, there are numerous people who have contributed to the development of the management plans for Avebury and Stonehenge and helped me indirectly in writing this chapter. Unfortunately, they cannot all be named here. I would like to acknowledge a special debt of gratitude to Amanda Chadburn, Melanie Pomeroy, and Nick Burton, who, in addition to making a substantial contribution to the projects I have drawn from, have also provided good company throughout. I must also thank Geoff Wainwright, who not only took a leading role in all the Avebury and Stonehenge projects but also actively supported the development of the GIS from the outset. And finally I must thank the conference organizers, Jeanne Marie Teutonico and Frank Matero, and

US/ICOMOS for the opportunity to make a presentation at the Managing Change Symposium on which this chapter is based.

This chapter has been written with the benefit of my years' experience working for English Heritage. However, the views expressed are mine and do not necessarily reflect those of English Heritage.

References

Avebury Archaeology & Historical Research Group (AA&HRG). 2001. *Archaeological Research Agenda for the Avebury World Heritage Site*. London: AA&HRG.

Batchelor, D. 1997. Mapping the Stonehenge World Heritage Site. In *Science and Stonehenge*, ed. B. Cunliffe and C. Renfrew, 61–72. Proceedings of the British Academy 92. London: British Academy.

Bell, M., P. J. Fowler, and S. W. Hillson. 1996. The Experimental Earthwork Project 1960–1992. CBA Research Report 100.

Cleal, R. M. J., K. E. Walker, and R. Montague. 1995. *Stonehenge in Its Landscape: Twentieth-Century Excavation*. English Heritage Archaeological Report 10. London: English Heritage.

English Heritage. 2000. *The Stonehenge World Heritage Site Management Plan*. London: English Heritage.

Kerr, J. S. 1996. *The Conservation Plan: A Guide to the Preparation of Conservation Plans for Places of European Cultural Significance*. 4th ed. Sydney: J. S. Kerr on behalf of the National Trust of Australia (NSW).

Olivier, A. 1996. *Frameworks for Our Past: A Review of Research Frameworks, Strategies and Perceptions*. London: English Heritage.

Pomeroy, M. 1998. *The Avebury World Heritage Site Management Plan*. London: English Heritage.

Sustainable Management for Archaeological Sites: The Case of Chan Chan, Peru

Carolina Castellanos

CHAN CHAN, ONE OF THE LARGEST earthen architecture cities in the Americas, is key to understanding the cultural evolution of the Central Andes in pre-Hispanic times. The archaeological site represents the remains of what was the capital of the Chimu kingdom between the ninth and fifteenth centuries A.D. It is located on the northern margin of the Moche Valley, five kilometers from the city of Trujillo on Peru's northern coast.

At the height of its development, the Archaeological Complex extended for twenty square kilometers; today only fourteen are preserved. Of the latter, six belong to the central urban zone, where nine palaces were built as independent units; the other eight square kilometers comprise the agricultural and rural zone (Fig. 1).

The cultural history of Chan Chan encompasses a period of six hundred fifty years and has been established mainly by archaeological investigations; the first chronology, provided by Topic in 1978, was revised by Kolata in 1982 based on additional excavations (see Topic 1980; Kolata 1982). In addition to information gleaned through archaeological research, ethnohistoric data—such as administrative and judicial documents from

Figure 1
General view of the archaeological site and surrounding agricultural fields. Photo by Carolina Castellanos.

the sixteenth century and the myths regarding the Chimor dynasties, recorded in the seventeenth century—have been useful for the interpretation of the site's cultural history (Fig. 2).

Based on this information, we can say that Chan Chan synthesizes the cultural evolution of the Central Andes, particularly on the northern coast of Peru. It illustrates the most significant aspects of Chimú society, such as social, ideological, political, and economic organization, including subsistence strategies. The interpretation of the site allows us to understand the evolution of the city and the cultural processes of the Moche Valley and the region, since it was the dominant center of an extended state that exerted powerful influence. This is revealed in the architectural and cultural vestiges of its subject cities and territories (Fig. 3).

Figure 2
Cultural history of Chan Chan

	Topic (1980)		Kolata (1982)	
A.D. 850	Local	Chayhuac	Early Chimú	Chayhuac
		Tello (NW)		Uhle
				Tello
	Early Imperial Phase	Uhle		Laberinto
		Laberinto		
A.D. 1100	Middle Imperial Phase	Gran Chimú	Middle Chimú	Laberinto
		Bandelier		Gran Chimú
				Squier
A.D. 1400	Late Imperial Phase	Tschudi	Late Chimú	Velarde
		Rivero		Bandelier
				Tschudi
				Rivero
A.D. 1470	Inca Chimú		Inca Chimú	
A.D. 1532	Colonial		Colonial	

Figure 3
General view of the Tschudi Palace, Audiencias sector. Photo by Carolina Castellanos.

The management and organization of space, which integrates architecture with decorated surfaces, as well as its construction, design, form, and peculiar features, reflects the ancient inhabitants' relationship with the environment. Earthen architecture was adapted to fit diverse needs and emphasized the vastness of space, elevated constructions, and the use of decorated surfaces (Fig. 4).

Scientifically, Chan Chan is an important reserve for the understanding of the evolution and history of the societies of the northern coast of Peru. Studies of agricultural development during pre-Hispanic times, as well as investigations into earthen architecture technology, provide information that is still useful for contemporary application. Chan Chan also represents for the various local and regional cultural groups a sense of identity and continuity and a direct link between the past and the present. Its significance survives in the construction techniques and the use of materials for earthen architecture, the use of land and water for economic and subsistence activities, and traditional customs and beliefs (Fig. 5). Likewise, it represents a prime potential for the social, cultural, and economic development of the region. Similarly, the site presents an important educational value for archaeology and earthen architecture conservation.

Conditions at the Site

Conserving the archaeological site of Chan Chan presents significant challenges that range from fabric deterioration to context-related issues. Because of its location, the Archaeological Complex is subject to the dynamics of environmental factors that continuously interact and contribute to the deterioration of structures and decorated surfaces and to the progressive loss of construction materials. Among these factors are wind and insulation, but it is perhaps the periodic phenomenon of El Niño that historically has caused the most extensive deterioration; torrential rains, flooding, and mud slides have affected considerable areas of the archaeological site.

Deterioration of the archaeological heritage of Chan Chan has also resulted from factors related to its management and social context, particularly on the periphery of the site. Urban encroachment and agricultural and industrial production have generated pressure from adjacent communities and have led to the destruction of archaeological vestiges.

Figure 4
Detail of decorated surfaces at Velarde Palace. Photo by Carolina Castellanos.

Figure 5
Local worker making a *tapial* wall. Photo by Carolina Castellanos.

Figure 6
Deterioration and loss of construction materials in the perimeter wall. Photo by Carolina Castellanos.

Also, soil is constantly extracted for the manufacturing of adobes, which affects the landscape (Fig. 6). The low income levels of adjacent communities has led to looting and deterioration of the site's structures, which has been exacerbated by uncontrolled access to the site. The area is known for the high quality of its ceramics and textiles, which unfortunately are highly valued in the external and private "markets." Also, new settlements in the area tend to use the construction materials from the site, particularly adobes, which leads to structural problems and eventual collapse or loss of structures. And, of course, tourism with no visitor management strategies in place has played a large part in the deterioration of the site.

To address some of these problems, over the past thirty-five years the Peruvian state has implemented several actions for the investigation, conservation, presentation, promotion, and defense of Chan Chan. Specific measures include the drafting of legislation for the protection of the site and interventions for the recovery of illegally occupied sectors used for agricultural and industrial activities. In 1986, under criteria C (i) (iii), the Archaeological Complex of Chan Chan was inscribed on the World Heritage List; the same year, it was designated World Heritage in Danger, because of the precarious state of the earthen architecture. The World Heritage Committee recommended that adequate conservation, restoration, and management measures be carried out and that all excavation work be halted unless it was accompanied by conservation. It also advocated that all steps be taken to control looting at the site (UNESCO 1986). Since these recommendations were issued, conservation and maintenance of Chan Chan's palaces and *huacas* (monumental truncated pyramidal structures associated with ritual and ceremonial functions in pre-Hispanic times) have been undertaken, frequently in collaboration with international and national entities. Among these, the preventive actions against the El Niño of 1982, 1989, and 1997 and the construction of the Site Museum in 1990 were especially important. Further, there has been a strong emphasis on the recovery of areas that had been invaded by farming and industrial facilities; this recovery was completed in 1998. However, these efforts did not result in broader social or political support or a commitment to conservation endeavors and did not have a long-term impact.

Regarding management of the site, in 1996 the Instituto Nacional de Cultura de Perú–Dirección Regional La Libertad (INC-DRLL) developed and presented to the Ministry of Education a proposal entitled "Plan integral para la defensa y conservación de Chan Chan Patrimonio Mundial," which called for protection, conservation, research, presentation, dissemination, and education, among other actions, at the site. As part of the plan, between November 10 and December 13, 1996, the Curso panamericano sobre la conservación y el manejo del patrimonio arquitectónico histórico-arqueológico de tierra (Panamerican Course on the Conservation and Management of Historical-Archaeological Architectural Heritage; PAT 96) was carried out at the site and the museum facilities. The course was developed as a result of international technical cooperation between the INC-DRLL, the International Centre for Earth Construction–School of Architecture Grenoble (CRATerre-EAG), the

Getty Conservation Institute, and the International Centre for the Study of the Preservation and Restoration of Cultural Property (ICCROM), with the collaboration of the World Heritage Fund and the support of other official and private entities.

The course, designed for professionals involved with earthen architecture conservation and construction in Latin America, promoted integrated training activities for the conservation and management of earthen architecture and placed a strong emphasis on planning. For that purpose, the organizing institutions advocated a methodological approach that fostered an interdisciplinary and participatory planning process (Getty Conservation Institute 1996). The course resulted in a methodology for designing Chan Chan's management plan and important recommendations from participants.

In 1997, during the general session of UNESCO's World Heritage Committee in Naples, Italy, it was recommended to the Peruvian government that a management plan be put in place for Chan Chan, as a requisite for its designation as a World Heritage Site and World Heritage in Danger. In this context, collaboration between UNESCO's representatives in Peru and the INC-DRLL was formalized so as to prepare the master plan for Chan Chan. The Peruvian governnment deemed the project a priority in its cultural policy, and between January and December 1998, the planning process was begun by the INC-DRLL, with the collaboration of the World Heritage Fund–UNESCO, ICCROM, and the Getty Conservation Institute.

The Planning Process

The management planning initiative was based on a holistic, participatory, value-driven approach that would address not only the conservation needs of the archaeological site and its decorated surfaces but also issues related to the natural setting and the social context. The main purpose of preparing the plan was to integrate actions carried out at the site in a comprehensive and programmed action plan that sought to conserve the values that make Chan Chan a significant place but also to promote heritage as an essential component for human well-being and development, by generating both material and nonmaterial benefits.

It was also assumed that a series of programmed actions would be beneficial to optimize the limited financial, material, and human resources by investing them in priority needs. Given the complex issues related to the conservation and management of the site and in accordance with the significance-driven process, planning for the site promoted the active involvement of different stakeholders, which would lead to broader commitment and support for both conservation endeavors and the overall implementation of the plan. The participatory approach enabled the negotiation and reconciliation of diverse issues, ranging from archaeological research to conservation, presentation, education, promotion, zoning, and land use according to the prioritizing of values.

The planning process for Chan Chan consisted of three phases: study and documentation, analysis, and response, which included, respectively, identification of the place, analysis of conditions, assessment of cultural significance, definition of policies for the site, and finally development of programs and specific projects. The process also involved the elaboration of an implementation scheme and the definition of monitoring parameters for the evaluation and revision of the plan (Fig. 7) (see Castellanos 1999).

In practice, the approach entailed different levels of negotiation and understanding of a variety of complex issues. Thus emphasis was placed on the critical analysis of diverse components, ranging from fabric conditions to context issues, and on identifying and recognizing interdependencies as the key to proposals that would be most effective in the long term. In this respect, comprehensive assessments were essential to garnering required information; these were undertaken by professionals from a range of disciplines, with tools and methods derived from each discipline and within the resources available. The resulting evaluations allowed for the definition and identification of key issues that have an impact on or contribute to changes at the site, so as to respond to vulnerabilities and to better anticipate changes in the future.

But not only were these conditions to be subjected to critical analysis; they were to be reconciled with the values of the site from many different perspectives and the needs of other interest groups, recognizing the diversity of values and uses that represent fundamental aspects of different cultures. Chan Chan is significant in many respects, to many different groups, but it also has very specific needs. For example, the adjacent communities and local governments expected that increased tourism would bring economic benefits to the site and to the region. It was important, therefore, that the various stakeholders reach a consensus on the

Figure 7
Planning process for the development of a master plan for Chan Chan

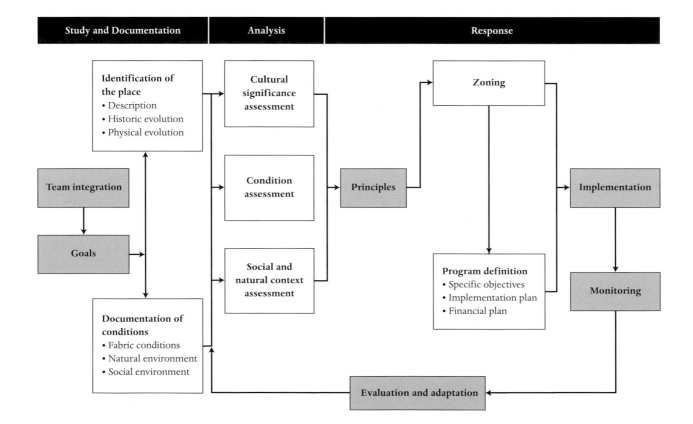

values of the site, but it was also essential to recognize the fundamental interdependencies and associated vulnerabilities of the site as well as their impact on the perception and valuing of the place. In this respect, from the beginning of the project, emphasis was placed on creating effective collaboration mechanisms and strategies that allowed the identification of other needs derived from the site and their potential articulation in the plan and to raise awareness of the needs related to the fabric of the site.

It was critical, therefore, to jointly plan and coordinate activities so as to build toward a vision for the future of Chan Chan, in which the proposed strategies and projects related not only to the conservation of the archaeological site but also to the ultimate end of human well-being and human development. Through discussions of the site's significance, it became clear that Chan Chan is essential to the lives of the local population in strengthening cultural identity, a sense of the past and its relationship to the present, and social cohesion. Specific issues were discussed regarding how to build on the importance of the site for the scientific community as well as how the development of the site could be accomplished in such a way that it would be integrated with the development of the Moche Valley more generally.

Examples of policies established in the management plan are

- integration of the Archaeological Complex with the economic activities of adjacent areas, including industrial and agricultural development;
- respect for and promotion of traditional practices and knowledge for cultural development and the fostering of educational and outreach activities;
- promotion of the Archaeological Complex as an axis of the cultural development of the region; and
- emphasis on minimum intervention in carrying out conservation and prioritizing conservation activities in the intensive- and extensive-use zones so that more areas would be opened to the public.

The implications of these policies and the means to implement them have been defined through various projects, which are described briefly below. A key provision of the plan is zoning, based on the initial proposal made by the INC-DRLL and examined by the various communities that would be affected by the proposal, not only physically, but also in terms of the proposed uses and regulations. The ultimate zoning project was approved by the Municipality of Trujillo, in accordance with its Metropolitan Development Plan, so as to make feasible certain proposed uses. Established zones were related to uses of the physical space and also to how actions and interventions were prioritized. Since infrastructure and specific management activities were jointly defined, there were initial solutions to conflicts regarding the space in the protected area and in the buffer zone.

The established-use zones were the following: restricted use, intensive use, extensive use, special use, and buffer zone. The latter two were particularly relevant to Chan Chan. In the special-use zone, it was agreed that the *huachaques*, areas designed in pre-Hispanic times for agricultural purposes, could continue to be farmed, and that *totorales*, a rush species characteristic of Peru's northern coast that grows in soils with a high concentration of salts, would be recovered to balance the needs of the agricultural communities with the conservation of the site; these proposals will be monitored by the INC and other involved entities. The project for the *totorales* is also linked to a major initiative proposed by the Ministry of Agriculture and Natural Resources to restore ecosystems along Peru's northern coast.

Projects were developed for each of the zones and in response to established policies, concentrating on the issues that were deemed priorities but also building on the long-term vision for the site. In the end, seven programs with twenty-four subprograms and one hundred forty projects were defined for the management and conservation of Chan Chan. Though proposed projects include the conservation of archaeological structures and decorated surfaces, future scientific research, and conservation of collections, projects were also defined for the conservation and promotion of other values, for example:

- a center for the recovery of traditional technology, proposed as as a joint venture between the National University at Trujillo and the INC, including traditional craftsmanship such as ceramics, textiles, and earthen architecture construction
- support for the cultural development of adjacent communities, including guidelines for housing, environmental issues, and urban planning
- strengthening of formal and informal education, through activities at the site but also through curriculum development at various educational levels, on subjects such as the cultural history of the place as well as the professional level of architects, agronomists, and engineers
- promotion of alternative uses and activities such as agriculture and rehabilitation of natural areas for production of resources

Special emphasis was placed on relating scientific investigations to other projects, so that results from these contribute effectively to the interpretation and understanding of the past and to the well-being and development of present and the future generations. In regard to tourism development, projects were proposed according to zoning, including research on and conservation and presentation of areas in the extensive-use zone (see Hoyle 1999).

Conclusion

As a result of the methodology used, the management of Chan Chan is now proposed as a more thorough articulation of the conservation of natural and cultural heritage and also as the integration of heritage with society to foster and contribute to sustainable development. By employing a value-driven process, the proposed plan was not limited only to the fabric of the site; it also addressed social and economic issues that influence the sense and meaning of heritage in the lives of different social groups, as well as means for making them direct beneficiaries of the site's conservation.

The plan seeks to establish the way in which various social, cultural, and natural factors are interrelated and also the relationship between change and continuity, so as to have the best means to manage future changes by adapting the proposed projects while continuing to invest in the natural, human, and social capital and by ensuring participation in the decision-making process for the developing cultural systems.

Another objective was to contribute to capacity building in order to not only implement the resulting product but also carry out further planning initiatives in the region. Constituting a team with local experience was important to guaranteeing the long-term multiplying effect of the initiative and also to designing a plan that would be in accord with the current political, technical, and administrative conditions of Peru. The monitoring of the planning process has allowed also for its adaptation for training purposes and has provided a baseline for adaptation of the methodology to planning initiatives at other earthen sites.

The participatory approach and consultation with a broad range of stakeholders permitted the goal of collaboration to be advanced; the active participation of diverse stakeholders allowed for reconciling many of the interests surrounding the site, particularly with respect to tourism and industrial development; and the project has fostered a deeper understanding of the significance of the site and its importance at the national level, particularly as an element that strengthens national identity. The methodology employed has also contributed to the sustainability of the plan by integrating social actors who will play an essential role in the implementation of projects.

Planning jointly for the future management of the site created a greater sense of responsibility and a shared commitment to conservation, both on the institutional and the personal level. This continues to be strengthened by the consolidation of working groups, by the constant collaboration in developing specific projects, and by the dissemination of results and progress.

Continuing relations have been established with local communities and the municipality to facilitate the preservation of the site. By making diverse stakeholders feel they are owners of the process and the resulting plan, a larger commitment to the site was engendered, which, in the long run, will guarantee long-term implementation and fulfillment of the plan's vision.

Since ultimately the implementation of the management plan cannot rest only with the Instituto Nacional de Cultura, provisions and policies have been established to define the roles and responsibilities of different stakeholders, to create adequate conditions for the holistic management of the site, and to provide means to address potential future conflicts and to better manage change.

Success will depend largely on the ability to adapt the existing plan to manage changes that will occur in time through strategies that ultimately contribute to the development and well-being of different social groups. Understanding the implications and challenges of employing a value-driven process will lead also to a closer examination of why we conserve cultural heritage—but most important, for whom. The feasibility of implementing the plan rests largely on this approach, but, in the end, so does conservation of cultural heritage.

Acknowledgments

I wish to thank all the institutions and individuals who have contributed to and supported this project. Among these are the Instituto Nacional de Cultura de Perú–Dirección Regional La Libertad, the World Heritage Center, UNESCO's representatives in Peru, ICCROM, CRATerre-EAG, and the Getty Conservation Institute.

References

Castellanos, C. 1999. Complejo arqueológico de Chan Chan: Proceso de planificación para el desarrollo del plan de manejo. Unpublished report. Getty Conservation Institute.

Castellanos, C., and A. M. Hoyle. 1998a. Complejo arqueológico de Chan Chan: Proyecto plan de manejo. Primer Informe de Trabajo a UNESCO. Unpublished report. INC-DRLL.

Castellanos, C., and A. M. Hoyle. 1998b. Complejo arqueológico de Chan Chan: Proyecto plan de manejo. Segundo Informe de Trabajo a UNESCO. Unpublished report. INC-DRLL.

Getty Conservation Institute. 1996. El enfoque de manejo. Unpublished working document. Los Angeles, California.

Hoyle, A. M. 1999. Complejo arqueológico de Chan Chan: Plan maestro de conservación y manejo. Tercer Informe de Trabajo a UNESCO. Unpublished report. INC- DRLL.

Kolata, A. L. 1982. Chronology and settlement growth at Chan Chan. In *Chan Chan: Andean Desert City*, ed. M. E. Moseley and K. C. Day, 67–85. School of American Research Advanced Seminar Series. Albuquerque: University of New Mexico Press.

Topic, J. R. 1980. Excavaciones en los barrios populares de Chan Chan. In *Chan Chan Metrópoli Chimor*. Lima: IEP.

Castles and Community in Cape Coast, Ghana

Gina Haney

BETWEEN 1992 AND 2000 THE UNITED STATES Agency for International Development (USAID) funded a two-phase project in Ghana's Central Region with the goal of stimulating economic opportunities relating to cultural and natural resources.[1] Phase 1 targeted the conservation and interpretation of "national monuments" as visitor attractions. Phase 2 addressed the long-term protection and development of the historic communities in which the monuments stood.[2] Here I want to examine the ways in which the project made the transition from the site-specific conservation of national monuments to the holistic protection and development of community, helped to empower the local population to join the heritage planning process, and encouraged a broader commitment to sustainability.

As we continue the discourse on the cultural relativity of heritage conservation, it is important to evaluate the juxtaposition of the conservation of monuments to the protection of historic communities, their interwoven belief systems and everyday life patterns. The Cape Coast project raised questions about the value placed on tangible, physical environments versus the intangible, often unseen structures and spaces that served to define them.

The Castles

Constructed in the fifteenth and seventeenth centuries as fortified containers for gold and later transformed into holding areas for enslaved West Africans, the World Heritage Sites of Elmina and Cape Coast Castles had fallen into disuse and disrepair by the second half of the twentieth century.[3] In recognition of their importance as landmarks of the transatlantic slave trade, Phase 1 of the project completed the conservation and interpretation of the castles as part of a larger effort to stimulate growth in Ghana's Central Region. Tourism, a new industry, was the catalyst for this economic development (Fig. 1, Color Plate 5).

By 1996 the castles of Elmina and Cape Coast had become popular destinations for those living in the diaspora and two of the most profitable attractions in Ghana. Domestic and international visitors alike came in great numbers to walk through restored dungeons and "doors of no return." Although successful on one level, the limitations of this site-specific, bricks-and-mortar approach became apparent.

Figure 1
Cape Coast Castle. Photo by Gina Haney.
(See also Color Plate 5.)

Visitors to the towns stayed only long enough to see the monumental castles, choosing to sleep, eat, and purchase crafts at beachside resorts. Moreover, municipal and traditional authorities had little incentive to capitalize on the industry as moneys generated from admission fees went to the Ghana Museums and Monuments Board, a division of the national government. The communities of Cape Coast and Elmina continued to rely on a sluggish economy based on fishing.

In addition to undertaking substantial conservation efforts, a strategic step of Phase 1 was the creation, with a U.S. $2 million endowment, of a regional nonprofit, the Ghana Heritage Conservation Trust (GHCT). Charged with the long-term conservation, management, and development of cultural and natural resources in the region, the GHCT was only a vision of Phase 1 planning. By Phase 2, the GHCT was functional and operating with a staff of two full-time employees.

Recognizing the need to sustain their initial investment in tourism, USAID funded Phase 2 of the project in 1998. Phase 2, managed by US/ICOMOS in partnership with the GHCT, shifted the focus from the conservation of national monuments to the historic settlements, specifically Cape Coast, that grew around them. In the process, the idea of conservation took on new meanings, whereby the built environment became a venue for understanding cultural heritage.

The Community

Phase 2 began with the restoration and adaptive reuse of a very visible public building, Government House, embodying a long and complex local history (Fig. 2). It was constructed in the 1840s by a prominent local merchant family, then leased and eventually purchased by the British Gold Coast administration during the 1850s. At this time and until 1872, Cape Coast was the seat of the Gold Coast regime. On independence in 1957, Government House, situated in the heart of downtown Cape Coast, near Cape Coast Castle, was inherited by the government of Ghana.

Until the purchase of Government House, the Gold Coast administration had been centered in one building, the castle. From here, British

Figure 2
Government House, circa 1874. Courtesy
Military Museum, Kumasi, Ghana.

administrators who dominated the Gold Coast following the abolition of the slave trade in 1808 presided over their territory. As the newly renovated base of operations of the colonial governor, Government House marked the movement of the British out of the castle and into the town of Cape Coast, symbolically extending their power into the indigenous community.

It may seem ironic that the restoration of Government House was targeted as the first initiative of Phase 2. On the surface it seems like yet another instance, the castle being the first, of foreign aid supporting the restoration of a colonial monument. Yet, as we learned, Government House was more than a marker of colonialism to Cape Coasters.

During the 1960s, Government House accommodated a newly independent local administration, its large entrance hall and former domestic spaces serving as courtrooms and judges' chambers. Between the 1970s and 1998, when restoration began, Government House was a bustling bus depot, the center of the wide-ranging nexus of lottery ticket sales, and a formal backdrop for group photographs. Government House had taken on a new identity that extended beyond that of the Gold Coast regime.

The Central Region administration, a decentralized branch of national government in charge of Government House, officially endorsed and supported the restoration and adaptive reuse of the building. The program for reuse included retaining public and commercial functions while upgrading and renewing the building to make it the focal point of visitor services in Cape Coast. During the restoration process, the transformation of the building, its paved north and south courtyards, and its terraced garden raised public awareness about conservation efforts and the newly established GHCT. On completion of restoration, Government House was commissioned Heritage House.

Today Heritage House holds the offices of the GHCT, the Tour Guides Association of Ghana, the Cape Coast Development Association, and a satellite office of the Ghana Tourist Board. Local concessions for the sale of handicrafts and food, a business advisory center, and a telecommunications establishment are also located in the building. A boardroom and a small museum interpreting the history of the site and the restoration are open to the public, and the garden is available for social events such as funerals and weddings. Proceeds from rent are overseen by the regional administration and support the ongoing maintenance of the building.

The restoration and adaptive reuse of Heritage House within the townscape had an effect quite different from that of Cape Coast Castle. As high walls surrounded the castle, citizens rarely saw the large-scale restoration and construction of museum exhibitions. Furthermore, while the castle is a prominent feature in downtown Cape Coast and is often used as a point of orientation when giving directions, many Cape Coasters have never entered the building. Because Heritage House is sited in an open public space, restoration was visible and accessible to the larger community. Adjacent neighbors and passersby frequently watched the work and offered their firsthand descriptions of court cases, lottery offices, and bus schedules.

The transformation of Heritage House created wide-ranging enthusiasm and support for the sensitive management of additional cultural resources during Phase 2. Building on this enthusiasm, US/ICOMOS and the GHCT organized a forum for a cross section of people that included market women, imams, stewards of fetish shrines, municipal assembly members, and fishermen, to name a few, to meet and discuss their collective heritage in terms of long-term development (see Fig. 3). This diverse group mapped locations of significant resources, defined problems, and posed solutions.

One month later, this group of local residents was joined by architects, urban planners, landscape architects, preservationists, and tourism experts from Ghana and around the world who gathered in Cape Coast for a weeklong design charette with the charge of analyzing information generated by forum participants. The result was a five-year conservation and tourism development plan for Cape Coast. This plan

Figure 3
Community planning forum.
Photo by Gina Haney.

included possible content for new municipal legislation addressing heritage conservation, design guidelines for local planning authorities, suggestions for enhancing and maintaining shared spaces, and recommendations for tourism development compatible with the community's value systems, traditions, and beliefs.

Implementation of the plan depended on creating public awareness and acceptance. Three groups were crucial in garnering community support and realizing a number of development plan proposals. First, local government included many recommendations in their 2000–2005 action plan that officially endorsed the viability of the document and made a commitment to the sensitive management of change. Second, community associations began soliciting contributions from private individuals and enterprises for proposed civic improvement projects, reinforcing public support of the development plan. Finally, US/ICOMOS and the GHCT dedicated project funds to long-term planning goals emphasizing the ongoing commitment of the newly established nonprofit.

The move to plant two hundred quick-growth shade trees along major streets in the downtown area was a direct result of charette recommendations. Spearheaded by the Cape Coast Development Association and funded by a local citizen in conjunction with the Cape Coast Municipal Assembly, the tree-planting exercise involved many town residents. The regional government supported the initial, long-term investment of local government by charging the Department of Parks and Gardens and the Fire Department with the continued maintenance of trees over the next two years. The development association continues to oversee the project.

The inclusive nature of the charette and support for the development plan resulted in continued backing of project activities, including community theater performances. Highlighting rich, local traditions of drumming and dance, these performances, known as concert parties, were scripted by a local troupe in Fante, an indigenous language. Over the course of eight performances, in various neighborhoods, approximately eighteen hundred residents attended. In addition to fostering awareness of heritage conservation, concert parties became impromptu forums for community discussions. As municipal assembly and traditional council members attended each event, citizens used the occasions to question local officials and voice opinions about a number of issues, including heritage conservation, AIDS, and sanitation (see Fig. 4).

The establishment of community oversight committees in charge of planning and executing specific initiatives further enhanced individual and group investment in the planning process. Members of the Ghana Museums and Monuments Board, the Traditional Council, municipal authorities, and the Cape Coast Development Association formed teams to administer specific initiatives such as the installation of public art and a small grants program for cultural site rehabilitation.

Under the charge of the regional director of the Center for National Culture, the installation of public art called attention to living traditions and cultural sites in downtown Cape Coast. Seven local artists, assisted by young residents interested in craft production, created batik, sculpture, wood relief, and painted murals. The installations can now be

Figure 4
Community theater performance. Photo by Gina Haney.

seen at the local fish and seafood market, the main bus station, the Town Hall, and the municipal administration garden (see Fig. 5).

Committee members overseeing the small grants program for cultural site rehabilitation determined the criteria for site selection, reviewed applications, and sent a field inspection team to examine and report on each site. The committee then awarded grants in the form of materials only. The Ghana Museums and Monuments Board provided skilled labor, and some property owners supplied unskilled labor and utilities and minor building materials such as earth and sand. Traditional craft training programs targeted youth residing in selected buildings. US/ICOMOS staff prepared technical guidelines highlighting simple methods of building protection and distributed them to grant recipients and unsuccessful applicants.

Recognizing the importance of public and private partnerships in addition to international aid, the committee undertook a local fund-raising campaign to leverage the initial moneys allotted by Phase 2 for the small grants program. As a result, Barclay's Bank, Ghana, sponsored the rehabilitation of one site with a donation to the GHCT. The interest of local businesses such as Barclay's in partnering with the GHCT and the community committee has established a foundation for the long-term viability of the project (see Fig. 6).

To promote continued maintenance at rehabilitated sites, the committee, supported by US/ICOMOS, engaged a local business advisory center to hold a workshop for site owners and occupants interested in developing microenterprises. After this event representatives from the business center conducted assessments of the proposed on-site enterprises. Finally, the center developed business action plans with interested family members able to fund start-up initiatives. As owners and occupants recognized that the physical appearance of the establishment was crucial to success, each business plan included moneys to cover the continued maintenance of the site. While many participants chose ventures related to processing and selling food items, several developed business plans centered on the craft trade and other small-scale, tourism-related

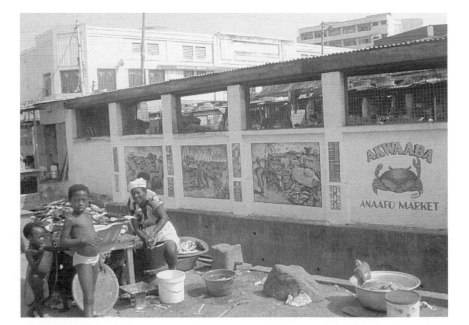

Figure 5
Public art installation, fish market. Photo by Gina Haney.

Figure 6
Project staff and representative of Barclay's Bank. Photo by Joseph Koomson.

businesses such as home-stay accommodations. By the completion of Phase 2, rehabilitated sites under this initiative included seven shrines expressing traditional religious practices, eleven family houses, and one cemetery.

To encourage local employment, the project undertook a guide training and licensing program for citizens of the Central Region. At the end of this program, twenty trained and licensed citizens of Cape Coast began leading walking tours, some beginning from Heritage House, of the downtown area and other nearby sites and towns. This microenterprise is flourishing as visitors, hoping to understand the larger town surrounding Cape Coast Castle, take these tours. The GHCT continues to support the marketing, sales, and promotion of this business.

Sustainable Conservation of the Built Environment

During the course of the project, it became apparent that while many Cape Coasters were interested in heritage conservation, some continued to replace traditional buildings and structures with those made of new and modern materials. The practice of considering building form as less worthy of conservation than the name, or family totem, attached to it, is indicative of a continued tradition of paying homage to and memorializing ancestors.

Addressing the protection of such intangible forms of cultural heritage and their contribution to memory may be critical to catalyzing a deeper understanding of the preservation of the tangible, or built, environment. The complexity deepens when we consider shrines that express traditional religious practices.

In Cape Coast, fetish or traditional gods live in natural resources, such as water, rocks, and trees, contained in or bordered by the built environment. Cape Coasters believe that during certain periods, fetishes inhabit people and animals, moving around and actively participating in ritual and parade. Fetish priests enshrine these sacred natural resources by constructing walls and shelters using contemporary materials (Fig. 7). As a result of marking and calling attention to fetish in this way, priests and practitioners place contemporary values on traditional religion—important in a town with an increasing number of Christian places of worship.

On the one hand, Cape Coasters continue the practice of honoring and commemorating their ancestry by creating new and modern buildings and structures. On the other hand, Cape Coasters preserve traditional religious values by protecting and augmenting ancient resources. Both methods demonstrate two rich yet conflicting ways of engaging the past through heritage conservation. Reconciling these and creating a model in which the conservation of the tangible and intangible coexist may achieve a more sustainable approach to the conservation of the built environment.

Amid these systems, community leaders led two unexpected initiatives that supported the sustainable approach of the project. First, the establishment of a historic core, or district, in the downtown area confirmed a long-term pledge to conservation of the built environment. Second, the move to obtain ownership of a historic site in Cape Coast by the paramount chief and leader of the Traditional Council demonstrated a commitment to implementation.

As community members and leaders participated in this project, an understanding of the rich, diverse, and overlapping layers of history began to emerge. In Cape Coast, the term "castle" has been appropriated and attached to several large family houses prominently situated on important streets in the downtown area. While a visitor to the town may be directed to the World Heritage Site, it is the smaller castles that serve to define the community. Similarly, one of the most well known structures in the town is London Bridge (Fig. 8, Color Plate 6). Constructed across a large stormwater drain, this structure, like the castles, deepens the connection between the community and its past.

Figure 7
Fetish shrine. Photo by Gina Haney.

Figure 8
London Bridge, Cape Coast. Photo by
Gina Haney.
(See also Color Plate 6.)

As a result of discussing, mapping, rehabilitating, and marking
some of these resources, community leaders enacted municipal legislation
to establish a historic core in the center of downtown. Bound by natural
features, the historic core includes religious and educational buildings,
markets, family houses, planted gardens, work yards, stormwater drains,
playing fields, bridges, streets, and footpaths. Although the castle is
included in the core, it is not the focal point. Nor is the built environment
the focus of the core's significance. It was clear in August 2000 when
opinion leaders, elected and appointed officials, and members of the
Traditional Council delineated core boundaries that the collective history
of this place is expressed in inextricable layers of the tangible and intangible,
natural and cultural, modern and historic, black and white. Together, these
public and private spaces embody a sense of what it means to share a
common past in this place, what it means to be a Cape Coaster.

The paramount chief, or Omanhen, whose position is passed
down through matrilineal lines, and his Traditional Council are the most
highly regarded authority in Cape Coast. For several years the paramount
chief had been without a palace or formal meeting hall for deliberations
and traditional court proceedings. Land had been obtained outside of the
downtown area and along a major road leading to Accra for the construction of a modern palace.

After observing the transformation of Heritage House and participating in subsequent community forums and planning sessions, the
Omanhen and the Traditional Council abandoned the plan for the new
palace and negotiated the ownership of a suitable historic site in the center
of downtown Cape Coast. Just after the close of the two-year project, the
Omanhen proudly announced that Gothic House, a large mid-nineteenth-
century compound constructed by a British merchant and later owned by
a well-known Cape Coaster, would become the palace.

At the end of the project it was evident that the sustainability of
conservation efforts depended first on a community base that was invested
in, engaged in, and empowered by the project. Second, sustainability
depended on the presence of a funded, well-trained, nongovernmental

organization, the GHCT, which since August 2000 has rehabilitated ten additional family houses under the small grants program. Finally, long-term conservation efforts resulted from a project that was able to recast itself to meet the changing needs of a community with a complex past and an unsure future. Conservation, in terms of both the tangible and the intangible, had to happen first for the community and second for the visitor. The idea that conservation, in whatever form it takes, expresses the past while contributing to the future is now integral to the dialogue in Cape Coast.

In conclusion, Cape Coast, like many towns around the world, represents layers of history and tradition. Each layer is significant. Traditional activities and landscapes are as important in the story of Cape Coast as its constructed colonial past. Members of the community of Cape Coast define their historic core as a place that accommodates the intricate, sometimes conflicting beliefs, sites, and activities that are distinctive. If the castle or other aspects of the built environment are to be understood and their conservation sustained, it must be in this context.

Acknowledgments

A number of individuals helped to shape the objectives and outcomes of the Cape Coast project. Foremost, Ellen Delage designed the comprehensive second phase, oversaw its management from Washington, D.C., and helped to reshape project initiatives as it unfolded over the two years. A number of US/ICOMOS board members, staff, and members provided invaluable insight, time, and energy both in the field and from across the Atlantic, and I am especially grateful to Doug Comer, Maurice Cox, Patricia O'Donnell, James Reap, Hisashi Sugaya, and Michael Tuite for their continued interest in and support of the Ghana Heritage Conservation Trust.

While all of these individuals have contributed greatly, the achievements of this project would not have been possible without the support and trust of the Cape Coast community. Osabarimba Kwesi Atta II, Omanhen of the Oguaa Traditional Area; the Honorable George Percy Eshun, Municipal Chief Executive; and Mr. Nkunu Akyea, Executive Director of the Ghana Heritage Conservation Trust slowly led me, and directed the project, through the complex, sometimes invisible, and ever-changing layers of the Cape Coast landscape.

Notes

1 Conservation International, a nonprofit organization concerned with the conservation of natural resources, managed the natural resource component of the Central Region Natural Resource Conservation and Historic Preservation project.

2 For more information on the Cape Coast project, see US/ICOMOS, *Conservation and Tourism Development Plan for Cape Coast* (Washington, D.C.: US/ICOMOS, 2000).

3 Elmina Castle was built in 1482 by the Portuguese and subsequently expanded and modified by the Dutch and, later, the British. Cape Coast Castle was built in 1652 by the Swedes and subsequently expanded and then modified by the Danes and the British.

Sustainability and the Planning of Historic Cities: The Experience of the Aga Khan Trust for Culture

Francesco Siravo

THE AGA KHAN TRUST for Culture's Historic Cities Support Programme (HCSP) was established in 1991 to foster and support conservation and development efforts in historic cities throughout the Muslim world by providing planning assistance to national institutions, local government bodies, and community groups. The HCSP's planning activities include projects in northern Pakistan (Hunza), Aleppo, Cairo, Zanzibar, Mostar in Bosnia-Herzegovina, and Samarkand in Uzbekistan.

All of these projects go beyond purely physical interventions and strive to improve living and working conditions as well as promote cultural, social, and economic development in the surrounding communities. At the same time, the HCSP endeavors to apply and disseminate international restoration standards and up-to-date urban conservation practices in its conservation activities. As we shall see, all of these aspects of the HCSP mission are relevant to sustainability.

What Is a Sustainable Historic City?

Achieving sustainability is central to the planning of historic cities, particularly in developing countries. In these parts of the world, because of the dynamics of often explosive urban development and rapid social and economic transformation, historic areas, often inhabited by the poor, have become unsightly and depressed and are considered an embarrassment by local planners and government officials. In fact, the solutions most often proposed by the administrations concerned revolve around two opposite and equally unsound alternatives.

The first alternative advocates sanitizing these areas and turning them into museums and commercial enclaves where visitors can enjoy the monuments and pay for their upkeep. This alternative, which I will call "the museum solution," cannot be sustained; there are not enough resources or visitors to any single country to make this option seriously plausible. And even if money were available, the result is unlikely to succeed. Visitors—so-called cultural tourists—travel to distant locations wanting to see and experience a special and unique place. Surely they will not be able to find much of anything inside empty shells devoid of real people.

The second alternative proposes modern redevelopment, clearing traditional buildings and spaces and replacing them with contemporary solutions, again following Western examples. The argument goes something like this. These areas are beyond repair and inaccessible to automobiles and modern transportation systems. With the exception of a few monuments, they are little better than slums, and, besides, nobody ever worried about transforming the remains of the past during previous eras, so why should we? Are we not entitled to our own creative expression, and to leave a visible manifestation of our times?

This second option, which I will call "the right to modernize," ignores a fundamental fact: our epoch is radically different from all previous ones. The gradual evolution of the urban landscape, where growth and change occurred within a system of cultural, religious, and technological continuity, has been interrupted and irreversibly lost. The turning point in Europe was the industrial revolution, and the rest of the world followed suit during the postcolonial period. The impact of Western ideas and models on traditional urban fabric around the globe has been profound. The exponential acceleration of the past two centuries has led to such a complete transformation in the way we live, build, and relate to our environment that traditional "preindustrial" urban forms and experiences have become unique and unrepeatable. The fate of our historic cities resembles more and more that of the planet's biological diversity, threatened all over the world.

What is clear in both of the alternatives described above is that they call for the expulsion of the residents living in the historic areas. This creates enormous physical upheaval and long-term social disruption, as we so sadly learned in Rome after Mussolini's pickax policies of the early 1930s. In fact, reluctance to uproot entire neighborhoods is one of the main reasons why, in spite of official arguments and intentions to modernize, very few governments have had the financial resources or political strength to go through with either alternative.

Unable to realize these grand schemes, however, governments abandon historic areas to their fate, thinking that there is no point in maintaining, much less in investing, precious municipal resources because some day it all will be cleared anyway. The result is a slow but insidious drift, whereby these areas are allowed to slowly but surely decay, and their inhabitants are left to increasing poverty and alienation.

This is clearly no solution, not for the fabric and not for the people. It is our job to look for a workable alternative, certainly different from the ones I have just described. And we must go back to the issue of sustainability. And, in particular, to the question: what is a sustainable historic city?

My answer is perhaps obvious, but I think it needs to be clearly stated as it is easily overlooked. Essentially, a sustainable historic city is a traditional urban context that survives and thrives because it has been handed down from generation to generation and its inhabitants are self-sufficient, have an acute sense of their past, and have enough resources to take care of their surroundings. In fact, this happy community cherishes its old houses and pedestrian environment because it feels secure and at home in its familiar, long-inhabited spaces.

I know of no healthy historic city where this essential symbiosis between an established, secure social base and its traditional environment is lacking. However, I can think of endless cases where the most persistent urban problems stem from the absence of this crucial synergy.

In today's developing countries, this all-important synergy between a self-sustaining social base and its urban environment cannot, as it was in the past, be taken for granted. Today, it can only be the result of careful planning and management of a finite resource—the traditional built environment. In addition, it requires that the fragile social fabric inhabiting the depressed historic neighborhoods be sustained and reinforced, if it is not to be wiped out together with the buildings and spaces that contain it.

In sum, the conservation and development of both the social and the physical fabric are the purpose of sustainable planning of historic cities—a loose discipline, in which one has to consider and act on many issues at once and whose success cannot be measured in the short term but requires sustained efforts over the span of years and indeed decades. There is no set recipe for success, only priority issues and activities that are crucial to the development of a long-term, self-sustaining strategy of urban rehabilitation. These activities are mixed and matched in the Aga Khan Trust for Culture's (AKTC's) work according to the various conditions and opportunities found in the field.

Examples from the AKTC's Portfolio

The priorities of any depressed historic area are first and foremost *social and economic*. We usually think that only big money and massive government interventions can produce results in these spheres, and forget that there are also relatively simple initiatives whose impact can be significant.

We have been implementing a minimalist socioeconomic approach in our project in Cairo's Darb al-Ahmar historic district with encouraging results. Our experience has been that you do not necessarily have to create new jobs to foster employment. A better strategy consists in connecting people with existing employment opportunities. With this in mind, we established a job placement and counseling service in our district office. We have also learned that acquiring on-the-job experience is the best and most direct way to prepare for and eventually find a job. We made agreements with a number of existing workshops in the area to train young people. Finally, the availability of credit can make a big difference in low-income areas, enabling people to engage in what they do best. With average disbursements of a few hundred dollars per loan, we have managed to give women and workshop owners tools and equipment that they needed to start or improve their businesses. (See Fig. 1.)

We also recognize the key importance of *building confidence and strengthening the identity of local communities*. This means making people aware of their cultural traditions, enabling them to share their problems and identify solutions, and essentially creating the confidence needed to act on their own behalf rather than passively waiting for outside intervention. For example, we enlist representatives of local nongovernmental organizations to talk to women about local crafts as well as discuss family health problems. Music and painting sessions for children have proven an easy way to introduce them to their surroundings, participate in common

Figure 1

Reinforcing the social and economic base. A small-credit program within the AKTC Cairo project enabled this woman to buy a new oven to prepare foods to sell to neighbors in the Darb al-Ahmar district, thus generating extra income for her family. © Milad Miawad, CDS.

projects, and learn about local history (Fig. 2). In the same vein, street theatrical events have been effective in getting residents to talk about common problems and neighborhood issues.

In the *institutional sphere*, we are helping to reorganize the planning process and the administrative setup in order to include a conservation agenda and resolve what residents perceive as long-standing stumbling blocks. More specifically, the AKTC has been working on two levels. First, we have been working with the national and local planning institutions to make sure that the historic areas are planned and treated differently than the contemporary city fabric, with finer-grain planning, closer monitoring, and special attention to the surrounding urban context. Certainly most developing country planning offices are not equipped for this kind of work. Therefore, the first step is to create a local team that with time can become the core of a specialized planning agency entirely focused on the historic area (Fig. 3). What we normally do is to work alongside our local teams, sometimes for several years until the new planning process is in place. In Samarkand, this led to the preparation of a plan for the city's central area. Unfortunately, for political reasons, it could not be implemented and we withdrew.

Figure 2

Promoting community awareness. The music and painting sessions organized in Darb al-Ahmar are an effective means of introducing children to their surroundings and of getting them to participate in common projects and hear local stories, thus reinforcing their sense of belonging to a special place. © Milad Miawad, CDS.

Figure 3

Strengthening the institutional and planning framework. A local planning team was established in Samarkand as a first step toward creating a specialized agency focused entirely on the city's historic area. Photo courtesy of AKTC.

In Zanzibar, we have been able to maintain a continued presence since 1992. We started by surveying and inventorying the old Stone Town, went through a full planning exercise culminating in the formal adoption of a new plan and building regulations, and prepared conservation and design guidelines. We are now helping with detailed planning of key open spaces. In fact, we are currently implementing some of these schemes.

But working with local institutions is perforce only one aspect. The second level of action is trying *to give more voice to the community,* playing the role of advocate and mediator between government and local groups (Fig. 4, Color Plate 7). Most problems in historic urban areas revolve around the use of public open space, the state of the infrastructure, the availability of services, and the related issues of secure tenure and better housing conditions. Governments often ignore or overlook residents' opinions, and when they do act, they tend to want massive interventions that disregard the real concerns of the people.

In Cairo, for example, we are addressing *the issue of tenure* along the medieval wall we are restoring and have obtained from the Egyptian Supreme Council of Antiquities a partial waiver of the demolition order that had condemned the traditional houses near the monument. As a result, the residents may continue to live in the area and the monument will be preserved in its living urban context.

Also, the issue of how to use and reorganize *public open spaces* requires talking to the users of these spaces, such as the vendors in the Tablita Market in Cairo, with whom we discussed the physical reorganization of the space with the help of scale models (Fig. 5). On these occasions one realizes the extent to which people's requirements are usually ignored by government planners.

Nowhere is the issue of participatory planning more relevant than in housing. In fact, we consider *rehabilitation of housing* the best long-term antidote to the chronic disinvestment and decline of historic areas. A housing improvement scheme can be the catalyst that sets in motion a positive chain reaction to arrest the decay and start a process of revitalization. Housing rehabilitation is also crucial to preserving the traditional urban fabric as a whole.

Figure 4
Giving more voice to the community. The AKTC often plays the role of advocate and mediator between government and local groups. Here the elders of Samarkand's Kom Said Imam neighborhood are discussing housing and neighborhood issues with local administrators. Photo courtesy of AKTC.
(See also Color Plate 7.)

Figure 5
Upgrading public open spaces. Using scale models, AKTC staff discuss the physical reorganization of the Tablita Market in Cairo with vendors and administrators. © Milad Miawad, CDS.

In our projects we concentrate on identifying prototypes and technical solutions that are low cost and low tech and on providing incentives for the rehabilitation of traditional housing using traditional materials and methods. For example, before withdrawing from Samarkand, we developed a pilot infill design and housing rehabilitation plan for one of the historic neighborhoods and initiated actual rehabilitation works (Fig. 6). We are going through a similar process in Cairo, where we are exploring possibilities for partial reconstruction as well as infill prototypes, and we have recently launched with the Ford Foundation a housing credit scheme for an area comprising one hundred fifty residential buildings. We discuss priorities with the residents, identify a building program, make funds available directly to the contractors approved by the local project management, and ensure repayment of loans to replenish the revolving fund.

Finally, introducing needed services and facilities in these neighboorhoods through the *reuse of old buildings*, preferably in public ownership, is an important component of our work as well. Successful adaptive reuse projects also serve an illustrative purpose for the communities concerned. They are a tangible demonstration that old is far from bad. It shows that old buildings need not necessarily be associated with poverty and neglect and that they are still capable of playing a useful role today. Completed adaptive reuse projects include the Baltit Fort in the Karakorum mountains of northern Pakistan, the Old Dispensary along Zanzibar's seafront (Fig. 7, Color Plate 8), and the restoration of several structures in the Mostar bazaar damaged during the recent war in Bosnia. Ongoing projects include the Customs House in Zanzibar, started by UNESCO a few years ago, and most recently an empty former school building near the medieval walls of Cairo, whose adaptive reuse as a community center started in 2001.

The rehabilitation of these structures also provides a very important chance to offer *training opportunities* to young apprentices and to promote local know-how and autonomous capabilities in traditional con-

Figure 6
Improving housing conditions. AKTC projects focus on housing rehabilitation as a means to arrest the flight of residents and preserve the traditional urban fabric. The figure shows a pilot housing rehabilitation initiative carried out in 1998 in the Gur-i Emir district of historic Samarkand. Photo courtesy of AKTC.

Figure 7
Reusing historic buildings. The rehabilitation of traditional structures, such as the Old Dispensary in Zanzibar, converted into a cultural center by AKTC in 1997, shows that old buildings need not necessarily be associated with poverty and neglect and that they are capable of playing a useful role today. Photo courtesy of AKTC.
(See also Color Plate 8.)

Figure 8
Training in traditional construction. All AKTC projects include a training component to promote local know-how and autonomous capabilities in traditional construction, such as the ongoing pilot restoration and training program on Cairo's medieval city walls. Photo courtesy of AKTC.

struction (Fig. 8). All of our projects include a training component and make use as much as possible of the local craftspeople and workforce, complemented by external trainers.

Conclusion

I would like to draw some conclusions from these examples and more generally regarding the approach my organization has taken with respect to urban conservation and its sustainability over time.

The complexity of harnessing a successful process of urban conservation can be reduced to the availability of a few fundamental ingredients.

- The process has to be fueled by an economically viable and *socially stable population.* Consolidating this bedrock may take several years, but there is no need to wait for all-encompassing solutions. The process of reactivating people's abilities to take care of themselves can be initiated almost anywhere with fairly simple strategies aimed at linking people with existing jobs, creating apprenticeship opportunities, and making available very limited credit to motivated residents, especially women.
- In order to advance, however, the urban conservation process needs not only fuel but also a reliable operating system. A conducive and supportive institutional climate is therefore very

important. This has to be based on a *conservation-specific planning framework*, coupled with incentives to facilitate rehabilitation and appropriate development. Some of these incentives should be financial; however, it is a mistake to dismiss nonfinancial incentives. Security of tenure, a streamlined and fair building permit process, good technical support, and help in avoiding the tyranny of an inefficient and demanding bureaucracy are incentives that residents will appreciate. They can be provided at a reasonable cost and by interacting decisively with the institutions that count.

- Another very important ingredient is the application of traditional construction methods. In many places, these are disappearing fast or have already been lost. No rehabilitation program, however, can be implemented without practical knowhow. And the gap between good intentions and accomplished facts usually becomes apparent once plans are to be implemented and practical work has to start. This is why *training in traditional construction and conservation* is so important and should be an absolute priority—not just training of craftspeople, however good or specialized, but also and more important of thinking builders, small entrepreneurs who understand the complexity of the traditional building process and the need to carefully coordinate a building site.

- The last and perhaps most important ingredient is also the least tangible—the *human and cultural dimension* that made the creation of what today we call historic cities possible. This dimension needs to be reappropriated, pieced back together—to regain the sense of community, the shared values, and the particular links to the traditions and cultures that are embodied in these special places. Indeed, historic cities are the repositories of these values, memories, roots, and traditions.

None of these ingredients can exist in isolation. Each has to be connected and integrated with the other in order that urban planning and conservation may work. Our tendency to separate and specialize different fields and activities must be overcome, as must the artificial and misleading separation between tradition and modernity, conservation and development.

Conservation planning cannot and must not be restricted to protecting historic property. If so narrowly defined, conservation is bound to fail. On the contrary, it must be seen as an intrinsic part of a broader economic and social development process, whereby it can bring out the all-important cultural dimension, a dimension too often lacking in city planning today.

This is the added value of conservation planning, a reminder that, to build sustainable communities and cities, we have to put people back in touch with their cultural identities and historic places—places that provide inspiration for the future and show that there is an alternative to the standardized, look-alike urban panoramas that we see today in so many parts of the world.

References

Aga Khan Trust for Culture, Historic Cities Support Programme. *Karimamad and Baltit Project Development.* Geneva, 1996.

Aga Khan Trust for Culture, Historic Cities Support Programme. *Planning for the Historic City of Samarkand.* Geneva, 1996.

Aga Khan Trust for Culture, Historic Cities Support Programme. *Reintegrating Historic Buildings into the Life of the Neighbourhood: The Adaptive Reuse of the Former Darb Shoughlan School.* Technical Brief no. 3. Cairo, 1999.

Aga Khan Trust for Culture, Historic Cities Support Programme. *A Plan for the Central Area of Samarkand.* Istanbul, 2000.

Aga Khan Trust for Culture, Historic Cities Support Programme. *The Darb al-Ahmar Project: Urban Rehabilitation and Community Development in Historic Cairo.* Technical Brief no. 5. Cairo, 2001.

Aga Khan Trust for Culture and the World Monuments Fund. *Reclaiming Historic Mostar, Opportunities for Revitalization.* New York: AKTC and WMF, 1999.

Bianca, S. *Urban Form in the Arab World.* London: Thames & Hudson, 2000.

Siravo, F. Il recupero dell'edilizia storica nei paesi in via di sviluppo: Il caso di Lamu. *Piano, Progetto, Città,* no. 5 (1987):48–61.

Siravo, F. A plan for the historic Stone Town. In *Zanzibar Stone Town Projects,* 34–47. Geneva: AKTC, 1997.

Siravo, F. Reversing the decline of a historic district. In *The Azhar Park Project in Cairo and the Conservation and Revitalization of Darb al-Ahmar,* 35–53. Geneva: AKTC, 2001.

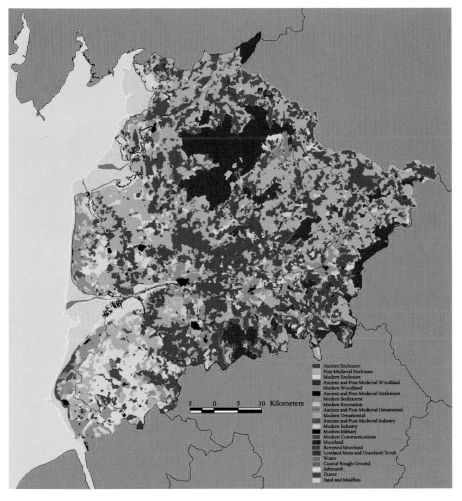

Ancient Enclosure
Post-Medieval Enclosure
Modern Enclosure
Ancient and Post-Medieval Woodland
Modern Woodland
Ancient and Post-Medieval Settlement
Modern Settlement
Modern Recreation
Ancient and Post-Medieval Ornamental
Modern Ornamental
Ancient and Post-Medieval Industry
Modern Industry
Modern Military
Modern Communications
Moorland
Reverted Moorland
Lowland Moss and Grassland/Scrub
Water
Coastal Rough Ground
Saltmarsh
Dunes
Sand and Mudflats

5   0   5   10 Kilometers

Plate 1

Lancashire HLC: Geographic Information System printout from using a "Broad Types" classification, an entry level to the GIS. Produced by Joy Ede and John Darlington; English Heritage/Lancashire County Council.

(See also Fig. 2, p. 34.)

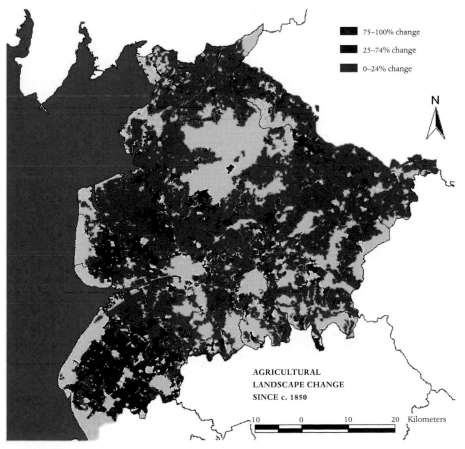

75–100% change

25–74% change

0–24% change

AGRICULTURAL
LANDSCAPE CHANGE
SINCE c. 1850

10   0   10   20 Kilometers

Plate 2

Lancashire HLC measuring landscape-scale change after comparison with nineteenth-century historic maps. Produced by Joy Ede and John Darlington; English Heritage/Lancashire County Council.

(See also Fig. 3, p. 39.)

Plate 3

Hampshire historic landscape types. Produced by Peter Atkinson after George Lambrick; English Heritage, Hampshire County Council, Oxford Archaeological Unit.

(See also Fig. 4, p. 40.)

Hampshire Historic Landscape Types

1.1 Small irregular assarted fields
1.2 Medium irregular assarted fields
1.3 Large irregular assarted fields
1.4 Regular assarted fields
1.5 Former strips and furlongs
1.6 Regular fields - wavy boundaries
1.7 Irregular fields - straight boundaries
1.8 Regular 'ladder' fields
1.9 Small regular parliamentary fields
1.10 Medium regular parliamentary fields
1.11 Large regular parliamentary fields
1.12 Variable regular parliamentary fields
1.14 'Prairie' fields
1.15 Irregular fields bounded by roads, tracks and paths
1.16 Small regular fields - wavy boundaries
2.1 Heathland commons
2.2 Downland commons
2.3 Other commons and greens
2.4 Wooded commons
3.1 Orchards
3.3 Nurseries with glass houses
4.1 Assarted pre-1810 woodland
4.2 Replanted assarted pre-1810 woodland
4.3 Other pre-1810 woodland
4.4 Replanted other pre-1810 woodland
4.5 19th-century plantations (general)

4.6 Pre-1810 hangers
4.7 19th-century hangers
4.8 Pre-1810 heathland enclosed woodland
4.9 19th-century heathland plantations
4.10 Pre-1810 wood pasture
4.11 19th-century wood pasture
5.1 Unenclosed heath and scrub
5.2 Enclosed heath and scrub
5.3 Purlieus
6.1 Downland
7.1 Miscellaneous valley floor enclosures
7.2 Valley floor woodlands
7.3 Marsh and rough grazing
7.4 Water meadows
7.5 Unimproved valley floor grassland
7.6 Watercress beds
7.7 Fishpond, natural ponds and lakes
7.8 Watermill complexes
8.1 Coastal wetlands
8.2 Salt marsh
8.3 Salterns
8.4 Reclaimed land
8.5 Harbours and marinas
8.6 Shingle and dunes
8.7 Mudflats
9.1 Scattered settlement 1810 extent
9.2 Scattered settlement post-1810 extent

9.3 Common edge settlement 1810 extent
9.4 Common edge settlement post-1810 extent
9.6 Post-1810 settlement
9.7 Village/hamlet 1810 extent
9.9 Town & city 1810 extent
9.11 Caravan sites
10.1 Pre-1810 parkland
10.2 Post-1810 parkland
10.3 Deer parks
11.1 Racecourses
11.2 Golf courses
11.3 Major sports fields
12.1 Chalk quarries
12.2 Gravel workings
12.3 Factories
12.4 Large-scale industry
12.5 Water treatment and reservoirs
12.6 Dockyards
13.1 Railway stations and sidings
13.3 Airfields
13.4 Motorway service areas
14.1 Prehistoric and Roman defence
14.2 Medieval defences
14.3 Post-medieval (1500–1830)
14.4 19th-century (1830–1914) defence
14.5 20th-century (1914–) defence

Plate 4
"Lutses" in Times Square. The Virgin Store,
circa 1998. Photo by M. Christine Boyer.
(See also Fig. 6, p. 73.)

Plate 5
Cape Coast Castle. Photo by Gina Haney.
(See also Fig. 1, p. 118.)

Plate 6
London Bridge, Cape Coast.
Photo by Gina Haney.
(See also Fig. 8, p. 125.)

Plate 7
Giving more voice to the community. AKTC often plays the role of advocate and mediator between government and local groups. Here the elders of Samarkand's Kom Said Imam neighborhood are discussing housing and neighborhood issues with local administrators. Photo courtesy of AKTC.
(See also Fig. 4, p. 131.)

Plate 8
Reusing historic buildings. The rehabilitation of traditional structures, such as the Old Dispensary in Zanzibar converted into a cultural center by AKTC in 1997, shows that old buildings need not necessarily be associated with poverty and neglect and that they are capable of playing a useful role today. Photo courtesy of AKTC.
(See also Fig. 7, p. 132.)

Plate 9
Street scene in the old city of San'a' (1997).
Sana'a' was declared a World Heritage Site by
UNESCO in 1984. Photo by Trevor Marchand.
(See also Fig. 1, p. 142.)

Plate 10
The seventh-century Jokhang, the holiest
structure in Tibet. J. Taring made accurate
drawings and a model to preserve its memory
for younger generations. Photo by Ernesto
Noriega.
(See also Fig. 2, p. 163.)

Plate 11
Students surveying Likir monastery.
Photo by Lucy Kennedy.
(See also Fig. 5, p. 167.)

Plate 12
Drawing of Likir monastery done by
students. Photo by Lucy Kennedy.
(See also Fig. 6, p. 168.)

Plate 13
Construction of experimental raised fields
during the dry season by farmers of Huatta,
Peru, 1986. Photo provided by Instituto
Geográfico Militar.
(See also Fig. 4, p. 187.)

Plate 14
The archaeology of development, 1986. The physical relicts of
failed international development projects promoting capitalist-based
and "appropriate" technology during the 1960s, 1970s, and 1980s at
the Illpa Agricultural Experimental Station, Puno, Peru. Photo by
Clark L. Erickson.
(See also Fig. 10, p. 196.)

Process over Product: Case Studies of Traditional Building Practices in Djenné, Mali, and San'a', Yemen

Trevor H. J. Marchand

THE INTERNALIZATION OF OWNERSHIP and responsibility by indigenous peoples is regarded as a vital component in conservation efforts, effectively guaranteeing the transmission of the object's "cultural essence" for the foreseeable future. This requires local populations to share, or adopt, Western definitions of "cultural property" as consisting of those material artifacts that are inseparable from identity. It also espouses notions of authenticity and beliefs about the irreplaceable nature of the "original," a subject I will come back to. In discussing the impact of the "museological view of culture"—described "as sensory experienced object rather than as meaning"—Rowlands (forthcoming) notes the pervasive influence of international legislation on late-twentieth-century notions of cultural property, fueled by the perceived threat of globalization to the survival of local cultures. Identity politics thrive in this climate. Claims to rights over cultural property instigate and perpetuate struggles to define and maintain bounded ethnic, linguistic, and nationalist enclaves. Rowlands is part of the wave of late-twentieth- and early-twenty-first-century anthropologists who embrace the discipline's return to a serious consideration of essentialist theories of material culture that no longer "oppose objects to persons or relations to things."[1] He believes that this perspective is "the key to understanding how a bridge can be made between the studies of the construction of persons and the value that is placed on the protection of culture and tradition."

This theory of culture, as embodied in the materiality of things, is highly complementary to the aims of the conservationist invested in the preservation of the "object." The object (whether artifact, architecture, or landscape) is bequeathed the status of "cultural resource," and resources are deemed to possess both a physicality and a value that may be claimed, owned, and cared for in the interests of the collective identity. It is not always clear, however, who this collective is and therefore who has the right to manage these resources. Despite claims that international guidelines (set forth by such bodies as UNESCO) serve to safeguard the local in the face of globalization, declarations of "world heritage" render the distinction between the two realms ambiguous. Struggles over the possession and conservation of these cultural resources are played out between the often disenfranchised populations of postcolonial locales and teams of Western-trained specialists (archaeologists, art historians, architects, engineers, scientists, conservators, museum curators, and government officials). This issue, however, is not my principal focus here. My aim is to draw attention to some of the serious consequences that result from underscoring the tangible, physical properties of cultural capital to the near exclusion of all else.

When the scope of cultural property is reduced to the physical, it can be thoroughly dissected and discerned. "Things," by virtue of their physicality, may be subjected to a positivist framework that classifies, quantifies, and qualifies, ultimately generating a specific, and scientific, form of knowledge (Feyerabend 1975). Those who control this knowledge command a privileged position from where decisions may be made and plans executed that directly affect the present and future state of the artifact, architecture, or landscape in question. Indeed, control over things is dangerously vulnerable to being wrested away from the original producers, owners, and inhabitants, and one must critically question which collective entity of people is ultimately the true and rightful possessor of the cultural resource: the locals, scientists, or global tourists. If the museological view of "culture as property" is prevalent, and culture is actually conceived as something that one can have more or less of, then, by extension, the declaration, conservation, and monitoring of World Heritage Sites must certainly (at least to some considerable degree) dispossess local populations of exclusive ownership and redistribute custody of that cultural resource within an international arena of competing interests. In short, it would seem that the practice of prioritizing the material by (largely) Western-trained specialists is vested with (potentially neoimperialist) ambitions to monopolize what has been constructed as a tangible resource. Cultures are effectively reduced to, and constrained by, a positivist discourse that reconfigures cultural resources as classifiable and quantifiable objects.

The issue of cultural-resources-as-objects is most pertinent to my thesis. In brief, my main objective is to counter this claim and illustrate that "process," not simply product, should be of (perhaps greater) concern to conservationists and be rightly regarded as a precious resource in its own right. Process is constituted by skilled performance and expert knowledge, both of which give rise to the production and reproduction of material entities. These qualities are possessed by people, not things, and they combine through normally complex regimes of socialization and training to generate competent agents with distinct roles and recognized status in a given society. For the most part, socially designated experts possessing skills and knowledge (i.e., artisans, builders, sorcerers, philosophers, etc.) are responsible for the transmission of their expertise to select members of younger generations. Thus, logically, the conservation of systems that produce and proliferate this knowledge, such as apprenticeship, and the maintenance of socioeconomic parameters necessary for production, equates to the most promising scenario for sustaining desirable cultural resources.

Practices and processes may not be tangible in the sense of being material artifacts that can be scientifically scrutinized and reduced to analytic descriptions of their chemical composition and physical properties, but they are nevertheless "sensibly experienced" and "passed along." As cultural resources, traditional processes are "regenerated" each time production and reproduction (of, for instance, the material object, the rite or ritual, the sacred word or incantation) takes place. Furthermore, traditional practices and processes—constituted by specialized trade and technical knowledge; engagement in skilled performance; the knowledge of one's identity, status, and social responsibility as an "expert" and moral agent; and the public manifestation of an expert discourse—are "historical" in the sense that they are rooted in a specific social, cultural, political, and economic history. Regeneration and historical constitution in no way imply a static reproduction of either the process or the product but instead indicate that both are anchored in a dynamic, living tradition that continues to harbor value for them, thereby sanctioning their survival. What has perhaps kept traditional practices and the processes of production peripheral to conservationist concerns is precisely their nontangible and dynamic qualities that render them elusive to effective control and manipulation.

As a trained architect and anthropologist, it is my intention to demonstrate by way of example the paramount importance of (in particular) building processes as a cultural resource and to consider ways that they may be sustainably conserved in the contexts of San'a', Yemen, and Djenné, Mali. The conservation of building processes (which are identified with the regeneration of both systems of knowledge and traditional built environments) must consider the following as aspects of the "process": the builders as social agents with culturally defined roles and status; their technical knowledge as embodied in their practices and performance, normally (but not exclusively) manifested in the construction of edifices; the transmission of their expert knowledge, often in the form of an apprenticeship system; and the builders' social, political, and economic relations with clients and suppliers. I will address these dimensions of the building process with reference to my fieldwork with builders in both settings. Before proceeding to specific case studies, I begin with a general overview of what an anthropology of space, place, and architecture has to offer and how it may contribute to more sustainable conservation efforts. As the warning reads above, this will require those specialists normally at the helm of conservation studies and programs to suspend their convictions that the object is primary and open their minds to a story of process.

An Anthropological Approach to the Built Environment

I have proposed elsewhere that the goal of anthropology is "to learn about what members of (other) societies and cultures know about the world, the manner in which people come to know what they know, and the ways that they represent and communicate their knowledge" (Marchand 2000b:301). In short, my interest is in knowledge, and it is "knowledge" that I am advocating as the primary interest for the field of conservation. This is not to discredit the immense importance of objects but rather to compel recognition of the factor that bestows those objects with importance in the first place: human thought, and the knowledge it yields. Without the knowledge that produces, uses, or even discards an object, the object, on its own, falls prey to new, decontextualized designations of meaning.

Meaning, like the knowledge that each of us possesses about the world, is a product of thought: it is derived from what we think about people, things, and other ideas, and it is amenable to change. Objects do not have meaning unto themselves because an object cannot think about what it is—an object cannot think about anything. Objects cannot "contain" meaning or memory because these belong to the realm of thought, and thought, as a property, belongs to humans (or other living species). If all this seems obvious and a little heavy-handed, then it should. I am merely reinforcing my position that in no conceivable way can objects be regarded as inherently containing values, essence, meaning, memory, or culture.

In discerning between the "spirit of the thing" and some conceived notion of its "essence," Law, inspired by Mauss's writings on the spirit (*hau*) of the gift, writes:

> [T]he 'original' knowledge (and by this I mean the knowledge alongside which the thing was conceived) of the object, its *hau* [spirit], comes to be confused with what is deemed to be its 'primordial essence' (i.e., a pre-existing, immutable truth). The *hau* of the thing is not anterior to its production. It is not a soul that transcends the object, surviving its destruction. Rather, the spirit of the object is (re)produced through its manufacture and subsequent (and continuous) circulation, and is subject to reinterpretation as the object moves through a complex network of exchange. (1999:107)

Following from this, if the ambition of governments, institutions, and conservation-related specialists is to effect sustainable conservation of culturally meaningful objects, then the "systems of knowledge" that render these objects meaningful must figure prominently on the program agenda. We must look to the people—the producers and users who, through their engagement in production and use, effectively generate knowledge about artifacts, architecture, and landscapes. The cultural memory is embodied "in" these practices, not in the object. As I asserted at the outset, a conservation of this knowledge, as it becomes manifest in the processes of production (and of use), is perhaps the most viable way of guaranteeing the renewal of salient resources. Anthropology provides an effective means of engaging with these more elusive cultural assets and would undoubtedly play a highly complementary role in relation to other conservation efforts.

More specifically, in dealing with the built environment, anthropology provides a framework for critically assessing the social, cultural, and historical significance of concepts such as space, place, and architecture. By considering the historical evolution of Western theories of space, from Aristotle through medieval Christianity and the Renaissance and via Descartes and later Enlightenment figures such as Newton, it becomes evident how space emerged conceptually as a reified, quantifiable entity in our society (Casey 1996; Lefebvre 1991). Its cultural construction becomes all the more evident in cross-cultural studies of spatial cognition (see, e.g., Gumperz and Levinson 1996; Marchand 2001; Senft 1997). Inspired by Heidegger's essay "Building, Dwelling, Thinking" (1977) and Merleau-Ponty's *Phenomenology of Perception* (1962), there has been mounting advocation by scholars during the past decade for recognizing the primacy of place over space (Casey 1996; Gregotti 1996:69; Hirsch and O'Hanlon 1995). As a result, space might be better understood as a conceptual extension of our emplacement-in-the-world as sentient beings: first and foremost, we are always "in place." Our emplacement is by virtue of our perpetual immersion in, embodied experience of, and engagement with our surroundings. Taking a theory of place seriously incites a closer examination of the processes that make place both a physical and a meaningful entity. An anthropology of space, place, and architecture investigates this "making" as comprising the competing discourses between builders, suppliers, architects, planners, governing bodies, conservationists (in the case of heritage sites), and inhabitants (whereby the notion of discourse encompasses engagement in all forms of practice).

My concern here is architecture, and more particularly building processes, at two UNESCO World Heritage Sites, Djenné, Mali, and San'a', Yemen. In both of these Islamic and urban settings, traditional builders—defined here as those employing indigenous materials and construction methods and deriving their expert knowledge through apprenticeship as opposed to a technical or formalized education process (Marchand 2001:73)—are still largely responsible for much (if not the majority)[2] of the construction in their cities, and they continue to transmit their expertise to younger generations of craftsmen in the trade.

Traditional Builders: Toward a Sustainable Conservation of Process

The Case of San'a'

Yemen's capital, unlike most other cities of the oil-rich Arabian states, has conserved a great deal of its preindustrial character and unique built environment despite increased contact with Western and modernized Arab countries following its 1962 revolution. During the 1970s, however, new surges of capital and a developing economy resulted in rapid urban expansion of San'a', and many of the city's established families with adequate financial means left their tower houses in the old historic core for modern villas in the more hygienic and convenient suburbs. The evacuation of wealthy patrons with the resources to erect and maintain the traditional San'a'ni-style architecture, combined with a nearly complete lack of municipal planning initiatives and building regulations and the consequent introduction of new construction materials and methods, posed a serious threat to the survival of historic buildings and associated practices. In response, the 1980 General Conference of UNESCO adopted a resolution to devise a plan for the preservation and restoration of the city. UNESCO's declaration of San'a' as a World Heritage Site in 1984 not only prompted wider international recognition of the city's rich architectural heritage but also bolstered local interest in architecture as a cultural resource. For city residents, the distinct indigenous building style came to be associated not only with the status of patrons but also with the tourism it attracts and, by association, the hard currency that foreign visitors inject into the local economy. (See Fig. 1, Color Plate 9.)

Traditional architecture has been tightly woven into the fabric of Yemeni national identity as the country increasingly comes to understand itself through its relations with other countries on the world stage (versus

Figure 1
Street scene in the old city of San'a' (1997). Sana'a' was declared a World Heritage Site by UNESCO in 1984. Photo by Trevor Marchand. *(See also Color Plate 9.)*

North Yemen's former isolation under the theocratic rule of the Zaydi imams). This identification with "tradition" is not straightforward and embodies contradictory sentiments for the preservation of old ways. As I have noted elsewhere (2000c:49), identity construction is significantly constituted by impressions that one harbors about the places "we" or the "other" inhabit. The historic core of San'a', like those of many Middle Eastern cities, is popularly conceived by outsiders as a conservatively religious enclave that perpetuates outdated values and practices. Such values and practices are thought to clash with the struggle to establish democracy and a modernized economy. Paradoxically, the Old City is simultaneously depicted in the national imagination as a reserve of Yemeni traditions and values that must be shielded against encroaching foreign influence and domination. The resident population is saddled with the custodianship of the virtuosity and moral order of the old ways.

In addition to rising international and local awareness of San'a''s architectural heritage and the issue of cultural identity, sluggish economic development has figured prominently in underpinning the survival of indigenous building practices and reproduction of the urban environment. The weak performance of Yemen's economy over the past two decades, exacerbated by economic sanctions imposed on the country by Saudi Arabia and the Gulf States after the Gulf War and a civil war between north and south in 1994, has meant that the importation of modern (read: Westernized) construction materials and techniques has become largely untenable for the majority of the population. Not only has much of the existing housing stock been maintained because of financial constraints, but the city's traditional master masons have continued to receive commissions for new constructions with more affordable and readily available local materials. Importantly, through the regeneration of the built environment, the traditional building trade has proliferated the necessary knowledge and skills, as well as the expert discourse associated with the master mason. These masons designate themselves as *taqliddi* (traditional), in marked distinction to those working in the city with modern materials and equipment, and they advantageously manipulate this identity through the discourse.

The flourishing of indigenous building practices has also renewed interest among the society's elite, who strive to appropriate San'a'ni-style architecture as a status marker. Much of this is realized in veneer applications of decorative motifs, carved plaster-and-stained-glass fanlights, and ornate interior plasterwork in the construction of new villas, office buildings, and government institutions. Some of the city's established families, however, have moved back to their ancestral homes in the Old City or have invested financially in their conservation. Others continue to extend the vertical height of their tower houses with additional stories, and several new tower houses have been raised in both the historic core and its peripheral neighborhoods. All consider the high-perched *manzar* (uppermost room of the house, highly decorated, and with window views across the city to the surrounding mountains) as the paramount male social space for afternoon *qat* chewing sessions. Another important source of building commissions that have served to sustain the traditional sector of the trade are those for religious edifices—mosques, minarets, and madrasahs. These are most often financed by patrons endeavoring to leave behind "good works" (*sadaqah*) as a (public) sign of their religious devotion, as well as their social standing (see Marchand 2001:225–30).

Between 1996 and 1998 I conducted extensive fieldwork with a team of traditional builders in San'a' who specialized in the construction of mosque minarets. During these studies, I actively participated in the building process as a laborer in order to better understand the social, political, economic, and technical aspects of the building process. A considerable component of my investigation was focused on the transmission of expert knowledge via the apprenticeship system. Of direct relevance to my position on conservation promoting process over product, it was determined that "it is not the particular objects produced by the trade, but rather the Master-apprentice relation which distinguishes traditional craft production" (Marchand 2001:246). The San'a'ni apprentice's training may be briefly summarized by the following passage.

> The training of the builder is deeply rooted in the formation of his person and not simply about teaching skills necessary for craft reproduction. . . . The formation of discipline in both mind and body is crucial for producing an individual who is capable of acting, thinking and understanding within the framework of their vocation. . . . Discipline, resolute attitude of superiority, and skilled performance, are integral qualities of the *usta* [Master Builder],

and it is the inculcation of all three during the course of the training that defined his expert status. (Marchand 2001:182)

The minaret of the al-Madrasah Mosque, erected in A.D. 1519–20, is thought to be the earliest example of its kind in Sanʿaʾ. Its form, proportion, and decorative brick style have served as precedents for minaret design in the city to the present day. The minaret is built entirely of kiln-baked brick and is adorned with decorative, mostly geometric, relief work from top to bottom. Like the al-Madrasah, nearly all minarets in Sanʿaʾ are freestanding, towering structures. Their component parts consist of an elevated square-planned base, supporting a high, circular or polygonal columnar shaft, terminated by a projecting calling platform, above which rises a slender octagonal tower of slenderer proportions than the shaft below; and the structure is capped by a hemispherical or fluted dome.[3] The minaret of the Musa Mosque, built in 1747–48, is renowned as the ultimate paradigm of Sanʿaʾni minarets by virtue of its pleasing proportions and brickwork, and it served as a guiding example for the early works of the al-Maswari family master masons with whom I worked.

The al-Maswari brothers began building minarets in the early 1980s, and by the mid-1990s they and their team of builders had erected nearly twenty-five in and around Sanʿaʾ. All of their minarets (with the exception of a couple that were built entirely of stone) consisted of kiln-baked brick towers supported on black stone plinths. Each structure was distinguished by its height (some rising more than sixty meters), by slight modifications in the proportional relation of elements, by variations in the decorative brick-relief patterning, and by either a hemispherical or gracefully fluted dome. Slight changes and innovations regarding greater height,[4] proportions, and decoration were all executed within a structuring framework of possibilities that the builder internalized in his understanding and practices and thereby came to master in the course of his training. Such a structuring framework is not static, nor is it prior to the builder's physical and intellectual engagement in his trade. It is, in fact, through his thinking (about) possibilities and his (possible) performance that such a structuring framework is produced and dynamically reproduced. His imaginative impulses to originate novel forms and decorations were constrained by a disciplined reason.

> The qualitative properties of [the Master Builder's] reasoning which guided his decisions and disciplined his creative imagination were rooted in a number of considerations including what could be practically achieved with the tools and materials at hand; what could be accomplished by his team in view of their capacities, both physically and vocationally; what was negotiated as desirable by his clients in terms of scale, style, and quality of construction; and, notably, what was ideally conceived as perpetuating "tradition" in Sanʿaʾni architecture [see Fig. 2]. For example, [the Master's] reasoning in relation to the latter harnessed his creative imagination for minaret design by focusing his creative intentions within the conceptual boundaries of what has been historically ordained "traditional" in the city. (Marchand 2001:235–36)

Figure 2
Construction of the minaret for the 'Addil
Mosque, San'a', led by the al-Maswari family
of masons (1996). Photo by Trevor Marchand.

The mastered balance between imagination and reason was considered the sine qua non of the builder's expert status (Marchand 2001:235–36). This competence enabled him to creatively regenerate the "traditional" built environment of San'a' and, through his engagement with his apprentices, sustain the knowledge involved in those regenerating processes (see Fig. 3). It was noted, however, that conveyance of the mastered balance between imagination and reason was not equivalent to the more straightforward inculcation of craft-related skills in young builders for simple reproduction purposes.

> Rather, the acquisition of this attribute is highly dependent on the inherent qualities of the apprentice, as well as on the intensity of the relation which evolves between the teacher and pupil during the course of the apprenticeship. The young builder must possess an inward vocation which is predicated upon his skilled aptitudes, motivations to secure a position, and aspirations toward attaining the highly focused level of intentionality for "doing what is beautiful" in his craft. (Marchand 2001: 245–46)

To conclude, the perpetuation of the apprenticeship system, and by consequence the master-apprentice relation, is vital to the conservation of

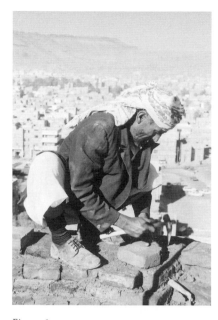

Figure 3
Ahmed al-Maswari, a master mason, perched
on top of the walls of the 'Addil Mosque
minaret laying bricks (1996). Photo by Trevor
Marchand.

trade knowledge and the regeneration of San'a''s architectural heritage. Therefore, it is the apprenticeship process—defined as the transmission of technical skills, social and moral responsibility, and professional status—that I am regarding as the legitimate object of conservation. Various planning specialists and architects concerned with the preservation of the built environment in San'a' have proposed the establishment of trade schools. The rationale for such government-run (or conservation organization–affiliated) institutions is the training of a younger generation of craftsmen to reproduce those building skills deemed at risk of disappearing (see Lewcock 1986:115; Marchand 2001:181–82 and notes 112, 113 [pp. 265–66]; Studio Quaroni in Piepenberg 1987:104). I hope that I have demonstrated, even in this summarized description of apprenticeship, that trade schools that aim to objectify and codify knowledge for efficient technical reproduction could not feasibly replace the complexity of knowledge inculcated in the young builder under the yoke of his master. The slow transmission of knowledge via the master-apprentice relation has the capacity to distill a fine balance between reason and imagination. This balance, in turn, fosters the possibility for a creative regeneration (of both the architectural heritage and the expert knowledge), configured within a discourse of continuity and tradition.

The Case of Djenné

At the start of 2001, I commenced new fieldwork with a team of traditional builders in Djenné in order to make a comparative study of building processes and apprenticeship. This was the first of several phases of projected research with Djenné masons. I will take the opportunity here to present some of this fresh material, focusing on selected episodes in the construction of a new traditional Tukolor-style house in order to draw out salient aspects of the process. I hope to demonstrate how the building process is inextricably linked to a number of the chief social and economic institutions of Djenné, including the practice of magic, religious scholarship, and the cyclical nature of the regional economy. Central to an understanding of building practices and the regeneration of the traditional built environment in Djenné are the (at times complex) social relations among the builders of the *barey ton* (the builders' organization), between the masons and their labor force, and between masons and clients. It is also important to briefly consider here the association between the masons and the (Dutch-sponsored) conservation efforts in Djenné. Though I believe that these efforts have been extremely well informed and that those at the helm have managed to successfully incorporate the practices and concerns of the local masons into their project objectives, I would advocate still greater decision-making autonomy for both the masons and the inhabitants in future interventions at Djenné.

Djenné is an ancient trade city located in the Inland Niger Delta of Mali and connected to the nearby Bani River (a major tributary of the Niger River) by a network of waterways. Historically, it served as a major junction for the trade in gold, ivory, kola, and slaves heading north from the southern forests and savannah and for the salt, copper, and Mediterranean goods coming across the Sahara via Timbuktu. It seems that the present site of the city succeeded the earlier settlement of Djenné-Djeno, three kilometers away, sometime between A.D. 1200 and 1400, when the latter was abandoned. Archaeological excavations at Djenné-Djeno have revealed continuous settlement there from the third century B.C. until about A.D. 1400, making this the oldest known city in sub-Saharan Africa (see McIntosh and McIntosh 1981:16; 1982:418). Until it was seized by the French in 1893, Djenné was known to the Western world from the fifteenth century onward only via the scant reports of merchants, chroniclers, and explorers. The first photographs of the city were taken shortly after the French conquest by a military doctor, Rousseau (Bedaux et al. 1996:7), and the documentary photographs taken by the journalist Félix Dubois before the turn of the century have served as a benchmark to monitor changes in the city and its architecture over the course of the last century (see Schijns 1992:15) and provided an "arbitrary model for restoration" (Bedaux et al. 2000:205) (see Fig. 4).

The French took a serious interest in the architecture of Djenné, which, along with that of Timbuktu, provided the inspiration for the design of the Sénégal-Soudan pavilion at the 1900 Exposition Universelle in Paris, as well as the citadel of French West Africa at the Marseille Colonial Exposition in 1922. Prussin (1986:18) notes that these examples "established the architectural prototype for France's entire West African Empire," which was coined the *style-soudanaise*. A precise definition of the

Figure 4
View over the crenellated rooftops of Djenné (2001). Photo by Trevor Marchand.

style-soudanaise, as it has come to be applied to the architecture of the region, is difficult to fix both stylistically and geographically, and the search for a definition is entangled by a confusing gamut of theories of origins. Denyer (1978:160) attempted a functional definition based on the style's central characteristics: "a courtyard plan; a flat or dome-shaped vaulted roof, and parapets pierced with gutter pipes or channels. Walls are constructed of mud bricks set in mud mortar; and the mud roofs are supported by palm frond joists and formers." She later suggests that if such a style can actually be said to exist in some cohesive sense, then it is likely that "it was primarily urban, and in existence before the spread of Islam" (p. 162). Prussin advocates Djenné as the center of origin and suggests that North African Islamic influences were married to the original Sudanic forms, writing that the "architecture consists of an indigenous savannah fabric into which select features of North African Islam are woven like gold or coloured threads" (1986:180; see also pp. 103–4). Domian (1989) also advances a theory that the originality of Sudanese architecture reached its apogee in Djenné, but he supports the hypothesis that the style is dominantly an indigenous creation due to the city's "relative isolation from the Saharan region and its merchant class that, unlike Timbuktu and Gao, was comprised mainly of a sub-Saharan population, not foreigners" (pp. 27–28).[5] In their article describing the Dutch-sponsored restoration of Djenné, Bedaux et al. (2000:205) also cite the popular academic conjecture of Djenné origins for the *style-soudanaise* and recognize that this architecture "has practically become a symbol of national identity" (see also Rowlands forthcoming).

The production of Djenné's built environment and the dissemination of the style throughout the region must be attributed to the city's organization of masons, the *barey ton*. The term *ton* is a Mande designation for either age set associations (Durán 1995:113; Imperato 1977:40) or professional organizations, such as that for hunters (*donson ton*) (McNaughton 1982:54), or builders. Fairhead and Leach (1999) note interestingly that the term is synonymous with the word for termite mound (*ton*); termites are revered throughout West Africa for their disciplined coordination. Domian (1989:26) remarks that the Djenné *barey* "form an association of elite artisans whose services are in high demand throughout the region,"[6] and Ligers (1964:41–42), in his account of the construction of a *saho* (boys' house) in a Bozo village, observes that the masons were often invited from Djenné, some who have "the reputation of being the best masons in the country."[7] It is thought that the builders' organization has existed for at least several centuries (Bedaux et al. 1996:12; 2000:204), and the mason's occupation has certainly been recognized as a distinct profession in the Inland Niger Delta since at least the late fifteenth century. According to the Tarikh al-Fattash, the ruler Askia Muhammad recruited five hundred masons at that time from the conquered town of Zagha to build up the Songhay capitals of Gao and Tindirma, thus indicating both an early recognition of the masons' status and the likelihood of a stylistic diffusion from the region of Djenné to the north (Saad 1979:15). Monteil ([1932] 1971:252), in one of the earliest detailed accounts of Djenné, notes the special artisan status of the builders and their organization within "la corporation des *bari*."

Serious drought throughout the 1970s and 1980s and the consequent impoverishment of the region, however, meant that there was little money available for new construction and building maintenance in Djenné during that period. Many of the town's former masons (along with a significant percentage of the male workforce) chose to leave in search of employment opportunities elsewhere, many making their way to Bamako or abroad to other West African nations. These circumstances dealt a serious blow to the *barey ton*, weakening the structure of the organization and the traditional mason-client relations and threatening the survival of the town's earthen architecture. Two other factors that continue to reshape the built environment are changes in the family structure and use of house space and the employment of imported building materials and techniques, most notably concrete and sheet metal (see Maas and Mommersteeg 1992:19, 86).

In an attempt to protect Djenné's heritage, UNESCO declared the city and its surrounding archaeological sites a World Monument in 1988, and the Malian authorities set up a Mission Culturelle with the aim of safeguarding the monument and educating the local population about heritage and conservation. Following from this, and based on an extensive body of Dutch research in the region (most important, the meticulous study of Djenné's architecture and urban environment by Maas and Mommersteeg [1992] and Bedaux's vast archaeological expertise), the Dutch Embassy in Bamako requested the Rijksmuseum voor Volkenkunde, Leiden, to draft a plan for the restoration of the city. The restoration project has been financed by the Ministry of Foreign Affairs (The Hague) for the period between 1996 and 2003 (Bedaux et al. 2000:203–4). Its initial objective to restore 168 houses in Djenné (of a total of some 1,850 houses) (Bedaux et al. 2000), has been scaled down to a more realistically attainable level of about 100 structures (Bedaux and Maas pers. com. 2001).

A full description of the restoration project aims and objectives can be found in the Plan de Projet Réhabilitation et Conservation de l'Architecture de Djenné (Bedaux et al. 1996), and more recent reflections by the project directors were published in a jointly authored paper for the Terra 2000 conference (Bedaux et al. 2000). Of main concern to my argument here promoting process over product is the project's astute regard for the role of the traditional masons and the transmission of technical knowledge as integral to the restoration program:

> A determining factor for this continuity [of building in banco] has been the association of masons, the *barey ton*, who may be properly considered the vehicle of Djenné's architectural tradition. Insofar as they are the creators and builders, it is they who transmit the specialized techniques in earthen construction that have made them famous beyond the borders of Mali. It is therefore crucial to implicate the *barey ton* in this project and to take the materials they use and the techniques they employ as the point of departure.[8] (Bedaux et al. 1996:15)

One criticism I reserve for the conservation efforts, however, is the continued reliance on a constructed notion of "authenticity" invested in the building-as-object over and above building-as-process. Despite a recognition by the project directors that the classification as a UNESCO World Heritage Site, in combination with protective Malian laws regarding classified monuments, immobilizes the "living city . . . in its own armour of architectural tradition," a rather "inflexible and rigid set of rules" is perpetuated for those houses chosen for restoration by their scientific committee (Bedaux et al. 2000:204). The project "proposes not to classify all of Jenné's buildings, but only those that are significant for its architectural image," in the hope that these will "serve as a source of inspiration for future developments" (p. 204). It is felt that "as much as possible of the original parts of any monument" should be retained, and the documentation produced for these houses should be used to ascertain a "reasonable control of future alterations" (p. 204). Original floor plans should be "reconstructed when possible" based on existing documentation and the coherent oral accounts of changes offered by house owners (p. 205). Also, despite the fact that traditional restoration methods entailed demolition and reconstruction (due to the inherent instability of the old-style cylindrical mud bricks), original walls should be retained whenever it is structurally feasible since there are "only a few really old walls left in the city" (p. 205; Bedaux, Diaby, and Maas pers. com. 2001).

Households that agree to participate in the project are expected to make no further structural or planning modifications to their homes. In theory, they are legally bound to the agreement and may be tried under Malian law for noncompliance. In my view, the house takes on the status of protected monument above and beyond its function as a home and is effectively rendered impotent in the face of changing family needs and transforming social values. It is therefore difficult to imagine how the already selected and restored houses will inspire other households to partake in a restoration agenda that is largely premised on an idealized authenticity arbitrarily rooted in Dubois's photographs and other turn-of-the-century colonial documentation (Bedaux et al. 2000:205). I suspect that a growing awareness of the threat of an imposed stasis on the evolution of their homes (in conjunction with other factors) has played significantly in the decision made by many households selected for the 2002 restoration schedule to be cautious about participating in the project.

The Dutch-financed restoration project for Djenné is sensitive to many of the issues I raise above, as evidenced in their published acknowledgments of the problems associated with "the restoration of a living classified mud town, in one of the world's poorest nations" (Bedaux 2000:204), and by their subsequent efforts to accommodate the needs of residents and participating masons. The project has endeavored to remain largely unintrusive by targeting "not more than 9% of the total number of houses" for restoration so as "not [to] hamper any future development in the city" and prioritizes traditional construction techniques and materials (p. 205). I would maintain, however, that a diminished fixation with freezing the architecture in some distant (and imagined) past and encouraging clients and masons to execute works in the absence of architect's plans and formalized directives would stimulate a more productive concern for the preservation of the masons' knowledge as something beyond mere technical expertise and as one that dynamically infuses local understandings of the built environment with deep (and changing) meaning. Below I briefly contextualize my own field site and highlight a few examples of magic practices that are integrated with the building process. Again, I am challenging the notion that authenticity lies primarily with the physical architecture of the building, and champion an emphasis on process.

The linguistic and ethnic mix at the building site I worked on was quintessentially Djenné in character, as was the mutual tolerance and relative easiness of social relations (see Fig. 5). Of the eighteen-member team, there was representation from eight ethnic groups, and five languages were regularly spoken of which Bambara, and to some extent Djenné Chiini (a variety of Songhay [see Heath 1999; Nicolaï 1981]), served as the lingua franca for interethnic communication. All four of the masons on site ascribed to a Bozo ethnic identity, perhaps the earliest inhabitants of the region and a people largely defined by their occupation as fishermen along the Niger and Bani Rivers. In Djenné town the Bozo constitute the majority of masons, along with representation from the Marka and some Hourso. The latter are a caste group who act as intermediaries for various rituals (including marriages and weddings), as well as at the meetings of the *barey ton*.[9] That some Hourso have become masons is contrary to Monteil's ([1932] 1971:252) observation that "les bari soient des gens libres non castes [the masons are noncaste free men]" but such (new) opportunities for casted groups may have surfaced in response to the need for masons during and following the drought in the 1970s and 1980s when many local masons were abroad as migrant laborers.

Not just anyone, however, can become a *barey*. The masons told me repeatedly that only boys from the town's stock of building families would be taken on as apprentices. Though the masons trace their genealogical origins to two legendary families, the Nassiri and the Yena (mason Bayre Kouroumantse pers. com.), access to the profession crosscuts ethnic group boundaries and, seemingly, social classes and castes. The

Figure 5
Construction of a new Tukolor-style house on the banks of the Bani River outside Djenné town (2001). Photo by Trevor Marchand.

Figure 6
Portrait of a young building laborer in Djenné (2001). Many of the young laborers are Qur'anic students who have come from abroad to study in Djenné and are sent out to earn money by their marabout teachers. Photo by Trevor Marchand.

main exclusionary factor barring members of nonbuilding families from the trade is the nature of the mason-client relation. A reciprocal agreement between the two parties ensures that the mason will be the first contacted if his patron-client requires any building works, and the mason will prioritize his patron's projects over other job opportunities. This relation is pervasive in Djenné, and a mason is bound to each family. Therefore, it is very difficult if not impossible for a mason without arranged or inherited connections to a patron family to find work. The possibility of usurping someone else's clients is curbed by the dominant discourse on magic. Encroaching on another mason's domain is dangerous and tethered to the very real risk of being afflicted by that mason's powerful defensive magic.

The laborers employed on building sites, with the exception of the apprentice(s), have a very limited future in the trade, and only a handful will persist in this occupation over the long term. Most of the laborers at my building site, as well as at others I visited in the town, were (predominantly non-native) Qur'anic school students who had been sent out by their marabout teachers to find work. The money they earned during the six-day workweek was handed over to their marabout in return for their board and lessons.[10] It should be noted that *maraboutage* has long been an important occupation in Djenné and sustains the town's historic reputation as one of the most eminent centers of Islamic learning in West Africa. Currently, the unskilled employment opportunities offered by the building industry in fact constitute an important source of revenue for Djenné's religious scholars via the student-laborers (see Fig. 6). The main building season is short, however, lasting roughly from the beginning of January until the end of March, and no one, including the masons, can rely on building as their sole source of income. Many of the Bozo return to fishing with the coming of the rains, and others attend to agricultural pursuits or operate small trading businesses. Several of the masons I knew also worked small commercial concessions at the Monday market throughout the year (Monday being the only day of repose from the building site).

Both Islam and magic play important roles in the building process. Aside from many of the laborers being Qur'anic students, midday prayers were regularly observed by the entire team, and the site's master mason requested that the client grant them every third Friday afternoon off so that they might attend the congregational prayer at the Djenné Mosque. More directly related to the actual building process at my particular site, a prominent marabout, who was a close acquaintance of the project client, blessed the site of the new house on the banks of the Bani River and identified three sacred trees (all attributed with medicinal properties) that were not to be felled. Horse bones were gathered by Djenné's chief hunter, and the marabout blessed these and ordered that they be buried at points along the perimeter line of the property, thereby extending his sanctifications to the property and protecting it against malice and ensuring the well-being of the occupant. I will not elaborate further here on the significance of this particular ritual but will proceed to a discussion of the magical practices employed by the builders themselves that "guarantee" protection.

The totem for all masons in Djenné is the *unbaka*, a small lizard found throughout West Africa and used by many other groups in their preparation of medicines for a variety of ailments, from coughs to male impotence. It is unlawful for builders to harm these little creatures, and children caught vexing them are severely reprimanded. The masons are believed to share the *unbaka*'s agility, balance, and capacity to cling to and scale vertical wall surfaces in the event that they stumble and fall from their elevated work station. Harming these lizards would compromise their own powers and invite harm onto themselves. Masons, in fact, take regular precautions to ensure the safety and well-being of their entire workforce and to guarantee the structural integrity of the building and the protection of their clients. New works, like any journey or new project, must commence on an auspicious day. These *jours ouverts* are calculated by the mason based on (among other things) the lunar calendar and constellations, and conferred by a gerontocratic neighborhood network that might include his own master, male members of his family, and marabouts. Initiation of work on that chosen day might include nothing more than hoeing topsoil at the spot where a foundation trench will be later excavated, as was the case at my site.

Following the rather nonceremonious site initiation and before the commencement of full-blown construction activity, the client's mason and the master mason appointed by him to execute the building work paid a joint visit to the site with a woven basket of mixed grains. They first selected four melon-sized stones from a pile that had been delivered earlier by truck and proceeded to bless them with benedictions. The benedictions muttered over the stones by each of the masons in turn comprised a mix of Qur'anic verses and magical incantations in the local Djenné Chiini language. Nearly inaudible levels ensured that the masons kept their own "secrets" concealed from each other and anyone else while at the same time providing a public spectacle of their power and expertise. After speaking the magic words, the mason, squatting down in front of the four stones, raised his right hand to his mouth and spat into his palm, then rubbed his open palm over the stones in a clockwise direction. He repeated this several times, thereby transferring the power of his benedictions to the stones themselves. The power of words in the West African context was already recognized by Mungo Park (1983:180) during his journey of 1795. Words, as Stoller (1989:100) remarks, "are not merely neutral instruments of reference [but] can be dangerously charged with the powers of the heavens and of the ancestors." A mason once said to me, "You know how to write, but in Djenné, people have knowledge of the plants and trees [referring to medicinal properties], and we masons possess the power of words. We know secrets and incantations."

Next, the basket of grains was similarly blessed by the masons (see Fig. 7). The client's chief mason justified that the grains are not a fetish (associated with pre-Islamic practices) because the grains come from God. He once told me, "God created man, but in order to procreate, God gave humankind the capacity to do so. Likewise, God also bestowed upon certain individuals the power to perform rituals and benedictions which

Figure 7

Mamadou Djennépo, a Djenné mason, displaying a basket of blessed grains that will be sprinkled into the foundations of the building's perimeter walls (2001). Photo by Trevor Marchand.

are always made in His name." The mixture of grains consisted of cotton-seed, sorghum, millet, maïs, fonio, and rice.[11] It was explained that the first produces the things we wear, and the others bring us nourishment, and therefore the placement of grains in the house foundations and at the corners of the property ensures prosperity and abundance of food for the inhabitants. "If the benedictions are made correctly," said the mason, "then God will lend His assistance; on the contrary, if they are not, God will end the work." Both masons proceeded to dig four shallow holes at the four corners of the property with their hoes. In each they placed one of the blessed stones,[12] and over these they sprinkled a little of the grain mixture before backfilling the holes by hand. A reserve of the grains would be kept on site to be sprinkled into the perimeter-wall foundations of the house as the project progressed.

Numerous rituals were performed during the course of construction, including the burial of an amulet in the foundations of the embankment wall along the river, the burial of the remaining horse bones blessed by the marabout, and simple recitations of "b'ism Allah" (In the Name of God) to initiate new stages of construction (see Fig. 8). Discreet and highly personal rituals were also performed by some of the individual masons on a daily basis. Before commencing work each morning, crouched on top of the mud-brick walls facing a fresh dollop of mortar placed there by a laborer and some bricks waiting to be placed, one mason

Figure 8
Boubacar Kouroumantse, a Djenné mason, burying blessed horse bones below the foundations of the building site's perimeter wall. Photo by Trevor Marchand.

performed his own ritual. Looking down to the open palm of his right hand, he murmured rhythmic, barely audible incantations while repetitiously touching each of his fingers with the tip of his thumb at about the inside center point of each digit, mechanically moving from his pinkie inward to his pointer. When finished, he would pause briefly, then pick up a brick and begin building. He refused to explain his secret, telling me simply that he had learned it from his father, and he from his father before him, and that the practice guaranteed good work and safety on the site throughout the day. The subject of a "guarantee" was highly charged with notions of expertise and the constitution of a professional identity. The client's mason, from the Kouroumantse family of builders, asserted that these rituals provide the public with a certainty of good works. He passionately proclaimed that he could personally guarantee that there will never be a problem with the house or for his client.

Legends of ancestry, exclusive admission to the trade, claims to magic powers and the performance of rituals, and proclamations of guarantees are all essential elements that make up the mason's expert discourse. This discourse serves not only to constitute a professional persona with ownership of specialized trade knowledge, but also a client-audience who invest faith in these social agents to produce and reproduce their built environment along with the status and meaning they attribute to it.

Conclusion

In my critique of a museological view of the built-environment-as-object, I have championed a conservation of process over product. Process, in the sense that I have considered it here, has been most notably defined by the knowledge possessed and transmitted by the traditional builder. I have not, however, advocated a fetishization of expert knowledge that would seek to "harness the exotic and cabalistic power of otherness . . . and veil it . . . in a shroud of mysticism" (Law 1999:101). Knowledge surely cannot, and should not, be preserved as a static objectified thing, alienated from its producer. Rather, it is knowledge recognized as a dynamic process responsible for regenerating social agents, architecture, and meaning that must be conserved.

I have offered examples of building practices in both San'a' and Djenné that illustrate the important role of masons for endowing popular conceptions of the built environment with status, meaning, and a sense of security. This is achieved in either place through an expert discourse derived from and responding to its particular social and cultural context. This context is historically constituted and therefore always in flux. It has been influenced by networks of trade, Islam, war, colonialism, globalization, and, most recently, the incorporation of both cities into the UNESCO framework of World Heritage Sites. The contemporary traditional builder, through his apprenticeship, is inculcated with the technical and social knowledge necessary for innovatively responding to change while simultaneously reproducing a discourse of locality, continuity, and tradition. In short, it is this expertise that sustains a sense of place. If through legislation and cultural politics (Western-inspired) conservation efforts incapacitate contemporary traditional builders and inhabitants in responding to changing needs and social values, their architectural heritage will inevitably lose its utility and meaning for the living local population, and thus also its authenticity as a valued cultural commodity.

Notes

1 Appadurai's book, *The Social Life of Things* (1986), played a major role in coercing an anthropological reconsideration of essentialist theories of material culture. Other important contributors to this wave of thinking include Gell (1998), Strathern (1988, 1990), Weiner (1992), and Godelier (1999). Gell advocates an appreciation of iconic objects as indexes of agency that, in particular, can occupy positions in the networks of human social agency. See Rowlands (forthcoming) for a more comprehensive overview of twentieth-century anthropological positions with regard to essentialism.

2 In Djenné, the traditional masons maintain (essentially complete) control over all building in the town. The building of government projects, such as the recently constructed hospital, may, however, be shared among teams of builders from other cities such as Bamako (the nation's capital) and Mopti (the regional capital) who are specialized in modern (read: Western) construction methods. In San'a', on the other hand, the traditional building trade has been heavily encroached on by architects, engineers, and Western-style contractors who employ (often unskilled) wage laborers. Despite the renegotiation of the power share, Yemen's traditional builders have nevertheless managed to preserve their upper hand in the competitive discourse (Marchand 2000a, 2001).

3 For a more detailed description of the history, design, and construction of the San'a'ni minaret, see al-Hajari (1942); Lewcock, Serjeant, and Smith (1983); Marchand (1999a, 1999b, 2001).

4 When I left San'a' for the last time in 1998, the al-Maswari masons were planning a seventy-meter-high minaret for the al-Mutawakkil Mosque, which would be the highest in southern Arabia.

5 "isolement relatif du monde saharien, et ou la classe des marchands se composait d'une majorité de Soudanais et non d'étrangers, comme à Tombouctou ou Gao." Here and below the translations in the text are mine.

6 "formaient un corps d'artisans d'élite dont les services étaient très demandés dans toute la region."

7 "la reputation d'être les meilleurs maçons du pays."

8 "Un facteur déterminant pour cette continuité [de construction en banco] a été la corporation des maçons, le barey-ton, qui peut être considéré comme le porteur de la culture traditionelle de l'architecture propre à Djenné. En tant que créateurs et bâtisseurs, ce sont eux qui transmettent la technique spéciale de la construction en terre qui le rend célèbres bien au-delà des frontières du Mali. Il est donc d'une importance cruciale d'impliquer le barey-ton dans ce projet et de prendre les techniques et les matériaux utilisés par eux comme point de depart."

9 The Hourso (or Horso) are described by Heath (1999:3) as members of the *griot* caste, who "assist in weddings and are notorious for their foul language and behaviour"; and defined by Stoller (1989:232) in his work with the Songhay of Niger as "the offspring of captives, who cannot be bought or sold." In Djenné, Hourso membership is not exclusive to any one ethnic group, and they are considered a servant class of sorts with low social status. Because of their low status, their harsh words cannot be considered insulting, and they often figure as intermediaries in disputes, as well as in social rituals. Interestingly, they can become masons, a profession that commands a considerable degree of respect in Djenné and throughout the Inland Niger Delta.

10 The student practice of paying for Qur'anic studies is also recorded by Monteil ([1932] 1971:154). Likewise, in the past building apprentices were obliged to make regular payments to their teacher-masons in the form of small gifts of money or kola nuts. This was done in return for their training and the knowledge they received. As McNaughton (1982:57) notes, paying for knowledge is a widespread practice in the Mande world (Djenné lies well within the borders of Mande influence), and "knowledge is always paid for." Maas and Mommersteeg (1992:187) also record that, at one time, the building apprentice was placed in the custody of a mason who provided board and secured a future wife and marriage for his young protégé. In return, the boy presumably labored for free and remained loyal to his master.

11 In discussing the ethnographic recognition of claims in oral tradition for the common origins of the Bozo, Dogon, and Nono, R. J. McIntosh ([1988] 1998:101–2) notes that "ethnicity is

expressed as a triumvirate of grains. Each recognizes the mythical quality and equivalence of grains of fonio (the Bozo), millet (the Dogon), and rice (the Nono)."

12 A consideration of masons' contemporary practices of burying blessed articles at property boundaries may furnish archaeologists with an important clue to their finds. Describing patterns of artifact distribution in archaeological finds at Djenné-Djeno, R. J. McIntosh ([1988] 1998:226) notes that "there appears to be a cardinal-point presentation of classes of materials offered in these ash-filled depressions" and asks, "[T]o what degree is this cardinal-point orientation to sacrificed objects merely happenchance? Or is it a reflection of an ancient Middle Niger material culture *imago mundi?*" I have also discussed the possible relation between the practices of contemporary masons and the distribution of artifacts in archaeological context with Susan Keech McIntosh (February 12, 2001).

References

al-Hajari, M. b. A. 1942. *Masajid San'a'*. San'a'. N.p., n.d.

Appadurai, A. 1986. *The Social Life of Things*. Cambridge: Cambridge University Press.

Bedaux, R., B. Diaby, M. K. Keita, S. Sidibe, and P. Maas. 1996. Plan de projet réhabilitation et conservation de l'architecture de Djenné (Mali). Bamako and Leiden.

Bedaux, R., B. Diaby, P. Maas, and S. Sidibe. 2000. The restoration of Jenné, Mali: African aesthetics and Western paradigms. In *Terra 2000*, 201–7. London: James & James Scientific Publishers.

Casey, E. 1996. How to get from space to place in a fairly short stretch of time: Phenomenological prolegomena. *In Senses of Place*, ed. S. Feld and K. Basso, 13–52. Santa Fe, New Mex.: School of American Research Press.

Denyer, S. 1978. *African Traditional Architecture: An Historical and Geographical Perspective*. London: Heinemann.

Domian, S. 1989. *Architecture soudanaise: Vitalité d'une tradition urbaine et monumentale*. Paris: Editions l'Harmattan.

Durán, L. 1995. Birds of Wasulu: Freedom of expression and expression of freedom in the popular music of southern Mali. *British Journal of Ethnomusicology* 4:101–34.

Fairhead, J., and M. Leach. 1999. Termites, society and ecology: Perspectives from West Africa. In *Cultural and Spiritual Values of Biodiversity*, ed. D. Posey, 235–42. London: UNEP and I.T. Books.

Feyerabend, P. 1975. *Against Method: Outline of an Anarchistic Theory of Knowledge*. London: Verso.

Gell, A. 1998. *Art and Agency: An Anthropological Theory*. Cambridge: Cambridge University Press.

Godelier, M. 1999. *The Enigma of the Gift*. Cambridge: Polity.

Gregotti, V. 1996. *Inside Architecture*. London: MIT Press.

Gumperz, S., and S. Levinson, eds. 1996. *Rethinking Linguistic Relativity*. Cambridge: Cambridge University Press.

Heath, J. 1999. *A Grammar of Koyra Chiini: The Songhay of Timbuktu*. New York: Mouton de Gruyter.

Heidegger, M. 1977. Building, dwelling, thinking. In *Basic Writings*, 319–39. San Francisco: Harper San Francisco.

Hirsch, E., and M. O'Hanlon, eds. 1995. *The Anthropology of Landscape: Perspectives on Place and Space*. Oxford: Clarendon Press.

Imperato, P. J. 1977. *African Folk Medicine: Practices and Beliefs of the Bambara and Other Peoples.* Baltimore, Md.: York Press.

Law, J. 1999. The storyteller. In *Liberated Voices: Contemporary Art from South Africa*, ed. F. Herreman, 92–109. London and New York: Museum for African Art.

Lefebvre, H. 1991. *The Production of Space.* Trans. D. Nicholson Smith. Oxford: Blackwell.

Lewcock, R. 1986. *The Old Walled City of Sana.* Paris: UNESCO.

Lewcock, R., R. B. Serjeant, and R. Smith. 1983. The smaller mosques of San'a'. In *San'a': An Arabian Islamic City*, ed. R. B. Serjeant and R. Lewcock, 351–90. London: World of Islam Festival Trust.

Ligers, Z. 1964. *Les Sorko (Bozo): Maîtres du Niger.* Vol. 3. Paris: Librairie des Cinq Continents.

Maas, P., and G. Mommersteeg. 1992. *Djenné: Chef d'oeuvre architecturale.* Eindhoven: Universite de Technologie.

Marchand, T. 1999a. Building traditional minarets in San'a', Yemen. In *Proceedings of the Symposium on Mosque Architecture*, vol. 4:127–38. Riyadh: College of Architecture and Planning, King Saud University.

Marchand, T. 1999b. Reconsidering the role of the mosque minaret in San'a'. In *Proceedings of the Seminar for Arabian Studies*, vol. 29:95–102. Turnhout, Belgium: Brepols.

Marchand, T. 2000a. The lore of the master builder: Working with local materials and local knowledge in San'a', Yemen. In *Traditional Knowledge: Learning from Experience.* IASTE Working Paper, vol. 137:1–17. University of California, Berkeley.

Marchand, T. 2000b. A possible explanation for the lack of explanation: Or "Why the master builder can't explain what he knows." In *SOAS Working Papers in Linguistics*, vol. 10:301–14. London: SOAS. [Also forthcoming in *Negotiating Local Knowledge*, ed. J. Pottier. London: Pluto.]

Marchand, T. 2000c. Walling old San'a': Reevaluating the resurrection of the city walls. In *Terra 2000*, 46–51. London: James & James Scientific Publishers.

Marchand, T. 2001. *Minaret Building and Apprenticeship in Yemen.* London: Curzon.

McIntosh, R. J. [1988] 1998. *The Peoples of the Middle Niger: The Island of Gold.* Oxford: Blackwell.

McIntosh, S. Keech, and R. McIntosh. 1981. Background to the 1981 research. In *Excavations at Jenne-Jeno, Hambarketelo, and Kaniana (Inland Niger Delta, Mali), the 1981 Season,* ed. S. Keech McIntosh, 1–26. Berkeley: University of California Press.

McIntosh, S., and R. McIntosh. 1982. Finding West Africa's oldest city. *National Geographic* (September):396–418.

McNaughton, P. R. 1982. The shirts that Mande hunters wear. *African Arts*, no. 3 (May):54–58.

Merleau-Ponty, M. 1962. *Phenomenology of Perception.* London: Routledge.

Monteil, C. [1932] 1971. *Une cite soudanaise: Djénné: Métropole du Delta Central du Niger.* Paris: Editions Anthropos.

Nicolaï, R. 1981. *Les dialectes du Songhay: Contribution à l'étude des changements linguistiques.* Paris: CNRS.

Park, M. 1983. *Travels into the Interior of Africa.* London: Eland.

Piepenberg, F. 1987. Sana'a al-Qadeema: The challenge of modernisation. In *The Middle East City*, ed. Abdulaziz Y. Saqqaf, 93–113. New York: Paragon House.

Prussin, L. 1986. *Hatumere: Islamic Design in West Africa*. Berkeley: University of California Press.

Rowlands, M. Forthcoming. Value and the cultural transmission of things. In *Commodities and the Value of Things*, ed. P. Geschiere. Durham: Duke University Press.

Saad, E. N. 1979. Social history of Timbuktu, 1400–1900: The role of Muslim scholars and notables. Ph.D. dissertation, Northwestern University.

Schijns, W. 1992. Djenné comme synthèse d'une conception spatiale architectonique. In *Djenné: Chef d'oeuvre architecturale*, ed. P. Maas and G. Mommersteeg, 12–19. Eindhoven: Universite de Technologie.

Senft, G. 1997. *Referring to Space: Studies in Austronesian and Papuan Languages*. Oxford: Clarendon Press.

Stoller, P. 1989. *Fusion of the Worlds: An Ethnography of Possession among the Songhay of Niger*. Chicago: University of Chicago Press.

Strathern, M. 1988. *The Gender of the Gift*. Berkeley: University of California Press.

Strathern, M. 1990. Artefacts of history. In *Culture and History in the Pacific*, ed. J. Siikala, 25–44. Helsinki: Finnish Anthropological Society.

Weiner, A. 1992. *Inalienable Possessions*. Berkeley: University of California Press.

Tradition and Innovation in the Tibetan Diaspora

Ernesto Noriega

IN 1959 THOUSANDS OF TIBETANS, forced to flee their country, crossed over the Himalayas into India. Today, there are approximately 130,000 living in exile, mainly in the almost fifty settlements scattered throughout India and Nepal but also in Bhutan, Europe, the United States, and Canada.[1]

Over the past forty years, the Tibetan exile community has been successful in organizing the resettlement process and meeting the basic needs of a growing number of refugees. Today, their biggest challenge is no longer physical survival but the survival of their endangered culture. Uprooted and dispersed, Tibetans undergo a painful process of adaptation and struggle to maintain the viability of their unique way of life. Time and again, community leaders have exhorted their people not to forget, to make efforts to integrate traditional values and knowledge into their changing lifestyles and their new professional activities—and to transmit their heritage to the next generation lest it be lost.

One of the most visible signs of this commitment to tradition is the presence of "Tibetan-style buildings" wherever a new community is established. A temple or monastery in the traditional fashion—sometimes smaller replicas of the ones left behind—or characteristic details adorning humble homes give these settlements some sense of identity and are concrete reminders of the community's perseverance.

I arrived in the Himalayas in 1990 and visited several of these Tibetan settlements, motivated in part by my interest in the role architecture can play in the process of cultural resistance and renewal, especially for indigenous peoples. There I found that a new generation of modern Tibetan builders was emerging. They had been born in exile and educated in India as civil engineers or architects. And in the face of the decline of old building practices and the destruction of the vast majority of historical monuments in Tibet,[2] these young professionals carried the responsibility of maintaining their building tradition.

But, predictably, their university education had not prepared them to meet this challenge. At best, their knowledge of their architectural heritage was superficial and fragmentary, and they had never been inside a genuine traditional building. This created a frustrating situation and a potentially dangerous one as well, since any attempt to practice Tibetan architecture without a profound understanding of its essence and deeper meaning would be a risky enterprise—one that could end up accelerating its death. A nostalgic approach, limited to the strict reproduction of old models and ignoring new environmental conditions and rejecting the introduction of appropriate materials and technologies, would render the tradition inflexible and nonadaptive. And the indiscriminate use of forms and symbols inappropriately and out of context, turning distinctive elements into mere decorative clichés, could finally reduce Tibetan architecture to a caricature of itself.[3]

At the same time, it seemed extremely difficult to effectively resume the interrupted tradition. The information was dispersed and of difficult access. Being an unwritten tradition passed on by example from generation to generation, the necessary knowledge existed mainly in the minds of the craftsmen and master builders who were now scattered about, who for many years had not been able to practice their craft, and who were growing old without transmitting their skills. Further, the main sources of learning, the monuments themselves—or whatever was left of them—remained off-limits in the homeland, and other examples outside Tibet were located in remote parts of the Himalayas.[4]

Against this background I was asked by the Tibetan exile administration based in northern India to serve as an architect and to collaborate on the design of buildings for the community. Instead, after long consultations with community members, I proposed a program to enable young Tibetans to regain access to their building tradition, as an effort to guarantee its development and continuity. Consequently, the Initiative for the Preservation, Development and Promotion of Tibetan Architecture and Construction Practices came into being in early 1991. The immediate aim of the project was to collect all information relevant to the built heritage and then to use this material to promote interest in it, especially among the young. A broader objective was to create conditions for the emergence of a social space where a new generation of Tibetans living between tradition and modernity could start to reconstruct the memory of their cultural heritage and make creative use of this recovered legacy in the process of redefining their identity and constructing their future.

The Last Architect of Lhasa

The project was launched with a symbolic act, a sort of pilgrimage. Its goal was to allow two young Tibetans, a civil engineer and an architecture apprentice, to make a two-day journey to visit Jigme Taring (Fig. 1). Mr. Taring had been a government official until 1959, when he had to flee Tibet, and was regarded as the "last architect" of Lhasa. He had designed the summer residence for the present Dalai Lama, an adolescent at the time. Soon after his arrival in India he drew a sketch map of Lhasa, including all important monuments and landmarks. Later in life, after retiring as director of a school for refugee children, he started work on his old ambition—to make a detailed plan of the seventh-century Jokhang, the oldest and most revered temple in Tibet (Fig. 2, Color Plate 10). Fearing the temple would be destroyed, he felt an urgent need to preserve its memory for younger genera-

Figure 1
Young Tibetan builders meet Jigme Taring, the last architect of Lhasa. Photo by Ernesto Noriega.

Figure 2
The seventh-century Jokhang, the holiest structure in Tibet. J. Taring made accurate drawings and a model to preserve its memory for younger generations. Photo by Ernesto Noriega.
(See also Color Plate 10.)

tions. He drew the plans from memory, as he knew the temple well. He then built a large scale model of it that was displayed in all Tibetan settlements.

To the young Tibetan builders, the old man incarnated the survival of the building tradition in exile. The meeting was momentous. Although several Western scholars and students of Tibetan architecture had visited and interviewed Taring previously, this was the first time young Tibetans had come to seek his knowledge. Although he was ailing, he talked to them for several hours. He told them how as a young man he had taught himself through observation of the old monuments and long conversations with traditional master builders and how he later learned from British army officers how to draw plans and sections. He brought out old photographs and drawings, told anecdotes, and made sketches of the way buildings were constructed in old Tibet.

When we told Taring about the project and our plans to visit the architecture of the Tibetan border regions, he was enthusiastic. With a tone of urgency, he said, "Yes, go and visit the monuments wherever you can, open your eyes and ears and make sketches, take photographs, ask questions, study the old stones. Even in ruins one can find precious information, small drops of knowledge here and there. But don't get discouraged, remember that small drops make a mighty ocean."

Arrangements were made for another visit in the future to record his memories. It was not to be; Jigme Taring died two months later.

Documentation Center

During the early stages of the project, our goal was to create a receptacle where all the recovered "drops of knowledge" could be collected, a place where the scattered fragments of memory could be assembled like a giant jigsaw puzzle in order to reconstruct the past. For this purpose, a specialized documentation center dedicated to the preservation and promotion of Tibetan architecture was established. It consisted of a small thematic library and an archives section where photographs, drawings, testimonies, historical texts, and research documents could be gathered, preserved, and organized so as to facilitate access by the general public, especially the younger generation.

The central feature of the archives was the photograph collection for which more than twenty-five hundred historical architecture photographs were initially gathered. Most were reproductions from private collections, museums, and colonial institutions in Europe that until then had been inaccessible to Tibetans.[5] The photographs show Tibet as it was before its destruction. Many are unique records of monumental buildings, religious complexes, towns, and villages that no longer exist.

Adolescents especially were enthusiastic users of the photo archive and would later contribute to its development. We built a darkroom where the young people could print and enlarge the photographs that had been brought to India, mostly in the form of negatives or contact sheets. During this process, their intense fascination was manifest each time an image was slowly revealed, like the opening of a magic window allowing them to rediscover valuable aspects of their stolen past. The young Tibetans realized that their ancestors had developed a rich architectural tradition well adapted to and in harmony with a difficult environment. They were exposed to a world populated by extraordinary structures, feats of engineering whereby countless monumental fortresses were strategically located atop inaccessible summits and giant monasteries resembled small towns in their size and complexity, sometimes accommodating up to ten thousand monks. They also learned how their built heritage extended far beyond monasteries and towns and permeated practically the whole landscape through the use of structures that marked historical events, defined boundaries, and ordered the ritual use of space, serving as focal points for worship or as stations along pilgrimage routes.

Young Tibetans also found that many lessons could be learned from the old tradition that offered relevant solutions to today's challenges. For example, monasteries that at some point in history had been confronted with a rapid increase in population, suddenly having to accommodate thousands of monks on a limited amount of land, developed sophisticated high-density housing that in many ways resembled housing developed in the West during recent decades. Surprised about the "modern" quality of these solutions, young Tibetans were excited about the points of coincidence between their own tradition and the prestigious and much admired contemporary architecture.

The historical photographs were complemented by a slide collection consisting of hundreds of recent and contemporary images showing the evolution of Tibetan architecture.[6] This collection was an important tool for comparative studies, reconstructing the biographies of monuments or towns, and monitoring the changes over the years, such as the level of destruction and successive stages of reconstruction (Fig. 3).

The photo collections encompassed the architecture of the various regions of Tibet and also of other areas within its cultural sphere of influence, from the old Buddhist kingdoms along the Himalayas all the way to Mongolia and south central Siberia. This material promoted the understanding that the Tibetan building tradition is flexible and has always been capable of adapting to diverse cultural and ecological conditions.

a

b

c

Figure 3
Using photographs from different periods one can reconstruct the biographies of monuments. Here are views of the monastery of Ganden, a main learning center of Tibet housing four thousand monks: (a) in full bloom in the 1930s; (b) destroyed during the Cultural Revolution of the 1960s; (c) reconstruction, which started in the early 1980s. Photos courtesy of Tibet Images.

Fieldwork

For any serious student of architecture, all the information acquired from photographs, books, and interviews can at best be secondary sources of knowledge, useful when the actual structures no longer exist or when they are inaccessible. Nothing can replace the direct experience of touching and walking through and around a building.

Consequently, during August and September 1993, we undertook our first field trip to the architectural monuments of Ladakh, a region within the Tibetan cultural realm but which today is part of India. We first visited several monasteries and traditional villages along the Indus valley (Fig. 4). This was the participants' first experience with genuine examples of their architectural heritage. Then we proceeded to the monastery of Samkar, where we stayed for four weeks measuring and documenting its buildings. It was the first attempt by the team to fully document a historical monument. A complete and meticulous survey of the monastic complex was carried out and accurate drawings were produced. Other documentation included photographs, sketches, and interviews with the resident monks. The extended stay at Samkar offered an opportunity to gain a deeper understanding of the organization and functioning of the monastery and the relationships between architectural space and the rhythms of monastic life and religious ritual.

Useful skills and methodological expertise were gained through this surveying exercise, and the documentation produced was a valuable record of a historical monument that would contribute to its preservation. But aside from these expected benefits, the expedition to Ladakh also revealed how such an event can provide the context for a unique and multifaceted learning experience.

Ladakh is probably the closest one can get to experiencing old Tibet, and the expedition was a valuable opportunity for young Tibetans to be exposed to a traditional way of life that closely resembles their own but which, unlike their own, has been spared the traumatic experience of rapid and violent change. In addition to the practical knowledge gained from the study of the monuments themselves, they were confronted with issues relevant to their development as both traditional and modern designers and builders. They could observe, for example, how remote villages were beginning to change under the first influences of modernity, the degree of change usually depending on their location in relation to the main road, or how monasteries were responding differently to new architectural challenges posed mainly by the rapid increase in tourism, as the sudden income was often reinvested in conservation or renovation work and in the conversion of old structures or the addition of new ones to accommodate visitors.

A series of unexpected encounters took place during this journey. At several places we met with groups of Western architects studying or documenting monasteries and conservation experts working on the endangered buildings and murals. Our young team members were surprised by the foreigners' high regard for Tibetan architecture and by their commitment to preserve it. This was a source of encouragement and a boost to their self-confidence. And there was some fruitful interaction as well. At the monastery of Ridzong we spent some days with a group of researchers from the University of Berlin who were making a full survey of the religious complex. It was an interesting and mutually beneficial exchange, in which the Tibetans could learn from the Germans' accurate surveying methodology and the Germans could gain insight through the Tibetans' familiarity with the religious and cultural background. A sense of partnership grew out of this relationship and for our team, the important realization that they as Tibetans not only have much to learn from others but also much to offer.

Architecture Club

The documentation resulting from the survey of Samkar monastery in Ladakh was used to promote another main objective of the project—to stimulate interest in Tibetan architecture among students. An exhibition of the drawings, photographs, and sketches, complemented by a slide presentation and lecture on architectural heritage, was organized at the Tibetan Children Village School. We invited students ages fifteen to eighteen to get involved in the project. Suddenly dozens of them wanted to become architects. Because of our limited resources and infrastructure, we could only choose eleven highly motivated boys and girls to form the architecture club.

In the following months, the student group, which named itself Nyampa Larso,[7] undertook a series of activities, for the most part scheduled on weekends and holidays so as not to interfere with their schoolwork. The students were introduced to the language of architectural drawing and to basic graphic communication skills, to the point where

a
b
c
d

Figure 4
In Ladakh young exiled Tibetans can visit several monasteries and traditional villages: (a) the monastery of Tikse; (b) the monastery of Ridzong; (c) the village of Spituk; (d) the interior of the monastery of Likir. Photos by Ernesto Noriega.

Figure 5
Students surveying Likir monastery. Photo by Lucy Kennedy.
(See also Color Plate 11.)

they could read plans and sections and were able to express their own ideas on paper. They learned how to use photo and video equipment and applied their new knowledge to document local buildings. They also made a field trip to Ladakh and surveyed a monastery, producing drawings that they later exhibited at other schools in various settlements (Figs. 5, 6; Color Plates 11, 12). They met with artists and traditional craftsmen and recorded their know-how. From monks and Buddhist scholars, they learned about religious symbolism in architecture and about the historical background of several monuments.

In addition, the students had access to publications dealing with diverse subjects related to construction, from conservation of historical monuments to the new currents in modern architecture. They were also exposed to information dealing with ecology, appropriate building technologies, and the way in which other traditional societies were struggling to create living environments in harmony with their cultural values and needs.

The group increasingly assumed new responsibilities and contributed actively to the development of the documentation center. The students learned how to develop film and print photographs in the darkroom and organized and cataloged archival material. They also identified potential sources of information, especially among elderly members of the community, recording their accounts and sometimes translating their descriptions into illustrations of the evoked building or village (Fig. 7).

Figure 6
Drawing of Likir monastery done by
students. Photo by Lucy Kennedy.
(See also Color Plate 12.)

Figure 7
A student from the architecture club speaking
to elderly members of the community. Photo
by Lucy Kennedy.

Creative Workshops

Our next step was to organize a series of design workshops in which the group would be encouraged to imagine what their house, neighborhood, or village would ideally look like if they could live in Tibet. At this point I would like to relate in some detail how one of these workshops unfolded because I think it throws some light on the kind of processes this project tried to facilitate.

This time the students were asked what would be the first thing they would design and build if they could return to a free Tibet. Initial suggestions ranged from the rehabilitation of historical monuments to proposals for structures without precedent in traditional Tibet, such as a house of parliament, an Olympic stadium, or the headquarters for a women's organization. Then somebody said, "Let's rebuild the Chagpori!" and everybody agreed immediately.

The choice was significant, not only because of the building's religious and historic importance—it had been founded by one of Tibet's most venerated saints and had later become the main center of learning for Tibetan medicine—but also because of its present-day political symbolism. Along with the well-known Potala palace, the Chagpori monastery had once towered high over Lhasa, and together the monuments had framed the main access to the capital city. In 1959 the monastery was razed and replaced by a large telecommunications tower that still stands today, looming over the city as a conspicuous reminder of the political status quo (Fig. 8). Knowing this, it is not surprising that the students felt that the reinstatement of the sacred monument was a priority.

Once the decision was made, we set out to find as much information as possible about the disappeared structure. Several old photographs from our archives provided details about the building's exterior. We could find no information about its interior, however. Scholars were consulted and investigations carried out in the community without any results other than a brief description of the main altar discovered in an old text. Then word came that a very old monk, a traditional doctor who had been trained at the monastery as a young man, was living in a settlement just a few hours away. A meeting was arranged, and the students interviewed him at length. At first the old doctor said it had all been so long ago that he remembered very little. But with the aid of the photographs, the young girls and boys led their informant through the different parts of the building, pushing him to strain his memory for useful information: How many columns were in the main hall? How many paces between columns? Were there any sources of natural light? And so on. Applying their newly acquired drawing skills, the students translated these fragments of memory into plans and sections until an overall configuration of the structure emerged.

Figure 8
The main temple on the Chagpori, the sacred mountain overlooking Lhasa: (a) before its destruction; (b) after it was destroyed and replaced by a communications antenna. Photo 8a courtesy of Tibet Images; photo 8b by Ulrike Roessler.

a

b

Walking in the night after the meeting with the old man, an atmosphere of solemnity surrounded our little group. Then someone said, "Hey, the old man could die anytime, and all that information would be gone. We just saved it somehow. We should be doing this at least once a week and everyone at school should do the same with their grandparents or with every old person they know." It was as if an awareness of the fragility of their culture had just sunk in and a new sense of urgency was germinating in their young minds.

After the virtual reconstruction of the monument was completed to the extent possible, the next step was to return to the original assignment of the exercise, to design the building that would replace the old one. What should this structure look like?

At this point different factions of opinion began to emerge, and before long a passionate debate broke out. The "traditionalists" insisted that the monastery should be rebuilt in exact conformity with the original model, arguing that their ancestors had been wise people who had still lived in a harmonious and intact world, and nobody living in the present times of confusion could pretend to improve on their creation. One girl was convinced that even if an identical replica of the sacred structure could be built, the power and sanctity of the place had been irreversibly lost. Then there were those who believed the new building should be modern in design and incorporate the latest construction technologies. They maintained that Tibet should be part of the twentieth century and that they should show the world they could also be "players" in the international arena.

All these opinions were legitimate, of course, and reflected many of the conflicting convictions, tendencies, anxieties, and aspirations that make up the collective psychological landscape of the community. Through their emotional involvement in the debates, the students were bringing these contradictions to the surface and facing them, inadvertently dealing with profound and difficult questions concerning their identity as contemporary Tibetans. And later, through their design choices for the new Chagpori, they were in a sense beginning to redefine themselves and their perception of their people's place in the world. They could do this creatively, almost playfully, through imagining, drawing, and modeling. In this safe and permissive context, conflicting positions were reconciled, compromises were worked out, and new syntheses began to emerge. This search for the ideal design was a search for the future, the striving to find—as one student put it—"a middle way that would take advantage of the best of both worlds." This adventure was sustained by their ability to draw on the works and knowledge of their ancestors that were now accessible to them.

Significantly, during this time, several of the students felt the need to discuss their feelings and uncertainties with elder family members, teachers, and religious counselors, asking for opinions and advice, engaging them in the debate, and opening the way for the process to move beyond the workshop and include different generations and experiences. Visions resulting from such an inclusive dynamic should not be dismissed as mere products of illusion without consequence. Once they enter the social realm and catch the imagination of the community, attention can shift to action and the search for concrete solutions.

And perhaps some of these boys and girls will become architects or town planners and realize their visions. But all of them, whatever they do, will carry with them the insights gained through their common experience: the renewed respect for the knowledge of their elders, a commitment to their cultural heritage, a greater capacity to evaluate critically the virtues and weaknesses of the Western model, the courage to imagine a better future, and the self-confidence to construct it on the foundations of traditional values while benefiting from the possibilities offered by modernity.

This project was motivated by the belief that if the process leading to the loss of the cultural heritage can be reversed, then endangered societies will be empowered to take their destiny into their own hands and be better equipped to envision and construct their future on their own terms. Likewise, it was guided by the certainty that some of the most valuable resources necessary to achieve this, such as memory and creativity, are already present in the communities themselves and can be reactivated by the simple recognition of their importance and the removal of the obstacles that currently hinder them. The way the project evolved has only served to reinforce this conviction.

Our initiative in India was a direct response to the specific set of circumstances encountered there, and I am not suggesting that this experience could be simply duplicated in other cultural contexts. Nevertheless, given the many parallels between the current challenges faced by Tibetans and those confronted by other indigenous peoples, it seems reasonable to expect that some of the lessons and insights gained from this experience might be relevant in a broad way to other groups as well. With this in mind, I would like to briefly supplement my account of the project with some general thoughts derived from my involvement with the Tibetan community and other traditional societies, in the hope that they might be of interest to others similarly concerned with these issues.

Paradox

One of the great tragedies of our times is the silent decline or downright extinction of the unique and rich cultures of indigenous peoples throughout the world. There are 250 million to 300 million indigenous people in about seventy countries. Discriminated against and exploited, in many cases persecuted, they usually are the poorest among the poor and the victims of "development" and modernization. Their cultures are not accepted by the dominant societies, and they are generally forced to assimilate by brutal or subtle means—through resettlement programs, prohibition of traditional customs, religious indoctrination, the education system, the media, economic dependence, and so on.

Under these immense pressures, the traditional mechanisms for adjustment to change are overwhelmed and the capacity to adapt to the sudden and radically new reality is disrupted. In many cases individuals and groups are presented with what appear to be the only possible choices: abandon the traditional ways and embrace the modern lifestyle and value system or retreat into a defensive position that rejects everything foreign and tries to prevent the culture from changing. Leading to disintegration, on the one hand, and stagnation, on the other, neither option offers a viable alternative to ensure the vital and dynamic continuity of the culture.

Great creativity is necessary to overcome this traumatic moment. Unfortunately, at this time of profound crisis, the creative potential within the community is often suppressed. In the fear that any further departure from the traditional way of doing things and solving problems will accelerate the loss of cultural identity, fresh and innovative thinking is discouraged. This creates a restrictive atmosphere in which young members of the community, not wanting to "betray" their tradition, sometimes practice a sort of self-censorship and avoid bold creative action. In this way, the spaces where open dialogue and the exchange of different experiences could generate authentic new visions are greatly reduced. It is a tragic paradox that the creativity that can guarantee the continuity of a tradition, helping it to move forward with imaginative new solutions, is perceived as dangerous by the very same people most committed to the preservation of the cultural heritage.

Only by bringing together the memories and experience of the old and the creativity and restless aspirations of the young can the dreams of possible futures be produced. It is these visions that can empower a threatened society to successfully face the challenge of maintaining its unique identity while finding its place as an equal and active partner in the world of today. Especially among traditional societies, where past and future, tradition and modernity, seem to be mutually exclusive options, it is vital to create and support the social spaces where this dialogue and creative work can take place.

Crossroads

As the Mexican writer Carlos Fuentes once said, "Without tradition, there is no creation; without creation, you cannot maintain a tradition."[8] And to be sure, tradition and innovation always work hand in hand in well-integrated cultural contexts. Even in dislocated societies, where this natural alliance has been disrupted, these old partners are just waiting to find each other again whenever there is a small space for this to happen. To generate such a "space" was perhaps one of the main virtues of our project. By integrating our main objectives—the preservation of the architectural heritage and the production of future visions for the built environment—as fundamental aspects of the same process, a dynamic context was created in which these valuable cultural resources, memory and the imagination, could start to converge and sustain one another once again.

The quality of this space was that of a crossroads, a busy intersection where different means, experiences, memories, potentialities, and aspirations could come together, triggering personal and social processes and preparing the ground for the emergence of new syntheses, new visions and strategies. Here, meaningful encounters took place that would not have easily occurred otherwise. People from different regions and disciplines met. The engineer and the craftsman, the university graduate and the monk, the old and the young. They became aware of each other, compared information, transmitted knowledge, and cooperated and found themselves engaged in a common cause. It was a point of confluence, where traditional values and modern developments—where the local and the global—could start interacting in new and critical ways.

At the center of it were the young girls and boys of the architecture club, absorbing it all, reactivating and drawing from the dormant reservoirs of knowledge in the community and taking advantage of the new sources of information about their heritage collected in the documentation center. In addition, this newly conquered space they now occupied was not only meant to be a repository of memories, but also a breeding ground for dreams. It offered them a safe domain that favored creativity and experimentation and eased the anxiety of having their visions rejected or proven inappropriate, because here these were not produced in isolation but in permanent dialogue with tradition and its custodians.

Finally, this space became a kind of safe base camp, from which the students started their many adventures and to which they could always return to elaborate and interpret and share their experiences. Reflecting on the liberating and formative impact of these "voyages," we are reminded of Stephen Dedalus and the celebrated entry he made in his diary as he was about to step out into the world: "I go for the millionth time to encounter the reality of experience and forge in the smithy of my soul the uncreated conscience of my race."[9] In these lines Joyce's young hero revealed how much he hoped the journey he was about to embark on would serve to advance his quest for a viable new identity not just for himself but also for his people. Whether trucking to Ladakh, navigating the memory of an elderly informant, time traveling in the darkroom, or, later, surfing the Net, the young Tibetans had the opportunity to explore unknown—and if once known, now forgotten—territory in search of the elements that would shape their identity as both the inheritors of their tradition and the producers of the new ways necessary for their tradition to move into the future.

Archives

In older times, indigenous peoples did not have access to the photographic or motion picture technologies that would have enabled them to make a visual record of their physical world. And even when they did, there were often cultural or religious constraints that limited their use. In Tibet, for example, the few people who could afford a camera were discouraged from using one, and it is reported that an aristocrat was once degraded for the "undignified posture" he assumed while taking photographs. So, ironically, most visual records that exist of the now-vanished living environments of traditional societies—and which today could be so valuable to these peoples' efforts to reconstruct their past—were produced by the administrators, soldiers, scientists, and explorers serving the very same colonial powers that brought about the collapse of those cultural habitats. And at present, most of this documentation remains in Western institutions and out of reach for the communities that could make the best use of them. During my own hunt for images of Tibetan architecture in

Europe, I came across tens of thousands of historical photographs depicting the monuments, towns, and villages of other ethnic minorities from all over the world. Only through lengthy negotiations and a series of fortunate circumstances did I manage to obtain permission to make new copies of the Tibetan material, and so realized how difficult it would be for any indigenous group to lay claim to these precious records of their heritage. Clearly, it is essential to find ways to expedite the return of this information to the peoples concerned.

Recovering and safely storing this documentation is an important task for the community, but it can only be a first step. We have seen how by inserting these images in a dynamic context they can become a unique learning instrument and a catalyst for vital social and creative processes, such as the reconstruction—and construction—of memory as well as the generation of future visions. They are also an extraordinary vehicle for communication, offering people from different generations and experiences a common ground to come together and remember, compare, interpret, and draw inspiration. Moreover, the photographs are an important source of material for promoting activities such as exhibitions, lectures, workshops, and consciousness-raising campaigns in the community. And given the rapid development of the digital technologies that facilitate the effective storage and transfer of images, the future possibilities for the use of historical photographs are even greater.

Looking Outward

Attempts by several indigenous societies to promote the preservation of their cultural heritage and the revival of their dying traditions have so often been unsuccessful because of the failure to capture the imagination and enthusiasm of the young. We must remember that many of these young people are, as is natural, intensely curious about the world and attracted to modern technology and popular culture. They will watch MTV whenever they have a chance. They want to be up-to-date and to "belong" to the contemporary global community. In some cases they perceive the skills and knowledge of their parents as increasingly inconsequential to the world of today, and they do not find many bridges linking the traditional and the modern.

Our experience was that simple technology can start to build such bridges. Through the use of photo and video cameras, tape recorders, darkroom equipment, and a small computer, the students participating in the project could gain access to fascinating technologies, not only in a passive way, as simple spectators, but actively, by commanding the processes themselves. They could use this technology discriminatingly, as an instrument to reclaim and preserve their endangered heritage. The discovery of the technology and the rediscovery of their own past became parts of the same fascinating experience. Older people, on the other hand, who are naturally suspicious of a modernity that usually robs them of the ability to control social change, could start feeling less the victims of unstoppable technological developments and more confident in the possibility of selectively appropriating aspects of technology in order to use them as part of their strategy to survive as a people.

Access to the outside world was also provided through books and other publications that offered a wider perspective on subjects relevant to the project's interests. Through this literature it was possible to enter a process of cultural comparison, to learn how other societies and cultural groups have dealt or are dealing with similar problems and questions: architecture and cultural identity, the appropriateness of new materials and construction methods, preservation of historical monuments, displacement and reconstruction, integration of the modern building professions, and so on. The diversity of outside information also served to balance a distorted and incomplete perception of modernity and its architecture and urban practices, replacing it with a more critical view that included the dissenting voices coming from the West, not least those that extol the benefits of the vernacular architecture of traditional societies.

During the project, we also realized the importance of establishing and maintaining links with outside institutions and individuals who can contribute to preserving the building tradition. A network of potential partners could include architecture faculties, museums, historians, archaeologists, conservators, and photo-researchers. These partners can play a beneficial role in the location of historical documentation and the transfer of skills and technical knowledge, and in the long term, cooperation in research and training can develop. Moreover, through these relationships indigenous peoples soon understand not only that they can benefit from the outside world but that they have much to offer as well. Because they usually inhabit extreme and fragile ecosystems—deserts, mountains, rain forests, islands—indigenous peoples have developed unique building traditions and settlement practices that are well adapted to these environments. And as the modern world is compelled to search for more ecologically sensitive solutions in architecture, the building heritage of these societies increasingly gains in esteem and admiration. This type of realization will give rise to more egalitarian partnerships based on a coincidence of interests and mutual respect.

Traditional Values

When studying the old monuments, the students from the architecture club soon found that measuring and analyzing the structures was not enough to fully understand them. The choice of site and orientation of the buildings, the use of colors and symbols, and the construction procedures themselves all seemed to obey rules set down by the spiritual tradition. Furthermore, practically all the architects of important structures appeared to have been religious practitioners.[10] Therefore, the students invited a respected religious leader and scholar to visit the documentation center. The high Lama spoke to them for a long time, associating the practice of architecture with the basic values, insights, and principles of Tibetan culture. He told them of the importance of understanding the act of creating physical forms and environments as belonging to a larger context, as part of the same process through which nature unfolds, and that a spiritual approach was essential not only for understanding their building tradition but also for becoming responsible creators themselves. A way was being pointed in which the students' creative adventures and professional futures would not lead them away from tradition. On the contrary, they were being told that to become effective professionals and better serve their people, they could turn to the wisdom of their elders for inspiration and support.

As is the case with Tibetans, among most indigenous peoples creativity is strongly linked to spirituality, and in some cultures art is almost exclusively religious. Artists are often visionaries who have undergone dream training and other techniques of the mind.[11] Consequently, the buildings they create must also be understood as manifestations of diverse and profound experiences of the spirit. If one is involved in the study or the preservation of the architectural heritage of traditional societies one cannot ignore this cultural aspect. A people who view impermanence and change as the intrinsic quality of reality, for example, might question the motivation to preserve just the material substance of a building without considering the importance of the social or spiritual role this structure has in the community.

Early Start

The main actors of our initiative in India were clearly the young members of Nyampa Larso, the architecture club. They quickly grasped the deeper implications of their various activities, and this was reflected in their growing eagerness to assume responsibility and in their consistent and dedicated participation throughout the project. This might seem surprising, given their youth, but in this type of endeavor I have found that there are in fact many advantages in working with adolescents and young adults. Their selfless enthusiasm, creativity, and thirst for knowledge are essential requisites for such an initiative to succeed. Moreover, the inquisitive mind and resourcefulness characteristic of their age and a spontaneous capacity to relate to the elderly make these young people effective agents in the race to detect and record the rapidly vanishing memory.

Young people are also great disseminators, given their capacity to bring the issues and debates into the homes and schools, building communication channels between the project and different sectors of the community. They are also freer than their older cousins, who by the time they are in their late twenties or thirties have already developed allegiances—cultural, professional, or political—and assumed positions of responsibility and tend to be less flexible and adventurous as a result.

I think there is another strong argument that speaks for involving young people in this type of work. They are at a critical juncture in which they start to become increasingly dissatisfied and impatient with their living conditions. This restlessness is at least in part a result of their intense capacity to envision other, more desirable realities. When this visionary impetus cannot find an outlet for expression, as a way to—at least symbolically—close the gap between the real and the imagined situations and move toward the ideal alternative, a deep frustration sets in, often turning into apathy or into violent and self-destructive behavior. But if this and other youthful energies can be channeled at an early age, if the uninhibited creativity, the risk-taking attitude, the openness to innovation, and the willingness to welcome and reconcile contradictions can be recognized and furthered by the community as valuable resources, then the same young men and women can eventually make an invaluable contribution to their people's struggle for cultural survival.

This process needs to start early on, preferably before these youngsters leave the community for technical training or a university education. Once they return to the community as professionals they frequently find themselves at odds with their society, often entering into conflict with the traditional authorities. In the case of architecture, sometimes the transition from a traditional construction practice to a professional-oriented one has been an impoverishing experience. Enthusiastic young graduates, eager to demonstrate what they have learned, ignore time-proven traditional ways and dismiss the knowledge of the craftsmen, displacing them from the decision-making process. Sometimes even when they are aware of their own limitations, they are prisoners of their new status, believing that as modern professionals they are expected to know everything and fearing they would lose face if they were to go to an illiterate mason for advice.

In addition, we must remember that for indigenous young men and women the experience of going to college is often a traumatic one. There they find themselves confronted with an education system that does not recognize their cultural specificity and in which their traditional worldview can find no place. The deep distress produced by this situation is eloquently described by Adrienne Rich: "[W]hen someone with the authority of a teacher, say, describes the world and you are not in it, there is a moment of psychic disequilibrium, as if you looked into a mirror and saw nothing."[12]

The early acquisition of a deep understanding of their building heritage and its relationship to traditional principles and values can provide the future students with a strong basis that will guide and sustain them through their later university studies or technical training. Furthermore, a lasting commitment to the preservation of that heritage can also be expected from returning graduates who were previously involved in such an endeavor from an early age.

The Monuments

Finally, the monuments themselves can play an extremely important role in the struggle to maintain cultural identity. Many indigenous peoples live today in reservations, slums, or government housing projects, in homes and neighborhoods that do not reflect their social and cultural needs. Although in many cases they are the descendants of great building traditions, today these groups have little power to influence the shaping of their physical environment and must often passively comply with schemes produced by outside technocrats and alien bureaucracies. Their own old construction practices are often long forgotten, and in some cases there is not even an awareness of their rich architectural heritage.[13]

As we found out during the expeditions to Ladakh, reconnection with the old monuments is vital and can become a great source of inspiration and learning. Not only the active involvement of the community in their study and preservation can invest the historical buildings with social purpose once more. Their present significance will be especially enhanced if one can manage to sustain their continuing capacity to inspire and motivate younger generations in their quest to create better and more appropriate living environments for their community.

John Dewey wrote that "every important structure is a treasury of storied memories and a monumental registering of cherished expectancies for the future."[14] Indeed, the old structures not only reveal much about the forgotten ways of life and habits of a society, but they also tell us a great deal about its dreams. It seems to me very important to emphasize this future-oriented element implicit in the historical monuments, this utopian quality that shows that the building tradition was not one of mechanical reproduction of old models but rather one of transformation and permanent search for the ideal. Young people who are themselves engaged in creative and visionary work can then develop a sense of complicity with the old builders and will see themselves as belonging to the same tradition of dreamers. They will be empowered by the realization that their heritage does not need to be a limiting burden but, on the contrary, can be a source of liberation because it is part of that heritage to be inventive.

A Navajo teacher compared indigenous history to a bow and arrow: "The farther back you pull the bowstring, the farther the arrow flies. The same is true with historical vision: the farther back you look, the farther you can see into the future."[15] Most people will agree on the importance of not losing sight of the past in order to move into the future in a healthy manner. But my own experience is that we also need to have the courage to look into the future in order to develop a healthy relationship with the past. After all, without having a destination for his arrow in sight, the hunter will not feel a need to reach for the bowstring in the first place. Similarly, it is in the process of dreaming the future that we are always confronted with the need to look back to understand where we come from—and in doing so, we realize the value and relevance of our heritage and develop the willingness to protect it. By encouraging such visionary processes, we will not only promote the preservation of the heritage, we can also guarantee its continuing influence in the creation of the future.

Notes

1 India, 100,000; Nepal, 20,000; Bhutan, 2,000; Switzerland, 2,000; the United States, 1,500; Canada, 500.

2 It is calculated that more than 95 percent of the approximately six thousand monasteries were destroyed.

3 Signs of this tendency are already visible. An example is the insistence on the use of traditional flat roofs with which Tibetans so strongly identify and which are perfectly appropriate to the dry climate of central Tibet but are doomed to fail in the new environment where the monsoon is exceptionally strong.

4 In Ladakh, Sikkim, Bhutan, Sanskar, Spiti, Lahoul, Mustang, Dolpo, etc.

5 Some of the institutions the historical photographs came from are the British Museum, the Royal Geographical Society, and the India Office Library in London; the Pitt Rivers Archives in Oxford; and the Völkerkundemuseum in Zurich. A particularly interesting collection of about one hundred rare photographs depicting Tibetan-Buddhist architecture from the central Siberian provinces of Tuva and Buryatia were acquired from a private collector in St. Petersburg.

6 Photographs from the 1950s and 1960s could be found in publications from the former eastern bloc countries, especially East Germany and Czechoslovakia, which at the time had access to the region. Newer images were provided by independent Tibet travelers and organizations such as the Tibet Image Bank (today Tibet Images), based in London.

7 Nyampa Larso means regeneration or revival, in the sense of recovery from languor or neglect. Nyampa = decline, dissolution; Larso = to promote, to uplift.

8 From his lecture "Crucible of Fiction," delivered at George Mason University on April 14, 1988. Quoted by C. D. Kleymeyer, *Cultural Expression and Grassroots Development: Cases from Latin America and the Caribbean* (Boulder, Colo.: Lynne Rienner, 1994), 25.

9 J. Joyce, *A Portrait of the Artist as a Young Man* (Middlesex: Penguin Books, 1978), 253.

10 The most famous of these is probably Thartong Gyalpo, a fourteenth-century sage and meditator who is sometimes referred to as the Tibetan Leonardo da Vinci. He is credited with the design of numerous important and innovative buildings in Tibet and Bhutan. He also constructed iron bridges, developed important esoteric rituals, and is considered the father of Tibetan theater and medicine.

11 The present State Oracle of Tibet, who is recognized in exile as a creative sculptor and designer of religious structures, claims to draw most of his inspiration from his visionary disposition.

12 From "Invisibility in Academe," quoted by R. Rosaldo, *Culture and Truth* (London: Routledge, 1993), ix.

13 I once heard an anecdote from an old Maya expert about a visit he made to one of the ancient archaeological sites in southern Mexico. On this visit he took along a young man from one of the rural communities he was involved with. While he, along with dozens of other tourists, admired the old structures, his companion seemed bored and completely indifferent to the wonderful architecture. Toward the end of the visit the young man saw a carving detail in which he recognized a familiar symbol. He inquired why this symbol, used by his people today, was on this building. When told that it was his ancestors who had constructed the monuments, he was astounded. In a state of excitement he wanted to go once again through the buildings that until then he had considered only a sort of recreation ground for foreign tourists. Once back in his community, he told everyone about the magnificent monuments their people had once built and how these were admired by the whole world.

14 J. Dewey, *Art as Experience* (New York: Minton, Balch & Company, 1934), 222.

15 From a speech at a public forum on intercultural education on the Navajo reservation in October 1985. Quoted in Kleymeyer, *Cultural Expression and Grassroots Development*, 22.

Agricultural Landscapes as World Heritage: Raised Field Agriculture in Bolivia and Peru

Clark L. Erickson

S AN ARCHAEOLOGIST WHO STUDIES agrarian landscapes of the past and present, I am concerned about the low value placed on cultural landscapes by national and international agencies charged with promoting, protecting, and managing cultural heritage in the developing world. My research in Bolivia and Peru focuses on a particular class of unappreciated cultural landscape, the mundane, traditional agricultural landscape (Fig. 1).[1] It is difficult to convince governments, international development agencies, conservation groups, funding institutions, and my archaeology colleagues that this class of cultural heritage is important and worthy of attention. In contrast to cultural landscapes associated with traditional monuments, important buildings, archaeological sites, and sacred natural features, the very characteristics of agricultural landscapes work against their receiving attention and protection. Most traditional agricultural landscapes are (1) cultural, in that they "exist by virtue of . . . being perceived, experienced, and contextualized by people" (Ashmore and Knapp 1991:1); (2) large scale, usually covering entire regions; (3) without clear boundaries; (4) products of a long historical trajectory (Denevan 2001; Piperno and Pearsall 1998); (5) heterogeneous (Crumley 1994), resilient (McGlade 1999), engineered (Lansing 1991), and highly patterned (Erickson 1996); (6) increasingly "contested" (Bender 1998); (7) dynamic,

Figure 1
Rehabilitated pre-Columbian raised fields, a class of traditional agricultural landscape, on the lake plain near Huatta, Peru, 1986. The earth platforms (5 m wide and 50 cm high) are planted in potatoes. Photo by Clark L. Erickson.

that is, continuously under construction and transformation (Ingold 1993; Tilley 1994); (8) anthropogenic, or human made, the antithesis of the wilderness so beloved by conservationists (Erickson 2000; Redman 1999; Stahl 1996); (9) intensively used and densely inhabited by native and other peoples (Denevan 2001; Erickson 1996; Netting 1993); (10) associated with poor, rural peoples who are lacking in political power (Denevan 2001; Netting 1993); and (11) structured by local, non-Western principles of design and hence underappreciated by non-natives.

Many intensively farmed agricultural landscapes in the Andean region of South America are highly patterned and formally designed (Fig. 2). I refer to these landscapes as anthropogenic and consider them a form of built environment (Erickson 2000). These built environments are equal in complexity and design to any traditionally recognized building architecture or monuments. Most are truly engineered, with landscape capital and the accumulated infrastructure of fields, walls, paths, roads, canals, and other land improvements, the knowledge of which is passed down from parents to children over many generations (Erickson 2000; Lansing 1991:12). Many traditional agricultural landscapes support large rural populations and have been farmed sustainably for thousands of years.[2]

The built engineered environment, or landscape capital, of individual rural farming communities is often more monumental than the works created by centralized nonindustrial states. Computer modeling of the farmed landscapes of single ethnographic and archaeological communities in the Lake Titicaca basin of Peru and Bolivia provides volumetric calculations of construction fill for terrace platforms and the lengths of facing walls. The volume of soil moved and linear walls constructed within the spatial footprint of single communities dwarfs that of monumental sites. These studies show that the total energy expended in earth movement alone by single farming communities is up to two hundred

Figure 2

Aerial photograph of the complex formal patterning of pre-Columbian raised fields at the edge of Lake Titicaca, Peru. Old canals (dark lines) between the raised field platforms (light lines) are clearly visible. Photo by Clark L. Erickson.

times greater than that which was expended at individual monuments at ceremonial and administrative sites (Erickson n.d.).

Landscapes also have "cultural capital" or "social capital" (see Throsby and Low, this volume). Agricultural landscapes are the product of many generations of farmers applying their indigenous knowledge and technology to what are often considered marginal lands. The lifeways of present and past peoples are embedded in landscape: their settlements, technology, land tenure, social organization, and worldview have material expression in the physical patterning and palimpsest of landscape features (field morphology, house compounds, walls, networks of paths and roads, field boundary markers, and rural shrines). Through the reading of landscapes, archaeologists glean insights about "the people without history," those who are ignored by traditional archaeological research and historical analysis (Wolf 1982). The archaeology of landscapes is about *peopling* the landscapes of the past and present (Erickson 2000; Ingold 1993; Tilley 1994).

What is the real economic and cultural value of "relict," "continuing," or "lived in" agricultural landscapes? I argue that agricultural landscapes have significant tangible and intangible values for local peoples, the nonlocal public(s), national governments, and the international community (see Fairclough, Siravo, Noriega, and Haney, this volume). But value means nothing without advocates. In contrast to other categories of cultural landscapes, agricultural landscapes have few advocates in the world heritage and cultural resource management communities. Archaeologists should be the primary advocates of traditional agricultural landscapes, but, unfortunately, traditional archaeology is still firmly committed to the "site concept" (Dunnell 1992; Fotiadis 1992). Archaeologists find, excavate, analyze, interpret, and protect sites, which tend to be large urban settlements with significant buildings and monuments of stone and brick. Landscape, often equated with environment, is simply considered the context or background for sites and monuments. Surprisingly, the most vocal advocates of agricultural landscapes are cultural geographers (of the Berkeley school founded by Carl Sauer, e.g., Denevan 2001; Zimmerer 1996), cultural anthropologists interested in indigenous knowledge systems (e.g., Brokensha, Warren, and Werner 1980; Lansing 1991; Netting 1993; Warren, Slikkerveer, and Brokensha 1995), local travel agents involved in eco- and cultural tourism, native peoples and local residents, and private landowners.

The Problem of Traditional Definitions of Cultural Landscape

In 1992 UNESCO included cultural landscapes in its *Operational Guidelines for the Implementation of the World Heritage Convention*. While this is a positive step, monuments, groups of buildings, and sites continue to dominate the registry. As of 1998 UNESCO included 522 properties as World Heritage Sites (418 cultural properties, 114 natural properties, and 20 considered mixed cultural and natural sites) (Cleere 2000:99). Of these, only 14 are cultural landscapes, most of which were already registered because of their association with important buildings, monuments, or natural features rather than their intrinsic value (Cleere 2000:9, 102).[3] Agricultural landscapes remain the most underrepresented category of World Heritage. According to UNESCO,

> *Cultural landscapes* represent the "combined works of nature and of man" designated in Article 1 of the Convention. They are illustrative of the evolution of human society and settlement over time, under the influence of the physical constraints and/or opportunities presented by their natural environment and of successive social, economic and cultural forces, both external and internal. They should be selected on the basis both of their outstanding universal value and of their representativity [*sic*] in terms of a clearly defined geo-cultural region and also for their capacity to illustrate the essential and distinct cultural elements of such regions. (2002:9)

The *Operational Guidelines* (UNESCO 2002:9) state, "The term 'cultural landscape' embraces a diversity of manifestations of the interaction between humankind and its natural environment." The document recognizes three main categories of cultural landscapes:

(i) The most easily identifiable is the clearly defined landscape designed and created intentionally by man. This embraces garden and parkland landscapes constructed for aesthetic reasons which are often (but not always) associated with religious or other monumental buildings and ensembles.

(ii) The second category is the organically evolved landscape. This results from an initial social, economic, administrative, and/or religious imperative and has developed its present form by association with and in response to its natural environment. Such landscapes reflect that process of evolution in their form and component features. They fall into two subcategories:

—a relict (or fossil) landscape is one in which an evolutionary process came to an end at some time in the past, either abruptly or over a period. Its significant distinguishing features are, however, still visible in material form.

—a continuing landscape is one which retains an active social role in contemporary society closely associated with the traditional way of life and in which the evolutionary process is still in progress. At the same time it exhibits significant material evidence of its evolution over time.

(iii) The final category is the associative cultural landscape. The inclusion of such landscapes on the World Heritage List is justifiable by virtue of the powerful religious, artistic, or cultural associations of the natural element rather than material cultural evidence, which may be insignificant or even absent. (UNESCO 2002:9)

The site concept permeates the definitions and categories of cultural landscapes. I believe that the unique nature of cultural landscapes is not easily subsumed under the epistemology of the site concept that dominates archaeology and World Heritage management. Association with a sacred natural feature (i.e., a place) recognized as religiously important characterizes "associative landscapes" protected as World Heritage, not the landscape itself. As Church (1997:26) points out, "Landscapes are not merely large areas, nor are they aggregates of sites as most regional archaeological studies are structured."

Traditional agricultural landscapes of the Andean region, as a subcategory of cultural landscape, seem to fall between the cracks of contemporary definitions provided by UNESCO. Agricultural landscapes, although not specifically mentioned, would be considered "organically evolved landscapes."[4] UNESCO (2002:9) attributes this category to "an initial social, economic, administrative, and/or religious imperative" that organically evolves "by association with and in response to its natural environment." The statement seems to imply that (1) top-down demands were made on people occupying the land and (2) the landscape develops through an evolutionary process of interaction between culture and nature. The formation of landscape is attributed to the unintentional result or by-product of human occupation and use of the land over long periods. As such, there is little room in this definition for human agency, decision making, and historical contingency. According to UNESCO's categorization, in the Andes, abandoned archaeological terraces and raised fields would be classified as relict landscapes; and currently farmed terraced fields would be classified as continuing landscape. In this case study, I argue that the distinction between "relict" and "continuing" is artificial, because all cultural landscapes exist in the present and are part of the living, inhabited contemporary world.

The organically evolved landscape is contrasted to the categories "clearly defined landscape" and "associative cultural landscape." Clearly defined landscapes specifically include formal gardens and parks. As ideal forms of the Western cultural landscape, gardens and parks embody formal design, monumentality, and elite aesthetics, which are often contrasted with vernacular, unstructured, farmed landscapes or rural countryside. The clearly defined landscape again highlights the influence of the site concept in UNESCO's definitions of cultural landscape. These landscapes "are often (but not always) associated with religious or other monumental buildings and ensembles" and thus should be valued because traditional buildings, monuments, or sites are found on them. Why can't cultural landscapes be appreciated as cultural landscapes?

UNESCO's perception of cultural landscapes as "manifestations of the interaction between humankind and its natural environment" implies an association with nature. Agricultural landscapes are much more than simply the product of interaction between nature and culture. UNESCO's categories reify the artificial distinction between natural and cultural landscapes. As a consequence, the pervasive myth of the pristine environment and the concept of wilderness continue to shape World Heritage policy. Recent edited volumes promoting cultural landscapes as World Heritage (Lucas 1992; von Droste, Plachter, and Rossler 1995) reproduce the perception that human activities are bad for the environment.[5] This literature ignores the important insights of New Ecology that stress that chaos, disturbance, patches, and change are necessary for environmental health (e.g., Botkin

1990). Historical ecologists point out that no landscape of the Americas is natural or pristine (e.g., Denevan 1992; Stahl 1996). All landscapes are anthropogenic to some degree. Land recognized as natural or wilderness is the product of thousands of years of native agroforestry, farming, herding, burning, and other cultural activities. Landscapes that have been "domesticated" to some degree by past and present farmers or hunter-gatherers are now the ubiquitous landform on earth.

The association with nature is most evident in the third category of cultural landscape, "associative cultural landscape." Here, significance is linked to "powerful religious, artistic, or cultural associations with the natural element rather than material cultural evidence" (UNESCO 2002:10; see also Carmichael et al. 1994). The category is clearly intended to protect significant natural features and the immediate viewshed around them. The associative cultural landscape is reduced to a backdrop or natural setting for a place or site. As Bradley (2000) points out, landscapes with natural places of religious significance are "marked" by subtle archaeological features and activities (shrines, alignments, orientations, and caches of offerings) that are important cultural resources themselves.

Andean landscapes are much more than simply the interaction between humans and nature. Their significance is independent of traditional monumental architecture, buildings, or sites. These agricultural landscapes have been transformed to the extent that they are completely anthropogenic and have become built environment. As this case study shows, Andean agricultural landscapes are highly patterned and intentionally designed according to practical, aesthetic, and cosmological principles; thus, they should be classified as "clearly defined landscapes" (although not necessarily "clearly defined" in terms of cultural or physical boundaries).

In Latin America, cultural landscapes are not currently protected as a distinct category of cultural heritage but rather through association with high-profile "natural" or "pristine" environments of high biodiversity (examples include the World Heritage "mixed natural and cultural sites" of Machu Picchu Archaeological National Park and the Rio Abiseo National Park). The concept of wilderness still dominates cultural and natural resource management in developing countries. In developing countries in Latin America where the concept of cultural landscape is poorly developed, the "coattailing" or "piggybacking" of agricultural landscape protection to national parks, nature reserves, indigenous territories, traditional sites, and monuments is one approach. The problem is that the anthropogenic characteristics of traditional agricultural landscapes are at odds with green politics and environmentalism, which prioritize protection of a pristine nature or wilderness.

I believe that many traditional agricultural landscapes are of sufficient significance to be considered World Heritage Sites. Below I make a case for present raised field agriculture.

Rehabilitation of Raised Field Agriculture in the Lake Titicaca Basin

The Lake Titicaca basin in the south central Andes of present-day Peru and Bolivia is one of the most impressive engineered landscapes in the world (Erickson 2000). Much of the pre-Columbian agricultural infrastructure is still in use, although poorly maintained. Abandoned raised fields, sunken gardens, and various hydraulic earthworks are found throughout lake and river

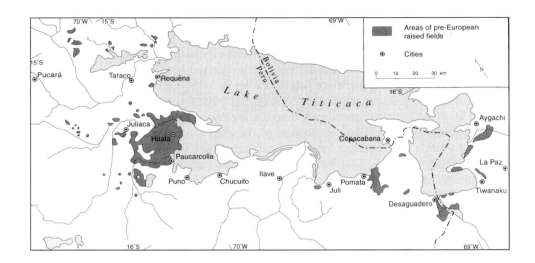

Figure 3

The distribution of pre-Columbian raised fields in the Lake Titicaca basin of Peru and Bolivia (after Denevan 2001:Fig. 13.1)

plains. The mountainous slopes are covered with stone-lined terraces, boundary walls, and canals. In the early 1980s I began a study of one abandoned farming system, raised field agriculture. The goal of the investigation was to describe; map; date origins, use, and abandonment; and determine the functions, carrying capacity, and sustainability of raised field agriculture. Raised fields (Spanish: *camellones*; Quechua: *waru waru*; Aymara: *suka kollus*) are elevated planting platforms of earth (1 to 20 meters wide, 10 to hundreds of meters long, and 0.5 to 1 meter high). Adjacent to each platform are canals that provided the earth for construction. My Peruvian colleagues and I estimate that raised fields cover more than 120,000 hectares of the Lake Titicaca basin, most of which now lie abandoned (Fig. 3). Archaeological excavations of raised fields demonstrated that farmers began constructing them by 1000 B.C. The production from raised fields and other intensive forms of agriculture underwrote the complex societies that developed within the basin.

Raised field agriculture was abandoned before or soon after the Spanish conquest, and most of the fields were converted into pasture for colonial haciendas and became government cooperatives in 1968. We found that rebuilding and using the fields was the best way to understand raised field agriculture (Fig. 4, Color Plate 13). From the beginning, local

Figure 4

Construction of experimental raised fields during the dry season by farmers of Huatta, Peru, 1986. Photo provided by Instituto Geográfico Militar.

(See also Color Plate 13.)

farmers were active participants in this experimental research. Through archaeological investigation and agronomic experimentation, we determined that raised fields resolved many of the problems facing farmers at high altitude (Fig. 5). Through raising the platform, farmers doubled the depth of topsoil for crops. The elevated platforms created dry surfaces in the waterlogged and flooded lake and river plains. The water-filled canals beside the platforms provided moisture for droughts during the growing season. Heated by the sun during the day, the water in canals protected crops against the killing frost that is common at high altitude. In addition, the canals captured nutrients and produced organic-rich sediments that could be incorporated into the fields for sustained harvests. During the first few years after reconstruction, the experimental raised fields produced harvests two to three times that of nonraised fields (Fig. 6).

Based on the success of the experiments, between 1981 and 1987, my Peruvian colleagues and I began a small-scale, grassroots development project to rehabilitate pre-Columbian raised field agriculture in several native communities (Erickson 1996; Erickson and Candler 1989). By working with larger groups of farmers, we could expand the scale of the agronomic experiments and reach the people who could benefit from the knowledge (Fig. 7). Agronomists and development agents working in the Lake Titicaca basin, initially resistant to raised field rehabilitation, began to support the technology. By the late 1980s many nongovernmental organizations (NGOs) and government agencies in Peru and Bolivia were promoting raised field rehabilitation (e.g., Kolata et al. 1996; PIWA 1994).

Figure 5
Andean crops (potatoes, ocas, ullucus, isañucus, quinoa, and cañihua) growing on rehabilitated raised fields at Illpa, Peru, 1986. Photo by Clark L. Erickson.

Figure 6
Harvest of potatoes grown on rehabilitated raised fields in Huatta, Peru, 1985. Photo by Clark L. Erickson.

Figure 7
Quechua farmers reviewing interviews for a raised field training video, 1985. Photo by Clark L. Erickson.

According to some estimates, farmers of several hundred Quechua and Aymara communities rehabilitated between 500 and 1,500 hectares of raised fields by 1990. Our textbooks, extension manuals, and training video on raised field and terrace rehabilitation were widely circulated with the larger corpus of NGO-produced materials on traditional agriculture, appropriate technology, and sustainable development (Fig. 8). After more than twenty years of investigation and promotion, *waru waru* and *suka kollus* are now integrated into public school curricula throughout Peru and Bolivia. The attention also inspired investigations of and a greater appreciation for other indigenous technologies and crops.

NGO and government personnel endorsed raised fields as home-grown sustainable development. The national and international press over-promoted raised fields as the solution to rural poverty in the Andes and elsewhere. By the 1990s criticism of raised field projects and reports of the

Figure 8

A selection of comic books and manuals about raised fields developed for public out-reach, extension, and training. a–b: Proyecto Agrícola de los Campos Elevados; c: Programa Interinstitucional de Waru Waru, NADE/PELT-COTESU.

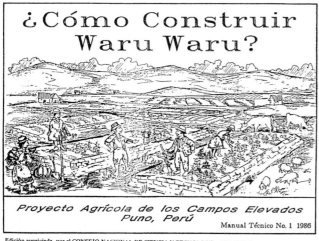

abandonment of recently rehabilitated fields began to appear and the sustainability and appropriateness of raised fields and other traditional Andean farming systems was questioned. I am convinced that if certain policies and strategies are promoted, raised field technology is sound and sustainable. The experiments demonstrated that raised fields have relatively high productivity and are probably capable of sustained yields under good management. Farmers that have continued to maintain rehabilitated raised fields in Peru and Bolivia are encouraging indications of success.[6] The archaeological record shows that raised fields sustained huge populations, provided the basis for complex sociopolitical institutions, and were used for more than two thousand years; thus raised fields are an indigenous, time-tested, environmentally appropriate technology. Detailed cost-benefit analyses show that raised fields are economically sound (PIWA 1994).

Technological and economic appropriateness does not necessarily mean that contemporary farmers of the region will or should adopt raised field agriculture. Surprisingly, some reasons for adoption of raised fields by farmers had little to do with appropriate technology and high productivity. During the 1980s, Huatta, Coata, and surrounding communities petitioned the Peruvian government for lands held by the government cooperative SAIS Buenavista. Pre-Columbian raised fields cover these lands, which originally belonged to these communities. When the government resisted the petitions, farmers occupied the lands, beginning a tense standoff between communities and police. The government finally ceded the lands to the communities in the late 1980s. Almost immediately, blocks of raised fields were built to mark the new boundaries between neighboring communities. Rehabilitated raised fields became a powerful political marker of a community's right to occupy and farm traditional lands (Erickson and Brinkmeier 1991).

Many farmers participated in order to receive incentives (food, wages, seed, and/or tools) provided by the agencies promoting the rehabilitation of raised fields. As we will see below, the use of incentives can have a negative effect on continued cultivation of rehabilitated raised fields and contribute to field abandonment. Some cases of spontaneous adoption (without incentives) by curious individual farmers are documented (Erickson and Brinkmeier 1991; Pari, Aguilar, and Cutipa 1989:35–36; PIWA 1994:52).

The social and cultural side of raised field agriculture is understood less than the technology. While most Quechua and Aymara farmers immediately recognize the benefits of raised field agriculture, the majority have not permanently adopted it as a production strategy. During a brief evaluation of raised field rehabilitation projects in 1989, we found that the reasons for nonadoption are complex and fascinating (Erickson and Brinkmeier 1991; Garaycochea 1988; Pari, Aguilar, and Cutipa 1989; PIWA 1994:169).[7] The most important factor is that the social, political, and economic environment today is different from that when the raised fields were first constructed and used. Other important factors are competing labor demands, traditional fallow cycles, crop genetic loss, competition with livestock, land tenure issues, limited NGO knowledge of the technology, misuse of incentives, political unrest, and emphasis on communal farming rather than the individual farmer.

Competing labor demands. The initial construction of large blocks of raised fields requires considerable labor (although total labor is relatively low when spread out over many years of continuous cultivation). By necessity, many farmers participate in migratory labor for temporary wage income in the cities and mines for part of the year, drawing labor away from the farm. In addition, competition between NGOs and government agencies for projects in well-organized communities has been intense. Farmers often have had to choose between projects offering substantial incentives.

Traditional fallow cycles. Farmers traditionally practice a three-year cropping period followed by a fallow (leaving fields uncultivated) period of up to twenty years. This cycling is an effective, low-cost means of cultivating the exhausted and eroded soils of the hill slopes where most farming is done. Although raised field agriculture under good management may not require long fallow cycles, farmers today apply the traditional cycle used for slope cultivation to rehabilitated raised fields. Many of the rehabilitated raised fields that appear recently "abandoned" may actually be in fallow.

Crop genetic loss. The specific crops adapted to the unique conditions of the cold lakeshore where pre-Columbian raised fields are found were lost with the abandonment of the field systems following massive depopulation of the region during the early colonial period. The crops grown on rehabilitated raised fields today are adapted to a radically different environmental zone: higher altitude slopes. The original crops probably produced consistent and higher yields than those now cultivated on rehabilitated raised fields.

Land tenure issues. Issues of land tenure are often central to farmers' decisions about whether to adopt raised fields. Most pre-Columbian raised fields are found on hacienda and government cooperative lands— lands that until recently were not controlled by indigenous communities in Peru. Since the colonial period, these lands were used exclusively for grazing sheep and cattle. Many communities in Peru maintain communal land for building raised fields; in contrast, few communities in Bolivia have communal landholdings. Thus in Bolivia, many rehabilitated raised fields built by communities were located on private lands "loaned" to them for an unspecified period. When the landowners realized the potential of the raised fields, permission to farm the land was withdrawn. Lacking sufficient labor to continue, the owners soon stopped cultivating the raised fields (Kolata et al. 1996; Kozloff 1994).

Competition with livestock. The raising of livestock is now an important source of income for Quechua farm families. Farmers who control areas of raised fields must often choose between rehabilitating raised fields and grazing livestock. Because of the relative higher market value of animals, farmers have chosen livestock over raised fields. Efforts to integrate livestock and crop production in raised fields have not yet been successful.

Limited NGO knowledge of the technology. In the beginning, it was difficult to convince local NGOs and government agencies of the importance of indigenous technology in development. After initial resistance to raised fields, in the late 1980s agencies began to support raised field rehabilitation. While many groups enthusiastically promoted raised field technology, their understanding of the technology was often limited. Their emphasis on making raised fields "look good" often required extra labor. Field platforms were often built higher than necessary, doubling the number of person-days of labor. Rather than simply rehabilitate preexisting raised fields, some NGOs promoted construction of new fields, again adding unnecessary labor. New fields were often built in inappropriate locations and constructed at the wrong time of the year, thus destroying old raised fields, inverting fertile topsoil with subsoil, and disrupting drainage. Crops inappropriate for local conditions were often imposed on the communities, resulting in harvest failures (Erickson and Brinkmeier 1991; Pari, Aguilar, and Cutipa 1989; PIWA 1994). In addition, those who promoted raised field agriculture promised results that were unrealistic and provided misleading information about harvests, sustainable yields, and risks.

Misuse of incentives. Most development groups rely heavily on the distribution of surplus food provided by the USAID PL480 program as an incentive. During the mid-1980s, the government of Peru promoted raised fields as "make-work projects" in which farmers were paid low daily wages to rehabilitate fields. The payment of incentives (wages, food, tools, and seed) to participants became the accepted means of increasing farmer participation in projects throughout Peru and Bolivia, often creating bidding wars among development agencies (Garaycochea 1988). This patronizing top-down approach is in sharp contrast to the grassroots approach of our original project. Rather than see the projects as rural community development, farmers felt they were "working for" the host development agency or NGO. After rehabilitating raised fields on their own lands, farmers often demanded additional wages to plant, harvest, and maintain them. These raised fields were soon abandoned when the NGOs refused to pay the additional wages and moved on to new projects. In other cases, agencies used a rotating fund of loaned potato seed whereby communities had to return the seed and 10 percent interest after harvest (some groups demanded half of the harvest).

Political unrest. Because of the war between the Peruvian government and the Shining Path during the late 1980s and early 1990s, most international aid agencies promoting raised fields left Peru. As a result, NGO funding for promoting raised field rehabilitation ended, projects were dissolved, and fields were abandoned. The political unrest, combined with the short duration of individual projects and the ever-changing missions of NGOs and funding agencies in good times, ended the golden age of raised field rehabilitation.

Emphasis on communal farming rather than the individual farmer. We found that most of the rehabilitated raised fields that were abandoned by the 1990s were those constructed by communities or large groups of farmers working together (Erickson and Brinkmeier 1991). Our project and most of the NGOs and government groups working in the region focused on communities rather than individual farmers. We believed that raised field rehabilitation would help to reinforce community development. We also found working with large community groups for the construction of large blocks of raised fields much more efficient than working with individuals. Poor organization and leadership, internal tensions, and land tenure problems within communities worked against long-term sustained commitment to communal farming of large raised field plots (Erickson and Brinkmeier 1991; Kehoe 1996; Kolata et al. 1996; Kozloff 1994; Pari, Aguilar, and Cutipa 1989).

In contrast, raised fields constructed by individual families, often without support and incentives from NGOs and other groups, continued in use and actually flourished through the 1980s and 1990s. These small blocks of fields were often intensively farmed as house gardens (Fig. 9). The family raised fields were well built and maintained for longer periods. The success of the "multiplier effect," the adoption and promotion by individual families, is difficult to track but remains an important means of diffusion and adoption of raised field technology.

In summary, the issue of sustainability of raised fields is complex and not simply one of technology, soil fertility, or labor requirements. There are no studies of continuous production on the experimental raised fields of Lake Titicaca because of the short life of development projects and the lack of long-term follow-up; thus sustainability has not been demonstrated. The archaeological record provides an important source of data on sustainability. Documented use of pre-Columbian raised fields for 2,000 to 2,500 years suggests that the technology was efficient, appropriate, productive, and sustainable. Settlement archaeology also shows that rural communities were rooted to particular geographic places for thousands of years (despite the periodic rise and fall of state societies in the region).

The experimental rehabilitated fields, as well as the pre-Columbian fields, were constructed for specific reasons and in specific historical contexts. Why they worked or did not is a complex matter and has more to do with social, cultural, and economic factors than with labor or technology issues. The factors outlined above are interrelated, and all work against the adoption of raised field agriculture by contemporary farmers.

Figure 9
A rehabilitated raised field built by an individual family in Huatta, Peru. Photo by Clark L. Erickson.

The Intangible Cultural Value of Traditional Agricultural Landscapes

Do raised fields have relevance to contemporary society beyond simply being used? Is the adoption and use of raised field agriculture by contemporary farmers a prerequisite for classification as having "outstanding universal value" and thus deserving of protection as World Heritage? Although current "living" use would better ensure survival, these agricultural landscapes may be valuable for other reasons.

To be nominated for World Heritage protection, UNESCO requires that a cultural landscape be of "outstanding universal value." As Cleere (1995, 1996) points out, this concept is problematic in theory and in practice. Cultural landscapes are less likely than traditional sites and monuments to meet the criteria of outstanding universal value and be considered for nomination. Cleere (1995:229) argues that appreciation of cultural property is not universal or homogeneous and that decisions are often based on "an aesthetic and historical perspective that is grounded in European culture." Responding to Cleere's critique, Titchen (1996) notes that the concept "outstanding universal value" is purposely vague and under continual construction.

Government planners, development agency personnel, and tourists look out over the rural Andes and see endless grinding poverty, backwardness, and ignorance. Anthropologists, archaeologists, and geographers see an idyllic, beautiful landscape filled with happy peasants employing a rich indigenous knowledge and sophisticated technology. Do traditional agricultural landscapes such as raised fields have outstanding universal value and thus merit protection as World Heritage Sites? Some important reasons for advocating, protecting, and managing traditional agricultural landscapes are these:

- Traditional agricultural landscapes harbor a rich gene pool of domestic, semidomestic, and wild species of landraces, an important resource that can be mined for new cultigens, enhanced resistance to diseases and pests, improved storability, and greater variety (recognized by UNESCO [2002:9]).
- Environmentalists, conservationists, and social and natural scientists are coming to recognize that the anthropogenic landscape will play an increasingly important role in the future of the environment of our planet. Scholars are beginning to understand that wilderness is a cultural construct and that all environments are to some degree anthropogenic.
- Agricultural landscapes are dynamic contexts for the expression of local, regional, and national cultures. The cultural diversity of living peoples within landscapes is often considered analogous to biological diversity. Cultural survival often depends on a strong sense of place, belonging, and identity rooted in local history and prehistory and embedded in the landscape, which connects past, present, and future.
- Agricultural landscapes, characterized by a complex stratified palimpsest of patterned human activity through time, are physical records of agriculture, risk management strategies, building technology, environmental change, and historical ecology. In

many cases, the archaeological record of human activity on the landscape is all that remains of past occupants.

- Agricultural landscapes provide local, time-tested models of appropriate technology and sustainable land use (recognized by UNESCO [2002:9] and the International Union for the Conservation of Nature, or IUCN [McNeeley 1995]). Archaeological and historical research can document resilience, long-term continuous use, high carrying capacities, and environmentally friendly practices.

- Cultural landscapes are both a model of and a model for society and thus play an important role in the transmission and reproduction of local culture. Local, national, and international appreciation of traditional agricultural landscapes reinforces native cultures.

- International appreciation and recognition of the cultural heritage and indigenous knowledge systems embedded in agricultural landscapes can empower native peoples in their efforts to gain political representation, promote economic development, reinforce local cultural identity, and win land disputes.

- The environmental, cultural, historical, and archaeological significance of agricultural landscapes for national and international tourism can be a source of income for local people. Native people benefit from increasing cultural tourism that focuses on the "lived in" agricultural landscapes of Bali, Cuzco (Peru), and the islands of the Sun, Taquile, and Amantaní (Bolivia and Peru), and the Ifugao (Philippines).

Some "values" of agricultural landscapes such as crop production and sustainability are measurable and quantifiable. Experiments and field trials of traditional agriculture provide critical information about function, ecological appropriateness, production rates, cropping frequency, carrying capacity, and sustainability. Cost-benefit analysis provides standards for comparing Andean traditional agriculture to Western and other non-Western agricultural systems (PIWA 1994). Issues of sustainability and appropriateness can be addressed through scientific study (Denevan 2001; Erickson 1996; Morlon 1996). In the case of raised fields, applied research of the 1970s and 1980s provided important scientific validation (experiments, cost-benefit analysis; production rates, management of resources, and social issues of adoption and rejection). This research by university students, professionals, and native peoples was presented and published in a variety of scholarly and public forums. Although the body of literature on raised fields and other Andean technologies is small compared to that available for Western agricultural systems, it demonstrates that raised field agriculture has potential as a sustainable technology under certain conditions and contexts.[8]

Many authors in this volume highlight the importance of cultural capital in considerations of determining the "value" and sustainability of World Heritage. Can monetary value be assigned to the natural, ecological, aesthetic, historical, archaeological, religious, and cultural significance of an agricultural landscape discussed above? Studies of the economy of the environment and the economy of art (Throsby, this volume) show promise.

The Interface between Sustainable Development and World Heritage

The abandonment of valuable farmland, rural to urban migration, increasing rural poverty, and the replacement of family farms by large commercial operations are significant problems throughout the developed and developing world. The causes and solutions for these phenomena are complex. Keeping people on the farm with an acceptable standard of living and putting abandoned farms back into production through sustainable development should be a major priority.

The attitudes of government and nongovernmental organizations financed by the World Bank, the International Development Bank, USAID, UNESCO, and others toward traditional agriculture often contribute to the problems. These organizations should reevaluate their current policies of imposing top-down, Western-based models of development on non-Western farmers (see also Cleere 2000:104–5). The arrogant "received wisdom" that drives contemporary development policy is often based on poor science and lack of understanding of local cultures, political economy, and historical ecology (Leach and Mearns 1996; Peet and Watts 1996). There is a long tradition in the development community of blaming environmental degradation and poverty on rural farmers. During my research in Peru and Bolivia, numerous international development projects were designed to replace "backward" traditional agriculture with Western "appropriate technology." Most projects ended in complete failure (although they were rarely officially recognized as such). The Lake Titicaca basin is a graveyard of development, a landscape littered with cracked cement-lined irrigation canals, rusted pumps, twisted windmills, and broken farm machinery, or what my colleagues Ignacio Garaycochea and Juan Palao refer to as the "archaeology of development" (Fig. 10, Color Plate 14). Development

Figure 10
The archaeology of development, 1986. The physical relics of failed international development projects promoting capitalist-based and "appropriate" technology during the 1960s, 1970s, and 1980s at the Illpa Agricultural Experimental Station, Puno, Peru. Photo by Clark L. Erickson.
(See also Color Plate 14.)

projects are introduced and fail with regularity, while Andean farmers continue to rely on the tried-and-true traditional agriculture practiced by their ancestors complemented by selective innovations. Advocacy for agricultural landscapes also requires setting the record straight about the pros and cons of native technology and practices (Dupuis and Vandergeest 1996).

I am convinced that traditional agricultural technology, indigenous knowledge, and rural lifeways, past and present, provide alternative models for development of cultural landscapes if certain strategies and policies are promoted. These might include

- acquiring formal land titles for individual farmers and native communities. As Netting (1993) argues in his cross-cultural study of smallholders, private family ownership of land plots being farmed has been and is the basis of sustainable agriculture throughout the world. The best way to keep farmers on the land and reduce the massive migration to urban centers is to ensure legal titles to the land they work and provide land to those without. Ownership of plots encourages continuity of occupation, reduces risks, and encourages improvements of the land (McNeeley 1995; PIWA 1994).
- improving access to economic resources. Most farmers would benefit from access to credit and tax incentives for family land improvements and risk reduction, opening of markets for traditional crops produced on these lands, and training in cooperative organization and small business administration.
- guaranteeing social justice or an acceptable quality of life for farming peoples in developing countries. These are important but often neglected elements of the original definition of sustainable development (CIKARD 1993). Reduction of the exploitation, violence, and racism against native peoples would help to ensure the survival of traditional agricultural landscapes.
- understanding and valuing strategies of risk management practiced by native farmers that enable them to adapt their traditional agriculture to the global economy. In countering the common stereotype of traditional agriculture as primitive, backward, stagnant, and inefficient, scholars have demonstrated that many farmers are constantly adapting, transforming, and adjusting their traditional strategies to meet new demands and challenges (Denevan 2001; Morlon 1996; Netting 1993; Zimmerer 1996).

Certain resources and policies that are already in place in the development community could be shifted to encourage, promote, and improve what already works or was known to work in the past: local indigenous knowledge and farming practices. To reduce bias against traditional agricultural practices, local historical ecology, indigenous knowledge systems, agricultural ecology, archaeology, history, ethnography, and local language should be part of the standard training for extension agents and development workers. Governments and international funding agencies routinely require environmental and cultural impact studies for large development projects (pipelines, roads, urbanization, irrigation, and dams). These mitigation studies, in addition to the traditional focus on historical and archaeological sites, monuments and wilderness, could become a primary source of new information about traditional agricultural landscapes and indigenous knowledge systems.

Value and Advocacy of Traditional Agricultural Landscapes as World Heritage

Throughout his life, the anthropologist Michael Warren promoted scientific research as the best way to validate and promote indigenous knowledge systems (IKS) (Brokensha, Warren, and Werner 1980; Warren 1999). To promote scientific and global appreciation of IKS, Warren advocated its incorporation into school programs, university education, and development training, in addition to promotion through traditional media and the Internet.[9]

Natural science critics point out that the advantages of IKS over development based on Western scientific knowledge have not been adequately demonstrated. Others highlight the problems of transferring specific IKS to other contexts. Social scientists argue that proponents of IKS stereotype farmers as static, ahistorical, exotic, and noble savages. Despite the critique, the development community is beginning to recognize that historically contingent IKS can benefit smallholder development (e.g., McNeeley 1995; Pichón, Uquillas, and Frechione 1999; Warren 1999; Warren, Slikkerveer, and Brokensha 1999). In other cases, IKS may contribute little to sustainable development because certain historical and traditional practices may not be relevant or adaptable to the contemporary world. Some indigenous knowledge systems can be combined successfully with Western scientific knowledge (DeWalt 1999). However, traditional practices that have little relevance today may become important in the future.

The traditional agricultural landscape is the cultural context for living, historical, and archaeological indigenous belief systems. They are physically embedded in settlements, fields, walls, canals, paths, and other features of the landscape. The conservation and management of the traditional agricultural landscape is the most effective means of protecting valuable IKS.

Conclusion

It will take time to bring the level of recognition of cultural landscapes and the subclass traditional agricultural landscapes to that enjoyed by outstanding natural landscapes, archaeological and historical buildings, sites, and monuments. The United States and Europe have established new institutions and enacted legislation to protect cultural landscapes. Some countries, such as England, include the agricultural landscape under this umbrella of protection and management. Unfortunately, I do not foresee similar developments in Latin America in the near future. Peruvians would never allow a bulldozer on Machu Picchu but think nothing of having one pull a huge plow over pre-Columbian raised fields and terraces in the Lake Titicaca basin (which has occurred in the course of development projects sponsored by the World Bank Project, the National Agrarian University, and the International Experimental Station Illpa) (Erickson and Candler 1989). UNESCO and other international organizations can influence national and local policies through active recognition and promotion of agricultural landscapes as World Heritage Sites.

Raised fields are physically embedded in the Andean agrarian landscape. The complex patterning, long period of use, high productivity and population carrying capacity, and local historical and ecological appropriateness documented for raised fields and other traditional agricultural strategies on the landscape demonstrate that Andean farming (past and present) is dynamic, resilient, time tested, and sustainable under certain conditions. Because of these characteristics, Andean technologies may provide viable alternative models for development at this critical time of global warming, overpopulation, political instability, and entrenched inequality. Agricultural landscapes have tangible and intangible value for the contemporary world. I would argue that agricultural landscapes such as the raised fields of the Lake Titicaca basin are of "outstanding universal value."

The traditional agrarian landscapes throughout the Andes are threatened, and the indigenous knowledge of the farmers that created them is in danger of being lost forever. After four hundred years of neglect because of rural depopulation, the introduction of Old World crops and animals, and government policies following the Spanish conquest, these landscapes are now under threat from all sides. Poorly planned urbanization encroaches on traditional fields; mechanization of agriculture increasingly erases fragile remains of pre-Columbian fields; the demands of agribusiness, cash cropping, and cultivated pasture are driven by national and international policy, the global economy, unchecked population growth, and the imposition of Western models of development. All have taken their toll on traditional agricultural landscapes.

UNESCO can be a powerful global advocate of traditional agricultural landscapes by helping to reshape development policy that is currently biased against indigenous knowledge systems. UNESCO's present definition and conceptualization of cultural landscapes as World Heritage is inadequate to protect traditional archaeological and lived-in traditional agricultural landscapes. Adherence to the site concept limits serious consideration of traditional agriculture landscapes except where they are incidentally included within the bounds of significant monuments, buildings, sites, or natural areas.

The first step is to ensure that farmers (i.e., smallholders) who are surviving on long-farmed landscapes and using traditional sustainable technology remain there by helping to assure them of an adequate standard of living, land titles, education, access to markets, and freedom from war and violence. In most developing nations, this is a daunting task. It is much easier to maintain an occupied "continuing landscape" than to resuscitate a "relict landscape." UNESCO's formal recognition of these landscapes as World Heritage may provide the catalyst to keep farmers on the land and encourage them to put land back into use when there is evidence that it has been intensively and successfully farmed in the past.

If traditional agricultural landscapes meet the criteria of "outstanding universal value," strict priorities will have to be established. Few would argue that all traditional agricultural landscapes deserve nomination as World Heritage Sites. Some cultural landscapes are "relict" because they failed for various reasons in the past. Some functioning traditional agricultural systems may have no place in the future. UNESCO and other agencies cannot protect, promote, support, and manage all traditional agricultural landscapes; thus a form of preservation triage is necessary. Traditional agricultural landscapes that were sustainable in the past or are still functioning today should receive priority. Many lived-in "continuing landscapes" exist because they are sustainable and can survive on their own. Farmers in some continuing landscapes are under threat from the outside world and need support. Landscapes with archaeological evidence of sustainable agricultural practices that are presently abandoned or utilized in nonsustainable ways should be studied, evaluated, and, if they meet certain criteria, protected and managed as World Heritage Sites. Priority should be given to unique agricultural landscapes that are in danger of being forever lost and those that show promise for sustaining present and future populations.

"Conservation" and "preservation" are probably the wrong terms to use when discussing a moving target such as a dynamic and complex agricultural landscape (Cook 1996). Any attempt to freeze an agricultural landscape, as a museum object or an heirloom, in some present state or moment in the past will condemn it. The goal should not be conservation or preservation but active management that involves the peoples who inhabit those landscapes. In cases in which the agricultural technology and knowledge have been lost, landscape management must draw on archaeological and historical approaches. The engineered agricultural landscapes of the Andes were produced by human agents, farmers making conscious decisions about the land for their own livelihoods and that of future generations, and represent an accumulation of landscape and cultural capital over considerable periods. The people, past and present, and the science, logic, and aesthetics of their indigenous knowledge systems must be understood and appreciated in order to effectively manage traditional agricultural landscapes. This management will require the active participation of many sectors of society.

Acknowledgments

I wish to thank the people of the Quechua communities of Huatta and Coata for their friendship and participation in this project. The National Science Foundation and the Social Sciences Research Council provided funding for various phases of the project. CARE, the Ministry of Agriculture, and NGOs provided potato seed and other materials. Ignacio Garaycochea, Kay Candler, and Dan Brinkmeier were co-investigators on this project. We also received help from Mario Tapia, Luis Lescano, and Hugo Rodriguez. I also wish to thank Jeanne Marie Teutonico, of the Getty Conservation Institute, and Frank Matero, of the University of Pennsylvania, who were co-chairs and organizers of the Managing Change Symposium, at which I presented a version of this chapter. I learned much from discussions with conference participants.

Notes

1   I do not mean to imply static, culture bound, ancient, or exotic in my choice of "traditional." By "traditional," I mean local, shared, historically contingent cultural practices embedded in the land, cultural memory, and practice of everyday life. I use the term "traditional" loosely to refer to categories such as native, peasant, indigenous, smallholder, vernacular, rural, and non-Western that are common in the literature. I recognize that all of these terms are cultural constructs that invariably categorize farmers as "the other" (Dupuis and Vandergeest 1996; Pichón, Uquillas, and Frechione 1999).

2   I use the World Commission on Environment and Development's definition of sustainable agriculture as "development that meets the needs of the present without compromising the ability of future generations to meet their own needs" (cited in CIKARD 1993:3). Although relatively imprecise, "sustainability" connotes the maintenance of high productivity over the long run while managing and protecting local environmental resources from degradation. Sustainable development also promotes an "acceptable livelihood," with connotations of justice and equitability.

3   The UNESCO Web site now lists twenty-three properties as cultural landscapes. Close examination of the descriptions of the new properties reveals a continuing bias toward monuments, buildings, and sites on cultural landscapes rather than an appreciation of agricultural landscape. Similar biases can be found in edited volumes on cultural landscapes sponsored by IUCN (Lucas 1992) and UNESCO (von Droste, Plachter, and Rossler 1995). I recognize that UNESCO and IUCN are attempting to become less Euro- and Anglo-American-centric in their consideration of World Heritage (e.g., Cleere 2000; Titchen 1996).

4   The Rice Terraces of the Philippine Cordillera and the Agricultural Landscape of Southern Öland, Sweden, are rare examples of cultural landscapes recognized as World Heritage Sites for their agricultural importance.

5   A small but growing World Heritage literature recognizes the role of human activity in shaping the environment and the paradigm of New Ecology (e.g., Cook 1996; Thorsell 1995).

6   My colleague Ignacio Garaycochea (1988) points out that local NGOs were the primary beneficiaries of raised field rehabilitation. The influx of funding supported a new middle class in Puno, Juliaca, La Paz, that benefited from salaries, importation of four-wheel-drive vehicles, purchases of computers, telephones, and fax machines, and office rental. Local university students received funding for original agronomic research on raised fields. Professional consultants were hired to write proposals, evaluations, and reports. A large number of extension agents, computer experts, educators, videographers, mechanics, secretaries, guards, and other professionals were employed by NGOs during this period.

7   Chapin (1988), Kozloff (1994), Kehoe (1996), and Swartley (2000) have also written about the adoption, rejection, and abandonment of rehabilitated raised fields in Mexico and Bolivia.

8   The Interinstitutional Program of Waru Waru (PIWA 1994), an NGO promoting raised field agriculture in southern Peru, is an example of sound, applied research and publication. PIWA has conducted social and agronomic research in raised field agriculture, prepared guides for extension agents and farmers, funded student thesis projects, mapped potential zones for raised fields, and published more than fifteen books, in addition to working directly with farmers to rehabilitate traditional agriculture and promote indigenous knowledge.

9   The Web is now the best source of information on IKS, some of it written by native peoples themselves.

References

Ashmore, W., and B. Knapp, eds. 1999. *The Archaeologies of Landscape*. London: Blackwell.

Bender, B. 1998. *Stonehenge: Making Space*. Oxford: Berg.

Botkin, D. 1990. *Discordant Harmonies: A New Ecology for the Twenty-first Century*. New York: Oxford University Press.

Bradley, R. 2000. *Archaeology of Natural Places*. New York: Routledge.

Brokensha, D., D. Warren, and O. Werner, eds. 1980. *Indigenous Knowledge Systems and Development*. Lanham, Md.: University Press of America.

Carmichael, D. L., J. Hubert, B. Reeves, and A. Schanche, eds. 1994. *Sacred Sites, Sacred Places*. London: Routledge.

Chapin, M. 1988. The seduction of models: Chinampa agriculture in Mexico. *Grassroots Development* 12(1):8–17.

Church, T. 1997. Ecosystem management and CRM: Do we have a role? *Society for American Archaeology Bulletin* 15(2):25–26.

CIKARD. 1993. Background to the International Symposium on Indigenous Knowledge and Sustainable Development. *Indigenous Knowledge and Development Monitor* 1(2):2–5.

Cleere, H. 1995. Cultural landscapes as world heritage. *Conservation and Management of Archaeological Sites* 1:63–68.

Cleere, H. 1996. The concept of "outstanding universal value" in the World Heritage Convention. *Conservation and Management of Archaeological Sites* 1:227–33.

Cleere, H. 2000. The World Heritage Convention in the third world. In *Cultural Resource Management in Contemporary Society: Perspectives on Managing and Presenting the Past*, ed. F. P. McManamon and A. Hatton, 99–106. London: Routledge.

Cook, R. E. 1996. Is landscape preservation an oxymoron? *George Wright Forum* 13(1):42–53.

Crumley, C. L., ed. 1994. *Historical Ecology: Cultural Knowledge and Changing Landscapes*. Santa Fe, New Mex.: School of American Research.

Denevan, W. M. 1992. The pristine myth: The landscape of the Americas in 1492. *Annals of the Association of American Geographers* 82:369–85.

Denevan, W. M. 2001. *Cultivated Landscapes of Native Amazonia and the Andes*. Oxford: Oxford University Press.

DeWalt, B. R. 1999. Combining indigenous and scientific knowledge to improve agriculture and natural resource management in Latin America. In *Traditional and Modern Natural Resource Management in Latin America*, ed. F. Pichón, J. E. Uquillas, and J. Frechione, 75–100. Pittsburgh: University of Pittsburgh Press.

Dunnell, R. C. 1992. The notion site. In *Space, Time, and Archaeological Landscapes*, ed. J. Rossignol and LuAnn Wandsnider, 21–41. New York: Plenum Press.

Dupuis, E. M., and P. Vandergeest, eds. 1996. *Creating the Countryside: The Politics of Rural and Environmental Discourse*. Philadelphia: Temple University Press.

Erickson, C. L. 1996. *Investigación arqueológica del sistema agrícola de los camellones en la Cuenca del Lago Titicaca del Perú*. La Paz: PIWA and Centro de Información para el Desarollo.

Erickson, C. L. 2000. The Lake Titicaca basin: A pre-Columbian built landscape. In *Imperfect Balance: Landscape Transformations in the Precolumbian Americas*, ed. D. Lentz, 311–56. New York: Columbia University Press.

Erickson, C. L. N.d. Agricultural landscapes as monuments. Unpublished manuscript.

Erickson, C. L., and D. Brinkmeier. 1991. Raised field rehabilitation projects in the northern Lake Titicaca basin. Unpublished report to the Interamerican Foundation, Washington, D.C.

Erickson, C. L., and K. L. Candler. 1989. Raised fields and sustainable agriculture in the Lake Titicaca basin. In *Fragile Lands of Latin America: Strategies for Sustainable Development*, ed. J. Browder, 230–48. Boulder: Westview Press.

Fotiadis, M. 1992. Units of data as deployment of disciplinary codes. In *Representations in Archaeology*, ed. J.-C. Gardin and C. Peebles, 132–48. Bloomington: Indiana University Press.

Garaycochea, I. 1988. Community-based organizations and rural development with a particular reference to Andean peasant communities. Master's thesis, Reading University, Reading, England.

Ingold, T. 1993. The temporality of the landscape. *World Archaeology* 25(2):152–74.

Kehoe, Alice. 1996. Participant observation with the Lakaya Centro de Madres. In *Tiwanaku and Its Hinterland: Archaeology and Paleoecology of an Andean Civilization*. Vol. 1, *Agroecology*, ed. A. L. Kolata, 231–40. Washington, D.C.: Smithsonian Institution Press.

Kolata, A. L., O. Rivera, J. C. Ramirez, and E. Gemio. 1996. Rehabilitating raised-field agriculture in the southern Lake Titicaca basin of Bolivia. In *Tiwanaku and Its Hinterland: Archaeology and Paleoecology of an Andean Civilization*. Vol. 1, *Agroecology*, ed. A. L. Kolata, 203–30. Washington, D.C.: Smithsonian Institution Press.

Kozloff, Robin R. 1994. Community factors in agricultural change: The introduction of raised fields in highland Bolivia. Master's thesis, University of California, Davis.

Lansing, J. Stephen. 1991. *Priests and Programmers: Technologies of Power in the Engineered Landscape of Bali*. Princeton: Princeton University Press.

Leach, M., and R. Mearns, eds. 1996. *The Lie of the Land: Challenging Environmental Orthodoxies in Africa*. London: James Currey.

Lucas, P. H. C., ed. 1992. *Protected Landscapes: A Guide for Policy-Makers and Planners*. London: Chapman and Hall.

McGlade, J. 1999. Archaeology and the evolution of cultural landscapes: Towards an interdisciplinary research agenda. In *The Archaeology and Anthropology of Landscapes*, ed. P. Ucko and R. Layton, 458–82. London: Routledge.

McNeely, J. A. 1995. IUCN and indigenous peoples: How to promote sustainable development. In *The Cultural Dimension of Development: Indigenous Knowledge Systems*, ed. D. M. Warren, L. J. Slikkerveer, and D. Brokensha, 445–50. London: Intermediate Technology Publications.

Morlon, P., ed. 1996. *Comprender la agricultura campesina en los Andes centrales: Perú y Bolivia*. Lima: Instituto Francés de Estudios Andinos.

Netting, R. 1993. *Smallholders, Householders: Farm Families and the Ecology of Intensive, Sustainable Agriculture*. Stanford: Stanford University Press.

Pari, P., P. C. Aguilar, and Z. Cutipa. 1989. Promoción de la rehabilitación de la infraestructura de waru-waru. *Waru Waru en la producción agropecuaria de las comunidades compesinas del altiplano. Agricultura Andina 1: Waru Waru*, Año 1, no. 1, 27–46. Instituto de Investigaciones para el Desarrollo Social del Altiplano-IIDSA, UNA, Puno.

Peet, R., and M. Watts, eds. 1996. *Liberation Ecologies: Environment, Development, Social Movements*. London. Routledge.

Pichón, F., J. E. Uquillas, and J. Frechione, eds. 1999. *Traditional and Modern Natural Resource Management in Latin America*. Pittsburgh: University of Pittsburgh Press.

Piperno, D. R., and D. M. Pearsall. 1998. *The Origins of Agriculture in the Lowland Neotropics*. New York: Academic Press.

PIWA. 1994. *Priorización de las Areas Potenciales para la (re)construcción de waru waru en el Altiplano de Puno*. Puno, Peru: Programa Interinstitucional de Waru Waru, INADE/PELT-COTESU.

Redman, C. 1999. *Human Impact on Ancient Environments*. Tucson: University of Arizona Press.

Stahl, P. 1996. Holocene biodiversity: An archaeological perspective from the Americas. *Annual Review of Anthropology* 25:105–26.

Swartley, L. 2000. Inventing indigenous knowledge: Archaeology, rural development, and the raised field rehabilitation project in Bolivia. Ph.D. dissertation, University of Pittsburgh.

Thorsell, J. 1995. How natural are World Heritage Natural Sites? *World Heritage Newsletter* 9:8–11.

Tilley, C. 1994. *A Phenomenology of Landscape: Places, Paths, and Monuments*. Providence: Berg.

Titchen, S. M. 1996. On the construction of "outstanding universal value": Some comments on the implementation of the 1972 UNESCO World Heritage Convention. *Conservation and Management of Archaeological Sites* 1:235–42.

UNESCO. 2002. *Operational Guidelines for the Implementation of the World Heritage Convention* (WHC.02/2:Revised July 2002). Paris: UNESCO Heritage Centre. http://www.unesco.org/whc/nwhc/pages/doc/main.htm

von Droste, B., H. Plachter, and M. Rossler, eds. 1995. *Cultural Landscapes of Universal Value: Components for a Global Strategy*. Jena: Fischer-Verlag.

Warren, D. M. 1999. Indigenous knowledge for agricultural development. In *Traditional and Modern Natural Resource Management in Latin America*, ed. F. Pichón, J. E. Uquillas, and J. Frechione, 197–211. Pittsburgh: University of Pittsburgh Press.

Warren, D. M., L. J. Slikkerveer, and D. Brokensha, eds. 1995. *The Cultural Dimension of Development: Indigenous Knowledge Systems*. London: Intermediate Technology Publications.

Wolf, E. R. 1982. *Europe and the People without History*. Berkeley: University of California Press.

Zimmerer, K. 1996. *Changing Fortunes: Biodiversity and Peasant Livelihood in the Peruvian Andes*. Berkeley: University of California Press.

Summary of Proceedings

Jeanne Marie Teutonico

SUSTAINABILITY IS A COMPLEX AND WIDE-REACHING concept that has become part of contemporary discourse but is difficult to define and risks being rendered meaningless from overuse. Yet it is clear from the many contributions represented here that sustainability is of widespread concern as we recognize that resources are not unlimited and that the world is certainly less rich (in cultural terms) and perhaps even destabilized socially by loss of memory, tradition, continuity, and increasing polarization and globalization.

In many ways, conservation has always been about sustainability: about traditional technologies that permit repair and reuse rather than constant wasteful cycles of destruction and rebuilding; about understanding the multiplicity of values that people attach to places and spaces, even if we have not always been skilled enough at recognizing the diverse stakeholder groups or interpreting their concerns; about managing change rather than freezing some kind of agreed fable that we call heritage; and about finding a way to have the past inform the present and future without compromising the need to improve and to assure a certain quality of life. In fact, it can be argued, too, that conservation has always been about development or, more generally, about the present and the future rather than a nostalgic attachment to a past that we can never completely understand.

And yet the general impression of conservation as a field and an activity is distinctly different from that described above. In part, the problem is undoubtedly that, until recently, the conservation field has not presented its work in a way that links it strongly to issues of sustainability and quality of life. Conservation professionals have also tended to speak among themselves and have not engaged often enough in dialogue with those who share their concerns but from different vantage points and disciplines.

With this in mind, the US/ICOMOS 2001 International Symposium was organized to bring together a diverse group of individuals, to explore new ways of thinking, and to challenge accepted wisdom. And though there were jarring juxtapositions at times, the points of connection outweighed those of divergence in the views expressed by the speakers from the standpoints of their respective disciplines and experience.

Conference Presentations

The first session of the conference was devoted to understanding the over-riding concepts and principles of sustainability. Jean Louis Luxen spoke of "integrated conservation" and the need to connect issues of culture and concern for the physical environment of the past to the needs of the present and future and to larger issues of human development and quality of life. He defined development as more than economic growth that must be measured by indicators that go beyond the GNP, such as health, education, life expectancy, and cultural values. Luxen was also the first to bring correlations with the environmental field, stressing the need to conserve cultural diversity (that is, the conservation not just of some aspects of the physical environment but of know-how and less tangible aspects of heritage). In addition, he made the case that sustainable conservation must be part of sustainable development and that it will never succeed without local democracy and the active engagement of the people who value and care for their environment.

Many of these ideas were elaborated by David Throsby, especially as they related to indicators of sustainability and the ways that value can be measured in other than strictly economic terms. He introduced the concept of cultural capital and offered a set of principles (rather than a single definition) for sustainability that included a concern for both material and nonmaterial benefits, intergenerational equity, and, again, the safeguarding of cultural diversity and cultural value. Throsby also articulated two concepts that were echoed by many later speakers, specifically that of the cultural ecosystem and of the need for increased interaction between economists and those engaged in the social sciences with the conservation community. He was cautiously optimistic that a paradigm shift was occurring among economists who were starting to be more comfortable with value measured in terms other than dollars and cents.

John Keene presented a less optimistic view of the current environmental and social sustainability of our planet, especially in view of climatic changes, population growth, and globalization. From the urbanist's perspective, though, he argued that managing urban growth and all that implies would do much to create a more sustainable environment. This led to an interesting discussion regarding gentrification and the need to balance market forces with social initiatives regarding, for example, low-cost housing, if diversity and balance are to be maintained in urban environments.

The second conference session addressed sustainability from the vantage point of different disciplines and scales of heritage, from the landscape to the city and building. Graham Fairclough began with a comprehensive overview of thinking and policy in Europe regarding the sustainability of cultural landscape and introduced "enough-ness" (that is, passing on enough to future generations to ensure that they, too, have options) as a central concept in attempting to define sustainability. He emphasized that the landscape is dynamic and noted that humans have never really had a peaceful relationship with the land. He expanded the concept of cultural capital to "quality of life" capital and emphasized the need for broad participation and consultation, the consideration of multiple values, and a long-term and holistic view. Fairclough also offered a methodology both for evaluation of landscape and for recording many features while stressing the difficulty with understanding and recording the perception of landscape, a factor that is extremely important but difficult to measure.

Setha Low introduced REAP (Rapid Ethnographic Assessment Procedure) as a way of understanding the values that various groups associate with places and spaces and also the impact on various groups of certain decisions. She attempted to provide indicators of social sustainability that included social diversity and inclusiveness; a concern for the self-perpetuating and self-generating characteristics of a system; and the preservation of social relationships and meanings that enhance cultural identity. The presentation concluded with two interesting case studies, Ellis Island and Independence National Historical Park, which showed quite clearly how different cultural groups value heritage in different ways and how the practice of historic preservation can actually disrupt cultural ecosystems. Implicit in these cases, however, was the challenge to move beyond analysis to decision making, since sustainability is ultimately about the implementation of sustainable policies and solutions.

M. Christine Boyer spoke eloquently of the importance of perception and cognitive significance, echoing some of the ideas that had been raised by Fairclough. She articulated the tension between history and memory and argued that sustainable conservation and development must allow for open-ended thinking and invention rather than simply the creation of static, fictionalized environments that, in fact, promote the passive experience of selective, stored memories. Boyer's three case studies showed three approaches to history: authenticity in the case of the South Street Seaport, nostalgia at Battery Park, and spectacle at Times Square. The latter was offered as a potential example of sustainability, an urban space that engenders memory and allows for multiple meanings and experiences.

Brian Ridout returned to the scale of the single building (and the tangibility of a material) with a consideration of ecologically sustainable approaches to wood infestation. Though at first this discussion seemed wildly different from what preceded it, the core message had many connections to previous presentations. Essentially, finding sustainable solutions to wood infestation is not simply a technical issue but is fundamentally about systems. It involves a comprehension of societal changes that have produced radically different wood products than those used historically, and then understanding the ecology of buildings so as to find benign and sustainable ways to manage infestation (perhaps, for example, by using the natural habits of insects to trap them rather than impregnating timber with chemicals that are better at killing the natural predators of insect pests than the pests themselves).

The final session of the conference was devoted to a series of case studies that brought the discussion from the realm of theory into the realm of practice. The first speakers considered archaeological sites in radically different cultural and socioeconomic environments. David Batchelor spoke of Stonehenge and Avebury, a World Heritage Site with a complex and contentious group of stakeholders. In developing a management plan for the site, he again stressed the importance of public participation and of multidisciplinarity in the management planning team and made a persuasive argument for the use of GIS in collecting data, resolving conflict, and managing change. Two of the strongest points to emerge from the presentation were the need for continuing research (since no solution is sustainable if it is not dynamic) and the notion that sustainability is really about creating a thought process at both the individual and the collective level.

Carolina Castellanos picked up many of these themes in her discussion of Chan Chan, where, again, a values-driven management plan was put in place. She also stressed the importance of public participation and the need for a holistic approach, stating that an archaeological site does not exist in isolation but as part of a social dynamic. Thus the management plan for Chan Chan dealt not just with the care of the physical fabric and the interpretation of the site for tourists but also with reconciliation of land use issues, cultural development of adjacent communities, education, and the sustaining of traditional craft. From the point of view of sustainability, it was also important that the project have resonance in the region and that local professionals have the ability to transfer knowledge and methodology to other sites. The issue of the "outsider" or "foreigner" and his or her role in such conservation and planning efforts became a general point of discussion.

Gina Haney used the example of the Cape Coast project in Ghana to make the case that a site-specific approach that does not involve local communities will not be sustainable in the long run. The Cape Coast project involved creating local ownership of and pride in heritage and also the economic base to permit its care and maintenance. Like other speakers, Haney emphasized that conservation must exist within social and cultural systems and that sustainability depends on a strong community and funding base, as well as a certain flexibility and ability to respond to the dynamic nature of any living place.

Turning to the subject of urban environments, Francesco Siravo was very clear in his definition of what makes a sustainable historic city: a traditional urban context that survives and thrives because it is handed down from generation to generation, and where the population has a profound connection to the past and enough resources to maintain the environment. In many cities today, where this urban tradition has broken down, planning is critical to the creation of a sustainable urban environment. In discussing the work of the Aga Khan Trust for Culture in Islamic cities such as Cairo and Samarkand, Siravo established several parameters for a successful urban conservation project. These include an economically viable and socially stable population, a supportive institutional environment, the application of traditional construction methods, and an emphasis on training. Crucial to all of this is, again, the view that conservation is an intrinsic part of larger social and cultural development. Cities will be sustainable when the population regains the shared values, traditions, and memories that made them in the first place.

Trevor Marchand's message was fundamentally about process over product. He criticized a Eurocentric focus on the materiality of things that pays little attention to the processes that create them. But more than just the conservation of "know-how" and traditional skills, he emphasized the importance of conserving the systems (such as apprenticeship) that create know-how, because these systems have social and cultural importance that extend far beyond the learning of particular technical skills. This was illustrated with examples of work in San'a', Yemen, and Djenné, Mali, where, it was argued, authenticity lies in authenticity of process rather than simply in the preservation of certain material forms. Of course, this discussion challenged some notions about the way that training is organized and delivered, often by "outsiders," in certain cultural environments.

The final presentations addressed even broader issues of tradition and agricultural landscape. Ernesto Noriega spoke movingly of his work with an exiled Tibetan population in northern India to reconstruct memory via indirect means (such as photographs, drawings, and discussions with elders) so as to help young builders create an architectural expression that reflected both their past and their aspirations. He spoke about creating "the space between tradition and modernity," a way to move forward without losing a sense of place and identity, in essence, perhaps, another definition of sustainable development where there has been an attempt at cultural genocide.

Finally, Clark Erickson's presentation focused on agrarian landscapes in Peru and Bolivia, challenging the idea that these types of landscapes are any less deliberate than buildings or what are usually considered designed landscapes. The work described bore similarities to Noriega's in that an indirect method—in this case archaeology—was used to reconstruct the system of "raised fields" that had been lost for nearly four hundred years. In many ways, this is an inherently sustainable type of farming, since it is environmentally friendly, increases production, is adapted to a small scale, and has a high carrying capacity. However, it was evident that sustainability also depends on other factors that had been mentioned previously in the context of cities, such as titles for small landholding, access to credit, guarantees of social justice, and access to information. The role of the "foreigner" was again explored in this context. Sometimes international appreciation for native lifeways can bring renewed pride and empowerment; alternatively, it can lead to an association of certain technologies with "outsiders" and hinder acceptance. In the end, though, it is clear that the best way to protect land is to use it and that the goal should not be arresting change but rather active management of a dynamic system.

Conclusion

Certainly, it is important to take a holistic view of conservation, to see it as part of larger processes of development and concern for social equity and the quality of life. Rather than create a fictionalized past, the conservation and stewardship of heritage is about managing change in a dynamic environment. This does involve attention to the safeguarding of material culture but not divorced from the cultural, social, and economic forces that both created it and continue to affect the way it is used and valued by diverse communities. Public participation is crucial to the sustainability of any conservation initiative, as is addressing economic and quality of life issues. And it is senseless to preserve "product" without attention to the preservation of know-how as well as the way in which skill is learned and passed down.

Clearly, too, it is crucial to work in a multidisciplinary and, indeed, transdisciplinary way, to look outside the confines of the conservation field to other disciplines such as economics and social anthropology so as to view issues from different perspectives and perhaps develop better tools for analysis, evaluation, and interpretation.

Finally, it is evident that we must articulate better what we do so that conservation is not seen as some sort of nostalgic, irrelevant, elitist activity but as a central and important aspect of sustainable development and the planning and management of the built and natural environment. This demands an integrated approach that looks at our physical environment in a holistic way in terms of interrelated systems, instead of drawing arbitrary boundaries between built and natural, tangible and intangible.

Much progress has been made, but there is still much to be done. Only by engaging in dialogue and challenging ourselves to think in more synthetic terms will we move forward in ways that permit the survival of memory, tradition, and a multiplicity of values, and that acknowledge limited resources and the fragility of our ecosystem, while promoting manageable change, sustainable development, and improved quality of life.

Contributors

David Batchelor has worked for English Heritage and its predecessor for more than twenty-five years, originally serving as an assistant field officer in the Central Excavation Unit at its inception in 1976. He has fieldwork experience in a range of projects and recently led the archaeological teams at the Hampton Court Palace and Windsor Castle following the fires there. He is currently based in the Policy Unit of the Archaeology and Survey Division, as liaison with local authorities in the management of the historic environment. In addition, for the past nine years he has been leading the team developing the application of Geographic Information Systems (GIS) in the management and understanding of World Heritage Sites. Initially this work focused on Stonehenge but has now expanded to include Avebury and Hadrian's Wall in the United Kingdom. He has also advised on the application of GIS on World Heritage Sites in Asia for the UNESCO World Heritage Centre.

M. Christine Boyer is Professor in the School of Architecture at Princeton University. Her books include *Dreaming the Rational City: The Myth of American City Planning; Manhattan Manners: Architecture and Style, 1850–1900; Cyber Cities: Visual Perception in the Age of Electronic Communication;* and *The City of Collective Memory: Its Historical Imagery and Architectural Entertainments.* The last of these was awarded the Lewis Mumford Prize for Best Book Published in American City and Regional Planning History, 1993–95.

Carolina Castellanos is an independent conservator specializing in the conservation and management of archaeological sites. She has developed management and conservation plans at Chan Chan in Peru, Joya de Cerén in El Salvador, and the Mimbres–Paquime Connection Project in Mexico and the United States, among others. Castellanos has served as consultant to the Getty Conservation Institute, the World Monuments Fund, the Instituto Nacional de Antropología e Historia (INAH), and ICCROM. She has also been an instructor in site management and conservation planning at the CRATerre-Getty-INC Panamerican Courses in the Conservation of Architectural Heritage and at other training workshops in management planning in Mexico and the United States.

Clark L. Erickson is Associate Curator of Andean Archaeology at the University of Pennsylvania Museum of Archaeology and Anthropology and Associate Professor of Anthropology at the University of Pennsylvania. He has more than twenty-five years of fieldwork experience in Latin America. His research focuses on the pre-Columbian cultural or anthropogenic landscapes of the Americas. Current projects include archaeological investigations of farming and settlement systems in the Amazon and the Andes. Using landscape features as artifacts, Erickson and colleagues are reconstructing the social organization, land tenure, technology, and lifeways of rural farmers. Information about past land use, indigenous knowledge systems, and historical ecology of landscapes can provide models for contemporary sustainable development. For example, Erickson and colleagues have identified an entire landscape of fish weirs, ponds, and dikes in the Amazon that was used to raise and harvest fish. His team is helping the Bolivian government to develop a plan for the conservation, management, and use of this cultural landscape.

Graham Fairclough is an archaeologist specializing and publishing in resource management, with experience also in the excavation and archaeology of standing buildings. He has worked with English Heritage and its government predecessor for more than twenty-five years. From 1995, he was Head of its Monuments and Countryside Protection Programmes, the long-term national review, characterization, and designation program for archaeology and historic landscape in England. Since 2002 Fairclough has been Head of the English Heritage Characterisation Team. He is an Honorary Fellow of the Department of Archaeology at York University. In recent years he pioneered English Heritage's links with nature conservation and landscape agencies, worked on the integration of archaeological conservation with land use planning, established Historic Landscape Characterisation as a national program, and spearheaded new thinking on sustainability and the historic environment. In 2000 he coordinated the review of government policies relating to the historic environment that led to the *Power of Place* report.

Gina Haney is an architectural historian specializing in community-based cultural resource management and planning. She holds an M.A. degree in architectural history from the University of Virginia. In addition to working as an archaeologist on prehistoric and historic sites, Haney has coordinated interdisciplinary design charettes in Paramaribo, Suriname, and Georgetown, Guyana. From 1998 to 2000 she resided in Cape Coast, Ghana, where she coordinated the historic preservation component of the Central Region Project for US/ICOMOS, a program that received broad recognition and regional awards in Ghana. Currently, she is assisting the Aga Khan Cultural Services–Egypt with the development and implementation of their urban revitalization project in Islamic Cairo.

John C. Keene, AICP, is Professor of City and Regional Planning at the University of Pennsylvania, specializing in the legal aspects of urban planning, growth management, and environmental policy. He teaches courses in the law of planning and urban development, historic preservation law, environmental law, Brownfield remediation, and emerging issues in environmental protection. He is currently chair of the doctoral program and a member of the Program Committee for the Historic Preservation Program. He is author and senior editor of two major national studies of farmland protection and two analyses of growth management techniques in New Jersey and Pennsylvania. He is a member of the Scientific and Technical Advisory Committee for the Chesapeake Bay Program. As partner in a small consulting firm, Keene has prepared plans for the protection of resource lands for county and municipal governments and has testified as an expert witness on matters of agricultural zoning. In 1999 he received a University Research Foundation award to study urban and regional planning in three regions of northern Spain.

Setha M. Low is Professor of Environmental Psychology and Anthropology at the Graduate Center of the City University of New York. She received her Ph.D. in Cultural Anthropology from the University of California, Berkeley, and spent her early career as Assistant and Associate Professor of Landscape Architecture and Regional Planning and City Planning at the University of Pennsylvania, where she became interested in cultural aspects of design and the anthropology of space and place. Among her published works are *On the Plaza: The Politics of Public Space and Culture; Theorizing the City; Children of the Urban Poor* (with F. J. Johnston); *Place Attachment* (edited with I. Altman); and *Housing, Culture, and Design* (edited with E. Chambers). Low has been awarded a National Endowment for the Humanities Fellowship, a Fulbright Research Fellowship, a John Simon Guggenheim Fellowship, and grants from the Wenner-Gren Foundation for Anthropological Research, the Canadian Social Research Council, and the National Science Foundation. In 2000 she was awarded the Textor Prize for Excellence in Anticipatory Anthropology from the American Anthropological Association, a national career award. Low is currently writing and lecturing about gated communities and editing a volume entitled *Cultural Spaces* with Denise Lawrence. As Director of the Public Space Research Group at the Center for Human Environments (CUNY), she has completed studies of cultural diversity in New York City and National Park Service parks and consults on cultural values in historic preservation for the Getty Conservation Institute in Los Angeles and the Municipal Arts Society of New York City.

Trevor H. J. Marchand is a lecturer in anthropology at the School of Oriental and African Studies, University of London, where he teaches the anthropology of urban space, place, and architecture. He received a Bachelor of Architecture degree from McGill University and a Ph.D. in social anthropology from the University of London. Dr. Marchand's research has taken an anthropological approach to the study of architecture and the built environment. He has conducted fieldwork with traditional masons in northern Nigeria, Mali, and Yemen, and his studies have focused on skilled performance and the transmission of expert knowledge. He is the author of *Minaret Building and Apprenticeship in Yemen* (2001).

Frank Matero is Associate Professor of Architecture and Chair of the Graduate Program in Historic Preservation in the Graduate School of Fine Arts as well as Director and founder of the Architectural Conservation Laboratory at the University of Pennsylvania. Since 1988 he has been on the faculty of the International Center for the Study of the Preservation and the Restoration of Cultural Property (ICCROM) in Rome. From 1981 to 1990 he was Assistant Professor of Architecture and from 1985 to 1990 Director of the Center for Preservation Research in the Graduate School of Architecture, Planning and Preservation at Columbia University. His teaching and research focuses on historic building technology and the conservation of building materials, with an emphasis on masonry and earthen construction, the conservation of archaeological sites, and issues related to preservation and appropriate technology for traditional societies and places. He has published numerous articles and is the author of two forthcoming books, on the technical history of the stone industries of North America and on the history of site preservation in the American Southwest. He is regional editor of *Conservation and Management of Archaeological Sites* and the *Journal of Architectural Preservation*. He is also a member of numerous professional boards, including US/ICOMOS, the Frank Lloyd Wright Building Conservancy, and the AIA Historic Resources Committee. His current work includes conservation plans for the Neolithic site of Catalhoyuk, the Al-Darb-Al Ahmar district of Cairo, and Mesa Verde National Park, Casa Grande Ruins, and Bandelier National Monuments in the United States.

Ernesto Noriega, born in Lima, Peru, has pursued a multinational career that focuses on the struggle of indigenous peoples to preserve their threatened cultural heritage and the possibilities of capitalizing on local human resources such as memory and creativity to generate viable options other than assimilation and loss of their unique traditions. He has studied architecture at the Georgia Institute of Technology and the Ecole des Beaux Arts, Paris, and pursued development studies at the Institut Universitaire d'Etudes du Développement in Geneva. He has worked with nongovernmental and grassroots development organizations and independently with indigenous groups. This work has included projects with an organization of indigenous rural communities in the Peruvian highlands and the Tibetan exile community in northern India.

Brian Ridout received an M.A. in entomology and mycology from Cambridge University and a Ph.D. in entomology from Birbeck College, University of London, which subsequently elected him Honorary Research Fellow. In 1978 he established his own company and for many years has served as English Heritage's timber decay consultant. With a small, committed team, he has developed a scientific approach to timber decay and damp-related problems. These techniques have been successfully employed to conserve some of the nation's most important historic buildings. His company has completed a three-year, European Community–funded research project on the deathwatch beetle and the decay of oak. Subsequent research funded by the DTI (2000) has provided greater understanding of insect damage potential. He has lectured widely on timber decay and written numerous articles on dry rot and other decay fungi. His book, *Timber Decay in Buildings: The Conservation Approach to Treatment*, received the Lee Nelson Award for Best Publication, 1999–2000, from the Association for Preservation Technology in Philadelphia. He is currently a senior architectural conservator at English Heritage.

Francesco Siravo is an architect and town planner. He received his professional degrees in architecture and town planning from the University of Rome, La Sapienza, and specialized in historic preservation at the College of Europe, Bruges, and Columbia University, New York. Currently, he is Senior Project Officer for the Historic Cities Support Programme of the Aga Khan Trust for Culture, Geneva, Switzerland, with projects in Cairo, Samarkand (Uzbekistan), and Mostar (Bosnia-Herzegovina). His previous work includes collaboration on plans for the historical areas of Rome and Urbino. Subsequently, he was responsible for the conservation plans of Lamu, Kenya, and Zanzibar, Tanzania. Before joining the Aga Khan Trust, Siravo consulted extensively for international, bilateral, and governmental organizations including UNESCO, UNDP, ICCROM, the Kenya Wildlife Service, and the Italian Ministry of Foreign Affairs. He has taught conservation planning at the University of Pennsylvania Graduate School of Fine Arts Program in Historic Preservation, the Università di Cassino, Italy, and ICCROM, Rome (International Centre for the Study and Preservation of Cultural Property). Among his publications on architectural conservation and town planning are *Zanzibar: A Plan for the Historic Stone Town* and *Planning Lamu: Conservation of an East African Seaport*.

Jeanne Marie Teutonico is Associate Director, Field Projects and Science, at the Getty Conservation Institute (GCI). She is an architectural conservator with an A.B. (Hons.) in art history from Princeton University and an M.Sc. in historic preservation from Columbia University, Graduate School of Architecture, Planning, and Preservation. From 1983 to 1992 she was employed by the International Centre for the Study of the Preservation and Restoration of Cultural Property (ICCROM) in Rome where she was instrumental in developing the laboratory curriculum for the International Architectural Conservation Course and responsible for research and technical advice concerning the analysis and conservation of building materials. After a period as an independent consultant to UNESCO in Zanzibar, Teutonico joined English Heritage in 1995 as a senior architectural conservator in the Building Conservation and Research Team. Until her departure for the GCI in September 1999, she was responsible for the design and management of an extensive research program dealing with building material science. Teutonico is author of *A Laboratory Manual for Architectural Conservators* and has published widely in professional journals and conference proceedings. She maintains research interests in the conservation and sustainable use of traditional building materials and serves on the board of US/ICOMOS.

David Throsby is Professor of Economics at Macquarie University in Sydney, Australia. He holds bachelor's and master's degrees from the University of Sydney and a Ph.D. from the London School of Economics. He has published widely in the economics of arts and culture, the economics of cultural heritage, and cultural policy. He has been a consultant to a number of international organizations, including the World Bank, UNESCO, the UN Food and Agriculture Organization, OECD, and the Getty Conservation Institute. He is a former president of the Association for Cultural Economics International and is a member of the editorial boards of several journals, including the *Journal of Cultural Economics*, the *International Journal of Cultural Policy*, and *Poetics*. His most recent book is *Economics and Culture*.